Multiple Intelligences and Language Learning

A Guidebook of Theory, Activities, Inventories, and Resources

Mary Ann Christison

Teacher Art by Sharron K. Bassano

ALTA BOOK CENTER PUBLISHERS—SAN FRANCISCO

Acquisitions Editor: **Aarón Berman**

Content Editor: **Cherie Lenz-Hackett**

Content and Production Editors: **Jamie Ann Cross, Raissa Nina Burns,** and **Jayme George**

Cover Art: **Bruce Marion Design**

Interior Art: **Sharron K. Bassano**

Interior Art (Animals): **Clare Faulkner**

Interior Design: **Natesh Daniel**

Typesetting and Production: **Martha Bateson Sautter**

Alta Book Center Publishers–San Francisco
14 Adrian Court
Burlingame, California 94010 USA

Website: www.altaesl.com • Email: info@altaesl.com
Phone: 800 ALTA/ESL • 650.692.1285 (International)
Fax: 800 ALTA/FAX • 650.692.4654 (International)

ISBN 978-1-882483-75-4
Library of Congress Control Number: 2001095695

If we can mobilize the spectrum of human abilities, not only will people feel better about themselves and more competent; it is even possible that they will also feel more engaged and better able to join the rest of the world community in working for the broader good. Perhaps if we can mobilize the full range of human intelligences and ally them to an ethical sense, we can help to increase the likelihood of our survival on this planet, and perhaps even contribute to our thriving.

— Howard Gardner

Table of Contents

UNIT 3 Logical/Mathematical Intelligence   57

UNIT 4 Visual/Spatial Intelligence   113

UNIT 5 Bodily/Kinesthetic Intelligence   167

UNIT 6 Personal Intelligences   209

Interpersonal

Intrapersonal

UNIT 7 Musical Intelligence 269

UNIT 8 Naturalist Intelligence 301

Preface

This book is intended to be used as a resource for second and foreign language teachers who are interested in translating the theory of multiple intelligences (MI theory) into classroom practice. It is obvious from the size of this book that I have much enthusiasm for this topic and for the educational implications and applications of MI theory to the second language classroom. As a second language educator, I embrace MI theory because it provides conceptual support for what I know intuitively is good classroom practice. MI theory has been a springboard for designing lesson plans and curricula for both language and teacher education programs.

The Audience

Language learning environments and teaching situations vary dramatically. You may work in foreign languages, EFL, or ESL situations in public schools, private academies, at the elementary-, secondary-, or university-level. You may be a language teacher or a teacher educator. In selecting activities to include in the various units, I have kept diverse teaching environments in mind and chosen flexible materials that can be used successfully in a wide range of contexts for language teaching and for demonstrating particular principles of lesson planning and curriculum design for teacher education programs. I would like to see this book used as a resource for language teachers and language teacher educators. It can be useful in specific content areas, such as social studies, math, natural sciences, and language arts in the public schools. If you are a foreign language teacher, I am hoping that you can take the initial ideas presented in these units, adapt them, and create the language necessary to make them work for you in your foreign language classrooms.

The Units

Multiple Intelligences and Language Learning is divided into eight units. The first unit serves as an introduction to MI theory. In this unit you will find a summary of the intelligences, the theoretical bases of MI theory, suggested steps for teachers in applying MI theory, the importance of using MI inventories for language learners and language teachers, and a discussion of issues related to testing and assessment. This unit is intended for teachers who have little or no background in MI theory, but it can also be used as an overview for teachers who are familiar with the approach and for teacher educators who wish to incorporate MI theory into their teacher education programs.

Units 2 through 8 are devoted to the different intelligences—linguistic, logical/mathematical, visual/spatial, bodily/kinesthetic, personal (interpersonal and intrapersonal), musical, and naturalist. In these units, I have developed a unique way of looking at language activities and MI theory. I have mined each activity for its potential to develop multiple intelligences rather than view each exercise as representative of only one intelligence. This approach was important for a book dealing with MI theory for the second language classroom because all activities must necessarily develop linguistic intelligence. Each of these units contains activities for different age levels (pre-K to adult) and different language levels (beginning to advanced).

The Activities

Some activities in the units are actual lesson plans and are designed to take most of a class period or continue over several class periods. Other activities are meant to be supplementary to lessons and are designed to take only a portion of the class time (15-30 minutes). Of course, you must decide which activities are better suited to your students—you know your curriculum and content better than anyone else.

The directions for the activities are written with an inexperienced teacher in mind. If you are an experienced teacher, you may find some of the directions unnecessary or you may find that you have another process for that particular activity that will work better for you. I have written the directions for the new or inexperienced teacher because I believe it is easier for an experienced teacher to make changes and revisions to suit his/her teaching style than it is for an inexperienced teacher to create the process on the spot.

The Indexes

In order that you might sort through the activities easily and select the ones that are most appropriate to your teaching situation, all of the activities are indexed chronologically by age level and then subdivided by language level in the appendices. If you are looking for a beginning level activity for Grade 3 to develop the bodily/kinesthetic intelligence, simply go to the Grades 3 to 5 index, then the beginning level list within this index, and look for those activities labeled with a "5" for Unit 5, the bodily/kinesthetic unit. There is also a content index in the appendices to help you find the right activities to complement the content you are teaching. The goal is for all parts of lesson planning to be unified—the identification of the particular intelligences being developed, the level of the language, the appropriateness of the content for the age level, and the fit of the content for the overall lesson or unit.

Acknowledgements

The ideas presented in this book have come from many different sources. I would like to thank the hundreds of teachers in my teacher education courses at the University of Utah, the public school district bilingual/ESL coordinators, the school principals, the program directors of international language and binational centers with whom I have worked in many different countries all over the world in the past two decades, and the students who have been willing to allow me to try out the ideas in this book in the classroom. I have learned much from our shared experiences. Thank you for sharing your ideas with me and for giving me such useful feedback.

I would also like to thank TESOL, Inc. for sponsoring a TeleTESOL event and the three TESOL Academies where I have taught MI theory over the past few years. These experiences put me in contact with many wonderful language teaching professionals who were interested in MI and gave me useful feedback on applying the theory in the L2 classroom.

I must also thank Howard Gardner, the father of MI theory, for putting the theory "out there" and for giving educators the freedom to apply it and use it in the classroom as we see fit.

To Alta Book Center Publishers, Aarón Berman, Simón Almendares, and Jamie Cross, and my editor, Cherie Lenz-Hackett, I thank you for your patience and willingness to adjust schedules and personal lives to accommodate this project. To my longtime personal and professional friend, Sharron K. Bassano, I thank you for the wonderful teacher art throughout the book. It fits to perfection! To my partner, Adrian Palmer, and my son, Cameron Christison, I thank you for your understanding, enthusiasm, and support of my many projects. Without this support, feedback, and the ongoing technical assistance you have given me, this project would never have come to fruition.

MARY ANN CHRISTISON
UNIVERSITY OF UTAH

Introduction

An Introduction to Multiple Intelligences Theory

Views on Intelligence

How intelligence is defined within any society has a profound effect on the individuals in that society. It affects social status, educational opportunities, and career choices. Even though great importance is attached to the concept of intelligence, most people are unable to define exactly what intelligence is. There is no objective, agreed-upon referent either among the general public or contemporary psychologists.

The Traditional View

It is quite common for people to accept a definition of intelligence that is synonymous with a score on the traditional intelligence test—a test originally designed by Binet and Simon (1905) at the beginning of the twentieth century to predict which youngsters in Parisian primary grades would succeed and which would fail. The test that Binet and Simon designed later became known as the IQ (intelligence quotient) test and has enjoyed great success the world over. This view of intelligence is known as the traditional psychometric view of intelligence. Intelligence is defined operationally; in other words, intelligence is equal to the ability to answer certain test items correctly. Theoretically, how accurately one responds to test items is related to some underlying ability known as intelligence. This traditional psychometric view of intelligence is supported by statistical techniques that compare the responses of different subjects who are of different ages on these intelligence tests. The idea is that intelligence is a single, static construct, an innate attribute that doesn't change with age, training, or experience. We are born with a certain amount of intelligence that will not change as a result of our life experiences.

The general public seems to have adopted this traditional psychometric view of intelligence. For many people, intelligence is something that an intelligence test measures (Kail and Peregrino 1985). A good example of public acceptance of this theory is Marilyn Vos Savant, the individual with the world's highest recorded score on the IQ test. She is often referred to as the most intelligent person in the world and, as such, writes a weekly syndicated column for Parade magazine in the United States called, "Ask Marilyn" (Vos Savant 1995). Many people read her column and stand in awe of the logical and precise answers she offers to difficult questions. Whatever intelligence means, Vos Savant is regarded as having a lot of it (see www.marilynvossavant.com).

Developmental and Information Processing Views

Not all cognitive psychologists agree on this psychometric definition of intelligence. One of the problems with the traditional IQ test is that even though the IQ test predicts school performance with considerable accuracy, it is only an indifferent predictor of performance and success in a profession after formal schooling (Jencks 1977). This is one factor that has led some cognitive psychologists to put forth different psychological perspectives on intelligence. For example, within modern psychology, the term "intelligence" is often defined in two additional ways. The first way is to use intelligence to refer to intelligent acts, such as writing a book or designing a new computer program. This is the developmental view of intelligence (Piaget 1970). The second way is to use intelligence to refer to mental processes that give rise to intelligent acts, such as the mental abilities that underlie these acts (e.g., analyzing and synthesizing information). This is the information processing view of intelligence. At one extreme, there is the proposal that each intelligent act is associated with a unique mental process. The other extreme proposes that a single mental ability underlies all intelligent achievements (Kail and Peregrino 1985). One view says that, for example, Mozart was born with a specific talent to write his music. Writing music is an intelligent act, and Mozart was born with this intelligence. The other extreme says that Mozart's music was an accident of time and place. In other words, Mozart was in the right place at the right time to develop the unique mental processes he needed to write his music. Another person could have written what Mozart wrote. Both views are very attractive (Gardner 1993).

Other Views

In the past two decades, researchers in the cognitive and neural sciences have proposed different views of intelligence and have offered support for a pluralistic view of cognition, suggesting that the mind is organized into relatively discrete realms of functioning (Ceci 1990, Feldman 1980, Fodor 1983, Gardner 1985, and Sternberg 1984, 1985). Howard Gardner's theory of multiple intelligences (hereafter known as MI theory) is the best-known example among educators of this pluralistic view of the human mind. Howard Gardner's MI theory pluralizes the traditional concept of intelligence by defining intelligence as " . . . the ability to solve problems or fashion products that are of consequence in a particular cultural setting or community" (Gardner 1993, 15). The problem to be solved could be a computer error, deciding what move to make next in a game of Monopoly, or figuring out how to plant a garden or saddle a horse. Humans have a biological proclivity to solve problems, so MI theory is framed in light of the biological origins of the specific skills related to each problem being solved. According to Gardner, intelligence is not just a single construct applied in the same way to each task or problem. Rather, intelligence is made up of component pieces. For example, a person may be very good at playing chess and may have mastered all of the skills necessary to succeed in playing the game, but this person may not be very good at playing a Mozart sonata on the piano. Gardner's theory has been popular with educators because it accounts for the different ways in which humans can be intelligent. MI theory has helped educators by providing a useful framework for talking about the differences we see among the students we teach.

A Personal Perspective

My interest in the theory of multiple intelligences and its application to the second and foreign language classroom began in the early 1990s. Since my first year of teaching in 1970, I have been troubled greatly by the traditional concept of intelligence as a single, static construct. It didn't seem to make sense when I applied it to my own life and the lives of my students. My students demonstrated so many different individual strengths and skills; they were constantly changing, learning, and growing. I remember during the first year of teaching when I would sit in the faculty room at lunchtime and listen to my colleagues talk about the students we shared. I was so surprised to find out that my best student in Spanish and English was failing math. Another student was struggling in my courses, but was an extremely talented musician. If someone had asked me to select the most intelligent student in my classes, I could not have done so. My experiences as an educator taught me that intelligence was not just one form of cognition that cut across all human thinking. Rather, there were quite possibly different intelligences. It took me almost 20 years to find the theory that supported these beliefs and my own experiences.

Gardner's theory (1983) proposes different and autonomous intelligence capacities that result in many different ways of knowing, understanding, and learning about our world. As an L2 educator, it has been important for me to get away from defining intelligence in terms of tests and correlations among tests and begin to look more seriously at how my students from around the world develop skills important to their lives. As Gardner states:

> It is of the utmost importance that we recognize and nurture all of the varied human intelligences, and all of the combinations of intelligences. We are all so different largely because we all have different combinations of intelligences. If we recognize this, I think we will have at least a better chance of dealing appropriately with the many problems we face in the world. (Gardner 1993, 15)

Gardner's MI theory proposes an alternative definition of intelligence based on a radically different view of the mind. He proposes ". . . a pluralistic view of the mind, recognizing many different and discrete facets of cognition and acknowledging that people have different cognitive strengths and contrasting cognitive styles (Gardner 1993, 6). This view of intelligence states that some finite set of mental processes gives rise to a full range of intelligent human activities. This intelligence is most completely realized in the process of solving problems and fashioning products in real-life situations.

The problem-solving skill allows one to approach a situation in which a goal is to be obtained and to locate the appropriate route to that goal. The creation of a cultural product is as crucial to such functions as capturing and transmitting knowledge or expressing one's view or feelings. The problems to be solved range from creating an end for a story to anticipating a mating move in chess to repairing a quilt. Products range from scientific theories to musical compositions to successful political campaigns. (Gardner 1993, 15)

The Theory of Multiple Intelligences

Intelligences Defined

There is frequently confusion among educators about the relationship between learning styles and multiple intelligences. Many teachers all over the world have asked me if the concepts were one and the same. They are not. I believe that the confusion has resulted because as L2 educators, the learning styles that we are most familiar with are the perceptual learning styles, such as visual and kinesthetic. We use similar terms to talk about some of the intelligences such as visual/spatial and bodily/kinesthetic. There is bound to be confusion. Let me offer a short example that might be helpful in sorting out these two concepts—multiple intelligences and perceptual learning styles. Let's say there are two people who want to develop their musical intelligence. Musical intelligence is basic to all people even though it may be manifested in different ways. The first person goes to the music store and buys several of his favorite CDs. He takes them home, listens to them, and then tries to play what he hears. The second person goes to the music store and buys sheet music. She takes the selections home, reads the written music, and then sits down to play. Both of these individuals are working to develop their musical intelligence, but they are doing it in different ways. The preferred learning style for accessing music for the first person is auditory; the preferred learning style for accessing music for the second person is visual. A preferred learning style may vary from task to task.

When considering multiple intelligences and learning styles, it is also important to remember that there are many different ways to talk about learning styles. Perceptual learning styles form only one piece of the puzzle. There are other learning styles that describe how people prefer to process and perceive information (Christison 1998). Some people are impulsive learners. They like to process information quickly and take action to solve problems almost immediately. Other people are reflective learners. They like to take their time in processing information and prefer to wait and consider options before making decisions. There are also field independent and field dependent learners. The distinction between these two styles of learning and processing information is concerned with whether you see the forest first or the trees. Do you like to have the big picture first and then fill in the details, or do you prefer to work with the details first and then get the big picture? (For a more complete overview of learning styles, see Christison 1998 and Reid 1997.)

MI theory is framed in the light of biological origins. In order to arrive at the list of eight intelligences, Gardner gathered evidence from many different sources:

> . . . we consulted evidence from several different sources: knowledge about normal development and development in gifted individuals; information about the breakdown of cognitive skills under conditions of brain damage; studies of exceptional populations, including prodigies, idiot savants, and autistic children; data about the evolution of cognition over the millennia; cross-cultural accounts of cognition; psychometric studies, including examinations of correlations among tests; and psychological training studies, particularly measures of transfer and generalization across tasks. (Gardner 1993, 16)

Gardner identified eight basic criteria that must be considered for an official intelligence. He wanted to make a clear distinction between an intelligence with biological origins and a talent or skill. He was being purposely provocative in his choice of words.

The Eight Theoretical Bases

1 BRAIN DAMAGE STUDIES. When people suffer brain damage as a result of an injury, one intelligence is often damaged. For example, if a person has damage to Broca's area (the left frontal lobe), linguistic intelligence may be impaired. The individual could have trouble reading, writing, or speaking; yet, the person might still be able to do math, dance, play the piano, etc. Gardner is actually proposing the existence of eight autonomous brain systems. His premise is that as long as a person can lose ability in one area while others are spared, there cannot simply be a single intelligence.

2 EXCEPTIONAL INDIVIDUALS. In some people, we can see intelligences operating at high levels. Some individuals can calculate multi-digit numbers in their heads or can play a musical composition after hearing it only once. Savants are people who demonstrate amazing abilities in one intelligence while other intelligences are very low.

3 DEVELOPMENTAL HISTORY. Each intelligence has its own developmental history—its time of arising in childhood, its time of peaking during one's lifetime, and its time of gradual decline. Musical intelligence, for example, peaks early, but linguistic intelligence often peaks very late.

4 EVOLUTIONARY HISTORY. Each intelligence has roots in the evolutionary history of human beings. For example, archaeological evidence supports the presence of early musical instruments—evidence of musical intelligence. The cave drawings of Lascaux are good examples of visual/spatial intelligence.

5 PSYCHOMETRIC FINDINGS. We can look at many existing standardized tests for support of the theory of multiple intelligences. The Weschsler Intelligence Scale for Children includes sub-tests that focus on several of the different intelligences.

6 PSYCHOLOGICAL TASKS. We can look at psychological studies and witness intelligences working separately. For example, subjects may master a specific skill, such as an arithmetic problem, but may still not be able to read well. Also, individuals may have a superior memory for words but not for faces, hereby indicating that these tasks seem to be independent of each other.

7 CORE OPERATIONS. Each intelligence has a set of core operations. For example, with musical intelligence, a person needs to be able to discriminate between rhythmic structures and be sensitive to pitch. For bodily/kinesthetic intelligence, a person would need to be able to imitate movements by others.

8 SYMBOL SYSTEM. Intelligences are susceptible to being encoded. For example, there are spoken and written languages, graphic languages, computer languages, musical notation systems, ideographic languages, and dance notation systems.

Gardner (1983) states that " . . . it must be admitted that the selection (or rejection) of a candidate's intelligence is reminiscent more of an artistic judgment than of a scientific assessment." Only those intelligences that have satisfied all or a majority of the criteria mentioned above have been selected as bonafide intelligences.

The Eight Intelligences

Having sketched out the criteria for an intelligence, Gardner identified seven original intelligences and has since added an eighth. The list is not meant to be final or exhaustive. The point is not the exact number of intelligences, but simply the plurality of the intellect. Each person has raw biological potential. We differ in the particular intelligence profiles with which we are born and the ways in which we develop them. Weinreich-Haste (1985) claims that many people are surprised at some of the intelligence categories that Gardner has selected because they never think of the areas of bodily/kinesthetic, interpersonal, or intrapersonal, for example, as being related to "intelligence." They think of the categories more as talents or aptitudes.

1 LINGUISTIC INTELLIGENCE: the ability to use words effectively both orally and in writing. This intelligence includes such skills as the ability to remember information, to convince others to help you, and to talk about language itself. All of the activities in this book help students develop linguistic intelligence by creating a rich print environment—things to look at and write about—and by providing many opportunities for interaction—among students and between the teacher and the students. When students read, write, talk to each other, and communicate their ideas in any form, they are developing their linguistic intelligence.

2 LOGICAL/MATHEMATICAL INTELLIGENCE: the ability to use numbers effectively and reason well. It includes such skills as understanding the basic properties of numbers, developing the ability to analyze data, understanding the principle of cause and effect, and being able to use simple machines. You can help students develop logical/mathematical intelligence by providing manipulatives for experimentation with numbers and using simple machines or computer programs to help students think about cause and effect. When students are asked to analyze a problem and work with numbers, they are developing their logical/mathematical intelligence.

3 VISUAL/SPATIAL INTELLIGENCE: the ability to have sensitivity to form, space, color, line, and shape. It includes the ability to graphically represent visual or spatial ideas. You can help students develop visual/spatial intelligence by providing opportunities for visual mapping activities and encouraging students to vary the arrangements of materials in space, for example, by creating charts and bulletin boards. When students draw a picture and label it, talk about an art piece, imagine a scene and then write about it, or read a map, they are developing their visual/spatial intelligence.

4 BODILY/KINESTHETIC INTELLIGENCE: the ability to use the body to express ideas and feelings, and to solve problems. This includes such physical skills as coordination, flexibility, speed, and balance. You can help your students develop their bodily/kinesthetic intelligence by providing opportunities for physical challenges during the second/foreign language lesson, such as conducting an experiment, acting out an idea, performing a dance, or participating in a role-play.

5 **INTERPERSONAL INTELLIGENCE:** the ability to understand another person's moods, feelings, motivations, and intentions. This includes such skills as responding effectively to other people in some pragmatic way, such as getting students or colleagues to participate in a project. As a second language educator, you can help students develop interpersonal intelligence through activities that require them to work with others to solve problems and resolve conflict, teach each other new skills, and learn how to encourage other members of a group or team.

6 **INTRAPERSONAL INTELLIGENCE:** the ability to understand yourself, your strengths, weaknesses, moods, desires, and intentions. This includes such skills as understanding how you are similar to or different from others; reminding yourself to do something; knowing about yourself as a language learner; and knowing how to handle your feelings, such as what to do and how to behave when you are angry or sad. You can help students develop intrapersonal intelligence by giving them opportunities to express their own preferences, reflect on how they participated in an activity, set goals for their own learning, and help them evaluate their own styles of learning.

The two personal intelligences have been referred to collectively as "emotional intelligence" (Salovey and Mayer 1990; Goleman 1995, 1998). Emotional intelligence (EQ) includes features of both intrapersonal and interpersonal intelligence, such as self-awareness, impulse control, persistence, zeal, self-motivation, empathy, and social deftness. Goleman (1995) believes that these are qualities that mark people who excel in real life. These qualities are also the hallmarks of character and self-discipline. We must develop these basic human capacities if society is to survive. Goleman's belief is that lack of emotional intelligence can sabotage the intellect and ruin careers, taking the greatest toll on children. Risks to children include depression, eating disorders, aggressiveness, and violent crime.

7 **MUSICAL INTELLIGENCE:** the ability to have sensitivity to rhythm and pitch. Musical intelligence includes such skills as the ability to recognize simple songs and the ability to vary speed, tempo, and rhythm in simple melodies. You can help students develop musical intelligence by using cassette or CD players for listening, singing along, and learning new songs. When students relax to music and beat out a rhythm to a favorite tune, they are developing their musical intelligence.

8 **NATURALIST INTELLIGENCE:** the ability to find patterns and recognize and classify plants, minerals, and animals, including rocks and all varieties of flora and fauna. It is also the ability to recognize cultural artifacts like cars or sneakers. You can help your students develop their naturalist intelligence by focusing their attention on the world outside the classroom. When students work to identify parts of real plants or participate in field trips to learn about different trees or animals, they are developing their naturalist intelligence. The Naturalist Intelligence was the last intelligence added by Gardner.

Other Intelligences

In his book, *Intelligence Reframed* (1999), Gardner states that he is repeatedly asked about adding other intelligences to his list of eight. People have asked if there is a cooking intelligence, a sexual intelligence, an intelligence for humor, a spiritual intelligence, a moral intelligence, an existential intelligence, and an intelligence for creativity. So far, Gardner has added none of these proposed intelligences. However, the existential intelligence is currently a candidate intelligence. The strength of the evidence for this intelligence varies. The existential intelligence " . . . scores reasonably well on the eight criteria . . . . Although empirical psychological evidence is sparse, what exists certainly does not invalidate the construct." (Gardner 1999, 64) Gardner has also gone so far as to speculate on the core ability for this intelligence and provide a preliminary definition.

As far as a core ability, Gardner writes that it is an ability to " . . . locate oneself with respect to the farthest reaches of the cosmos, the infinite no less than the infinitesimal, and the related capacity to locate oneself with respect to the most existential features of the human condition, the significance of life, the meaning of death, the ultimate fate of the physical and the psychological worlds, and such profound experiences as love of another human being or total immersion in a work of art." This capacity has been valued in every known human culture. Gardner also offers a preliminary definition of the existential intelligence: Individuals who exhibit the proclivity to pose and ponder questions about life, death, and ultimate realities. Yet, Gardner does not add existential to the list at this time. He does find the proposed intelligence perplexing. He believes that the " . . . distance away from other intelligences is vast enough to dictate prudence" (64).

Implications of MI Theory for Second Language Education

MI Theory Among Educators

The theory of multiple intelligences was developed first as an account of human cognition that could be subjected to empirical tests (Gardner 1993, 27). When Gardner wrote *Frames of Mind* in 1983, he believed that his work would be of interest chiefly to persons trained in his discipline of developmental psychology. In truth, *Frames of Mind* did not arouse much interest within the discipline of developmental psychology; most developmental psychologists ignored it. The reception among educators, however, was quite different. Gardner writes:

> Some months after the publication of *Frames*, I was invited to address the annual meeting of the National Association of Independent Schools, the umbrella organization for American private or "independent" schools. I expected the typical audience of fifty to seventy-five persons, a customary talk of fifty minutes followed by a small number of easily anticipated questions. Instead, arriving at the auditorium a few minutes early, I encountered a new experience: a much larger hall, entirely filled with people, and humming with excitement. It was almost as if I had walked by mistake into a talk given by someone who was famous. But the audience had, in fact, come to hear me: it listened attentively, and grew steadily in size until it spilled out into the hallways on both sides of the room. The talk was very well received; thought-provoking questions poured forth, and after the session had concluded, I was ringed by interested headmasters, teachers, trustees, and journalists who wanted to hear more and were reluctant to allow me to slip back in anonymity. (1993, xiii)

Key Points for Educators

The theory of multiple intelligences seems to harbor a number of educational implications that are worthy of consideration. Armstrong (1994) has synthesized these ideas into four key points that educators find attractive about the theory:

1 EACH PERSON POSSESSES ALL EIGHT INTELLIGENCES. In each person the eight intelligences function together in unique ways. Some people have high levels of functioning in all or most of the intelligences; a few people lack most of the rudimentary aspects of intelligence. Most people are somewhere in the middle—with a few intelligences highly developed, most modestly developed, and one or two underdeveloped.

2 INTELLIGENCES CAN BE DEVELOPED. In the traditional view, intelligence is defined as an attribute that doesn't change with age, training, or experience. Traditional views of intelligence support the notion that we are born with a certain amount of intelligence and that intelligence will not change as a result of life experiences. MI theory, on the other hand, suggests that humans have the capacity to develop all eight intelligences to a reasonably high level of performance with appropriate encouragement, enrichment, and instruction.

3 INTELLIGENCES WORK TOGETHER IN COMPLEX WAYS. No intelligence really exists by itself. Intelligences are always interacting with each other. For example, in order to cook a meal, one must read a recipe (linguistic), perhaps double it (logical/mathematical), and prepare a menu that satisfies others you may cook for (interpersonal) and yourself (intrapersonal).

4 THERE ARE MANY DIFFERENT WAYS TO BE INTELLIGENT. There is no set standard of attributes that one must have in order to be considered intelligent. I remember a friend in high school who was completely awkward in dance class and yet a marvel in building construction. Both activities required bodily/kinesthetic intelligence.

It is important to remember that Howard Gardner was not designing a curriculum or preparing a model to be used in schools with his multiple intelligences theory (Hoerr 1997). Educators have taken the theory, put it together in different ways, and applied it to their lesson planning and program and curriculum development. The theory provides a framework within which teachers can use their imaginations and creativity in designing materials for the second language classroom. The four key points given here are all attractive to the second language teaching profession because they provide a framework to appreciate and value the diversity we observe in our students, and they provide us with a structure for addressing these differences in our teaching.

Applying MI Theory in the Second Language Classroom

Steps to Follow

Overall, there are few theories that have been embraced more enthusiastically by second language teachers in the past few years than MI theory. We have seen more papers being written on the topic (for example, Reid 1997 and Christison 1998) and more workshops and papers being offered at conferences (see TESOL Convention Programs 1997–2004). As second language educators, we want information and resources about the theory; we want to know how to apply the theory in the classroom. MI theory offers second language teachers a way to examine their best teaching techniques and strategies in light of human differences. There are several important steps to follow in applying the theory in your own classrooms.

1 **INTRODUCE YOURSELF TO THE BASIC THEORY.** If you are reading this introduction now, you are taking the first step in applying MI theory to your classroom. Once you have read through the basics, see if you understand them well enough to answer the simple and straightforward questions below. If you are working alone, you might use the questions to check your understanding. If you are able to work with other teachers, discuss the questions with them. If you are a teacher educator, you might use the questions in a "mix and mingle" activity with your students. Each student gets one of the ten questions and talks to five other people. After asking and answering a question with the first person, the partners switch questions and find other partners. So each time a teacher asks a question, he/she has a new question and a new partner!

Basic MI Theory Questions

List the eight intelligences and explain how each one is used.

Why are there only eight intelligences?

What are the theoretical bases that Gardner uses to determine an intelligence?

According to Gardner, what's the difference between a talent and an intelligence?

Why do you think MI theory has been popular with educators?

What are Armstrong's key points concerning MI theory for educators?

What is the traditional psychometric view of intelligence?

What is the developmental view of intelligence? The information processing view?

What is meant by the phrase "pluralistic view of the mind?"

What is Gardner's definition of intelligence? Do you agree with the definition? Disagree?

If you are a second language teacher educator hoping to make MI theory part of your teacher education curriculum, you have a challenge (Marzano, et al. 1988). Second language teacher educators are responsible for creating curricula for the programs that provide prospective second language teachers with a foundation for what they should know as professional language teachers. Much of what is traditionally included in second language teacher education programs (TESL/TEFL) is based on academic tradition. Because second language teachers are expected to know about methods, testing, L2 theory, as well as the teaching of grammar, reading, speaking, and listening, most teacher education programs include courses in all of these subject areas. Teacher education programs are also expected to keep current by introducing teachers to the newest and most creative ideas in second language pedagogy. When new concepts and ideas are embraced by the profession, second language teacher education programs are challenged with the notion of how to integrate them into the already existing program. When I am working with pre-service teachers (i.e., those teachers who are working to get their degree) or in-service teachers (i.e., those teachers who have a degree or certification and want to get a specialization or endorsement in teaching English as a second language or another language), I have had great success using a simple, interesting, and unique introductory MI theory activity. It has been my experience that before I can start talking about the details of MI theory, I need to capture the students' attention and interest. I have had success with an adaptation of the familiar second language teaching activity entitled "Find Someone Who . . . " (see activity 1.1).

The statements listed in the "Find Someone Who . . . " activity each represent one of the eight intelligences. In-service or pre-service teachers follow the directions and obtain the necessary signatures. Once all signatures have been obtained, the follow-up discussion should focus on the different intelligences needed to complete the activity (i.e., "likes to dance"—bodily/kinesthetic, "will sing part of a favorite song"—musical). With a little imagination and creativity, teachers and teacher educators will find many possibilities for introducing MI to their L2 students.

Armstrong (1994) suggests two activities to use when teaching students (in this case, L2 students) about MI theory. He offers a version of "Find Someone Who . . . " called "The Human Intelligence Hunt." Armstrong's list includes seven actions—one for each of the original intelligences. The student who signs the paper must actually perform the action to the other student's satisfaction. This version works well with ESL/EFL students. Armstrong also suggests the "Multiple Intelligence Pizza" for young children. The instructor draws a circle on the board and divides it into eight pieces. The instructor then asks the students to tell him/her the different ways in which a person can be smart (i.e., music smart, word smart, body smart, number smart, nature smart, etc.). Finally, students are asked to choose the different ways in which they are smart and write down the things they do to demonstrate the particular intelligences chosen. Showing L2 teachers how to introduce MI theory to their students is an important part of this first step.

2 **TAKE AN MI INVENTORY.** Armstrong (1994) believes that before teachers apply a model of learning to the classroom, they should apply it to themselves as educators. Therefore, the next step in applying MI theory to the classroom is for teachers to determine their own multiple intelligences profile. The "Multiple Intelligences Inventory" for prospective second language teachers appears in the appendices. Other inventories such as the "Teele Inventory of Multiple Intelligences" are also very useful (Teele 1992). I encourage L2 teachers and prospective teachers to complete an inventory and share the results with each other.

Inventories can also be used with L2 students. There are inventories for language students in the appendices. Choose the MI inventory that is the most appropriate for your students. If none of the inventories included in the appendices at the end of this book seems to work with your situation, you can create your own. Once you have introduced your students to the idea that they can be smart in many different ways and have presented Gardner's eight intelligences, ask students to write down three different ways in which they focus on each intelligence in their daily lives. Then collect the responses and create your own inventory, making certain that none of the items are repeated and that each intelligence has the same number of items. When you use this technique, you make certain that the inventory is personal and directly related to the lives of your students.

Once you learn more about your own multiple intelligences profile, you will become more confident in the choices you make that affect your teaching. The purpose of taking an MI inventory is to connect your life experiences to the ideas presented in MI theory. Inventories are not intelligence tests. Scoring high on an inventory merely gives you a sense of how much you are focusing on this intelligence in your daily life. The types of learning activities you select for your classes are often directly related to your experiences in the real world.

The choices you make as a teacher for your classroom can affect the MI profiles of the students in your classes. The same rule of thumb applies to teacher educators. You will choose classroom activities that complement your own MI profile. There is nothing inherently wrong with choosing classroom activities to complement your own MI profile, but it is important to understand that the choices you make as a teacher educator determine how you present information to prospective teachers. This, in turn, can affect their MI profiles and ultimately the MI profiles of the students they teach. The key for language teachers and teacher educators is to make informed choices. Both language students and language teachers benefit from instructional approaches that help them reflect on their own learning.

3 **LEARN TO CATEGORIZE FAMILIAR LANGUAGE ACTIVITIES.** In order to begin lesson planning, it is important for you to be able to identify the activities you normally use in your lessons as they relate to the different intelligences. This is another step in making informed choices. There are a number of ways in which you might identify activities. Campbell (1997) suggests creating menus (a linguistic menu, logical/mathematical menu, musical menu, etc.). When I first began working with MI, I found this suggestion very useful. I looked back at my old lesson plans and made a list of the different activities that I used in these lessons (see activity 1.2). After I had a list of commonly used activities, I used the list and the MI Menu Chart (see activity 1.2) and put the activities in the appropriate spaces.

If you are an L2 teacher educator, you can take this activity one step further and use the information as a mix and mingle activity. Write the activities you generated from your own practice on separate strips of paper. Tape the intelligence menus on the walls around the room (e.g., linguistic intelligence, logical/mathematical intelligence, spatial/visual intelligence). Then give teachers the strips of paper and ask them to decide under which menu the strips belong. Once all the activities have been placed under the intelligence menus, conduct a large group discussion. Many of the activities support more than one intelligence, so you should expect a healthy discussion. While all activities for the second language classroom will support the linguistic intelligence, the activities will develop other intelligences as well. For each activity type being used, it is important to get an overall MI activity profile. For example, consider the "Find Someone Who . . ." activity previously explained. This activity clearly helps students develop their linguistic intelligence, but it also develops interpersonal, intrapersonal, and bodily/kinesthetic intelligences. The MI activity profile for "Find Someone Who . . ." is linguistic, bodily/kinesthetic, interpersonal, and intrapersonal. When planning curricula, it will be important to recognize the chief intelligence being focused on as well as the other intelligences being developed.

4 **CONDUCT A PERSONAL AUDIT OF YOUR OWN TEACHING.** I have found this activity very helpful in applying MI theory in my own classroom and use these same techniques in my teacher education courses and workshops. The activity is reflective in nature and requires that teachers look at the activities they include in their lessons over a given period of time, say one week. The activities are then categorized according to the different intelligences, using activity 1.3. Other intelligences are also noted.

When I reviewed the results from one of my own classes, I was surprised. During the two-week period that I tracked, I did not use any activities in my classes that helped students develop their logical/mathematical intelligence or their musical intelligence; whereas, the other intelligences were equally represented. There were two things I could have done with this information. I could have simply considered it interesting and taken no action to change, or I could have used the information to explore ways of introducing these different intelligences in my lessons. I made a decision to do the latter and tried to think of ways to include these two intelligences in my language teaching.

In order to include opportunities for students to develop their musical intelligence, I taught my students the tunes and words to two very simple folk songs, "Skip to My Lou" and "Down in the Valley." They enjoyed singing these songs, and I managed to accompany them on the guitar. In a later lesson, I asked students to work in groups, take the information from the chapter, write a simple verse, and put the words to one of the tunes that I had previously taught them. The students continued to enjoy the activity. Most of the student groups performed the new songs for the entire class. They also commented to me later that the technique made it easy to remember the content of the chapter. Trying this new activity was a big risk for me. However, when I saw how much my students learned from each other, how much they were interacting and using English, how much they seemed to enjoy it, and how successful they felt about the activity, I was glad that I had taken the risk.

The above anecdote is an excellent example of how MI theory influenced language teaching and learning in my classroom. My decisions about activities as they relate to MI theory were made by choice and not by accident. This is perhaps the most important point I try to get across to the teachers in my own pre-service and in-service courses. If you are working through this material by yourself, it is also an important point to remember.

5 **DEVELOP ASSESSMENT TECHNIQUES THAT ADDRESS THE EIGHT INTELLIGENCES.** Another important component of applying MI theory in the second language classroom is assessment. Not only should you be concerned with integrating MI into your lesson plans, you should also be concerned with the assessment techniques you employ. The two paradigms—teaching and assessment—must evolve if you want to make any significant changes in your curriculum and in the ways in which your students learn and respond to your classes (Lazear 1994). There are a number of assessment challenges that a MI curriculum brings to the forefront.

First, an MI curriculum supports the idea that each student is unique and that instruction and assessment must be varied. It also supports a variety of assessment instruments so that we can get a more complete, accurate, and fair picture of what students know. In an MI curriculum, the lines between instruction and assessment are always blurred because assessment is occurring in and through the curriculum and daily instruction. For example, you are familiar with the concept of giving short, pen-and-paper quizzes as self-tests. If you are a classroom teacher, quizzes are designed to help students reflect on the material and concepts. If you are a teacher educator, you can use the same technique with the teachers with whom you work. Not all "quizzes" have to be of the pen-and-paper variety. Instead of using the traditional method, you might use the same information to create a "Find Your Partner" activity (see activity 1.4).

The left-hand side of the chart in activity 1.4 contains some sample questions that you might give after the first introductory lesson on MI theory. Rather than simply handing out the questions and having the students or teachers answer them, give half of the class the questions and half of the class the answers. Then ask them to find their partners. By changing the focus of the assessment component, you integrate assessment with instruction and expand on the number of intelligences that are being developed through assessment. Pen-and-paper assessment techniques work to develop the linguistic intelligence; the "Find Your Partner" version adds the bodily/kinesthetic intelligence as well as the interpersonal intelligence.

Secondly, an MI curriculum for either language education or teacher education should teach students or teachers how to learn, how to think, and how to be intelligent in as many different ways as possible. In developing assessment practices consistent with an MI curriculum, teachers face an enormous challenge. In many language programs, students are given standardized tests. This is true even in progressive settings. The basic premise of MI theory suggests that not all learning of content can be measured in a standardized way. In pursuing a new MI assessment paradigm, teachers must explore multi-modal testing practices based on the eight intelligences—not just the verbal/linguistic and logical/mathematical practices that dominate educational assessment.

I remember several years ago when two distraught students came to my office. They were students in a content-based ESL course that I was teaching on American culture and history. Both students had done poorly on the traditional pen-and-paper test that I had given in class. Their complaint was that they had studied hard for the test and believed they knew most of the information in the chapter; yet, the test had not given them a chance to demonstrate what they knew.

Because I had made such an effort to revise my course curriculum and because these students had done well in class activities and in small group discussions, I decided to regard what they were saying as true and find out what they wanted me to do. I said that I was interested in their perspective and would like them to put themselves in my shoes. Specifically, what would they like to do to show me that they knew and understood the content of the chapter? They agreed to think about the task and return the following day.

When they came back to my office the following day, they told me what they wanted to do. Since they were both musicians, they asked if they could write a song about the content of the chapter, perform the song, and teach the chorus to the other students in the class. The chapter had been about early European explorers in North America, so I felt that the content would lend itself well to this particular task. I gave them three days to complete the assignment and told them that the song had to be memorized. In three days, the students came to class with their guitars and performed the song for their classmates.

I must admit that I had expected a short song with perhaps one or two verses and a chorus that would be repeated. The students, in fact, created nine different verses that covered the contributions of twelve early explorers and included a clever refrain. They had memorized all of the verses, and they taught the chorus to their classmates who were delighted to sing along with them. Needless to say, I was surprised and pleased. This experience was a turning point for me in how I view assessment. I now encourage my students to participate in the assessment process and I focus on giving them options.

Finally, an MI curriculum should recognize that students are at varying developmental stages and at varying levels of language acquisition, even in a curriculum where students are tested and placed. Assessment practices must be individualized and developmentally appropriate.

The definition of successful teaching in an MI curriculum is about helping students develop skills for "solving problems and fashioning products" in their real lives. It is about preparing students for experiences outside of the classroom. Are students assessed in ways that are consistent with what they will be expected to know and do in the wider world?

In Conclusion

I realize that no two teachers who read this chapter will use MI theory in exactly the same way. Some teacher educators will use MI theory as an entry point into lesson content. Others will attempt to engage all eight intelligences. There is no correct answer or road to follow. What is important is to understand how MI theory informs your own teaching. Once you understand this concept, you can consciously apply the theory to your lesson planning and curriculum development. There are no hard and fast rules. You certainly do not need to have every intelligence in every lesson. Much of how you decide to balance the intelligences in your curriculum will depend on the circumstances in which you teach. For example, are you working closely with other teachers or is the class that you teach part of an overall program?

It takes patience, time, imagination, and creativity to bring a new theory into your teaching. In the case of MI theory, I believe that the effort will be worth it!

Find Someone Who . . . 1.1

FOR L2 TEACHERS

DIRECTIONS

Find someone who can do each of the activities listed below. When you find someone who can do the activity, get him/her to sign your paper. A person can only sign your paper once.

Find someone who . . .

likes to write articles and have them published. _____

can tell if someone is singing off-key. _____

can calculate numbers easily in his/her head. _____

likes to read books with many pictures. _____

likes to dance. _____

likes doing puzzles and mazes. _____

regularly spends time meditating. _____

can list three things that help him/her learn. _____

can draw a picture of his/her favorite food. _____

has a good joke to tell. _____

will sing part of a favorite song. _____

sings in the shower. _____

can easily identify at least 10 different kinds of flowers. _____

finds it hard to sit for long periods of time. _____

frequently creates new activities and materials for his/her classes. _____

is often involved in social activities at night. _____

loves to teach people new skills. _____

1.2 MI Menus

FOR L2 TEACHERS

DIRECTIONS

Look at the activities below. Place each activity under one of the intelligences on the chart. When you have finished, share your worksheet with a partner or a small group. Be prepared to justify your decisions.

Example Activities

lecture	singing songs	storytelling	group singing
visualization	using a video clip from a movie	logic puzzles	folk dancing
using charts and maps	optical illusions	word mazes	goal setting
scientific demonstrations	peer teaching	role plays	mood music
small group discussions	independent learning stations	classroom publishing	strip stories
word games	group brainstorming	making collages	writing short essays
creative movement	*Jazz Chants*	using student-created art	"Find Someone Who…"
field trips	classroom "cooking"	problem-solving	
mime	personal journal keeping	memorization	

MI Menu Chart

Bodily/ Kinesthetic	Interpersonal	Intrapersonal	Linguistic	Logical/ Mathematical	Musical	Naturalist	Visual/ Spatial

Lesson Planning Using MI Theory 1.3

FOR L2 TEACHERS

DIRECTIONS

Make notations to remind yourself of how and when to use each intelligence in your lessons. You can use one chart for each day or one chart per week. At the end of the selected timeframe, check to see if you have focused on all of the eight different intelligences. What changes, if any, do you want to make in your teaching? Why? Why not?

The Intelligence	The person . . .	In what class did I use it?	What's the name of the activity?	Which other intelligences are used?	What did students do?
Bodily/kinesthetic	• is good at activities involving fine or gross motor skills				
Interpersonal	• is sensitive to others • interacts effectively with others				
Intrapersonal	• is sensitive to one's own feelings • uses self-knowledge				
Linguistic	• uses language and words in many different forms to express meaning				
Logical/ mathematical	• approaches problems logically • recognizes patterns easily • uses reasoning skills				
Musical	• is sensitive to sounds in the environment • is aware of patterns in rhythm, pitch, and timbre				
Naturalist	• is sensitive to the natural world • sees connections in the plant and animal kingdoms				
Visual/spatial	• is aware of the relationship between objects in space • perceives or draws the visual world accurately				

1.4 Find Your Partner

Multiple Intelligences and Language Learning © 2005 Alta Book Center Publishers, San Francisco, California
www.altaesl.com Permission granted to photocopy for one teacher's classroom use only.

FOR IN-SERVICE AND PRE-SERVICE TEACHERS

DIRECTIONS

Photocopy and cut the questions and answers into strips. Give each student or teacher a strip. Persons with questions must find their answers and vice versa without showing their answers to anyone.

Questions	Answers
What is the difference between a talent and an intelligence?	An intelligence meets most of the eight criteria that Gardner sets forth.
Which intelligence is sensitive to nonverbal sounds in the environment?	The Musical Intelligence
What is the eighth intelligence?	The Naturalist Intelligence
What is the purpose of an MI inventory?	To relate one's life experiences to the theory.
Who is the originator of MI theory?	Howard Gardner
People who can easily create mental images have a strong _____.	visual/spatial intelligence
People with a strong _____ like to spend time outdoors.	naturalist intelligence
Name one idea for developing the Intrapersonal Intelligence.	One idea is to ask students to set their own goals.
Which intelligence is adept at gross motor skills?	The Bodily/Kinesthetic Intelligence
Murals, maps, and flowcharts are examples of activities that develop _____.	visual/spatial intelligence
Jazz Chants promote _____.	musical intelligence
Name three of the intelligences.	Interpersonal, linguistic, and logical/mathematical

Linguistic Intelligence

"A word is dead when it is said, some say.
I say it just begins to live that day."
— Emily Dickinson (1830–1886)

The activities in this unit help students develop their linguistic intelligence by:

reading

writing short essays

answering questions

writing poems

telling stories and jokes

communicating ideas

enjoying word games

completing puzzles and mazes

2.1 Alphabet Question Book

Age Group
Grades 3 to 5

Language Level
Intermediate

INTELLIGENCES DEVELOPED	OBJECTIVES

Linguistic

Interpersonal

Logical/mathematical

Naturalist

Visual/spatial

To develop logical thinking skills

To foster creative expression

To help students develop an understanding of the world around them

To give students an opportunity to work together

Materials Needed
- Colored markers
- Stapler
- Plain white paper

This is an activity in which the entire class can partici-pate. The class will make a 26-page "Alphabet Question Book" together.

1 First make the cover for the book. Fold a plain white piece of paper in half and write "Alphabet Question Book" on the outside cover. Send the cover around the classroom, asking each student to write his/her name on either the front or back. Use colored markers. The cover should ultimately represent a collage of names.

2 Make the interior of the book by folding 13 pieces of paper in half. Put the cover (created in Step 1) on the outside and staple through the "spine" to form a small book.

3 On the first page write a large letter "A" across the top. On the next page write the letter "B." Continue with sub-sequent pages until all the letters of the alphabet have been used.

4 Ask students to think of questions to which they would like answers. These might be questions they have asked adults at some point and perhaps did not get answers.

5 Together the class needs to decide where the ques-tions should be written in the book based on the focus of the question. For example, the question, "Why do birds fly?" could go under the letter "B" because the focus is on "birds" or under "F" because it's a question about "flying."

6 Once it's been decided where the question should be written, the student who asked the question writes it under the appropriate letter in the book and circles the "focus" word (in the example above this would be either "bird" or "flying"). Use colored markers.

7 Throughout the week, students compose questions until each page (and therefore letter of the alphabet) has one. Once all letters have questions, the "Alphabet Book" is complete.

8 As a follow-up activity, students vol-unteer to find an answer to one of the questions in the "Alphabet Question Book" and make a short report to the class.

Antonym Crisscross 2.2

Age Group
Middle school to adult

Language Level
Beginning

INTELLIGENCES DEVELOPED	OBJECTIVES
Linguistic	To reinforce work with adjectives
Interpersonal	To develop logical thinking skills
Logical/mathematical	To foster creative expression
Visual/spatial	To give students an opportunity to work together

Materials Needed
- One sheet of plain white paper or graph paper for each student
- Board or flipchart

1 Divide students into pairs. On the board, write antonyms that students know and have been studying. For example, some common antonyms might be: *young/old, sweet/sour, big/small, close/far, hard/soft, difficult/easy, noisy/quiet, fast/slow, good/bad, ugly/pretty, black/white, on/off,* and *happy/sad.*

2 Make certain that students understand the meaning of the words that you have chosen.

3 On the board, demonstrate how to do an antonym crisscross. Write the word and crisscross it with its antonym. For example:

4 Give students 10 minutes to make as many antonym crisscrosses as they can.

5 Conduct a large group sharing in which students write their examples on the board.

19

2.3 Family Matters

Age Group Grade 5 to middle school	

Age Group
Grade 5 to middle school

Language Level
Intermediate to advanced

INTELLIGENCES DEVELOPED

Linguistic

Intrapersonal

Visual/spatial

OBJECTIVES

To help students understand and value their families

To give students an opportunity to evaluate what is important to them

Materials Needed
• Plain white paper
• Colored markers

1 Tell students that they are going to have a family party. The party includes all of the people they think of as their family—parents, aunts, uncles, sisters, brothers, close friends, and neighbors. Their job for the party is to create an original t-shirt with a family motto and symbol. The motto should be a short statement that best describes what their family represents to them. The logo should be a symbolic representation or picture of what their family represents to them. The logo design they create will be placed on the back and the motto on the front of a family t-shirt. Everyone at the family party will receive and wear a t-shirt.

2 Students write a motto and design a logo for the t-shirt.

3 Follow up with a large group sharing. Use the following question and statement to guide students: "What is your motto? Tell us two things about your logo."

Family Trees 2.4

INTELLIGENCES DEVELOPED	OBJECTIVES
Linguistic	To give students an opportunity to think about and appreciate their families
Interpersonal	To develop vocabulary for talking about families
Intrapersonal	To give students an opportunity to think about their own family structures
	To give students an opportunity to work together

Age Group
Grade 5 to middle school

Language Level
Beginning to intermediate

Materials Needed
- One copy of handout 2.4 for each student
- Board or flipchart

1 Conduct a discussion with students about their families. Help them brainstorm the vocabulary needed for talking about their families. Write a list of useful words on the board, such as *mother, father, sister, brother, aunt, uncle, cousin, grandma, grandpa, stepbrother (-sister, -mother, -father), relative, family, etc.*

2 Give each student a copy of handout 2.4. Have students research their family and complete the family tree as best they can.

3 Ask each student to choose a person on his/her family tree, find out something interesting about that person, and write a short paragraph or story.

4 Encourage students to show their family trees and share their stories with the entire class.

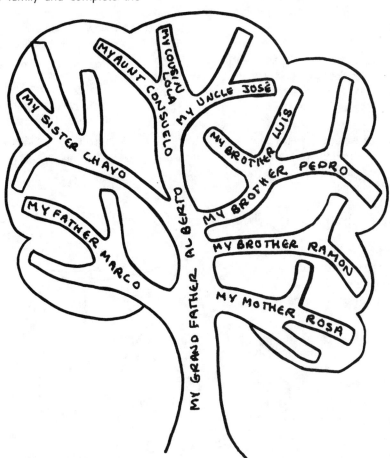

2.5 Fashion Show

Age Group
High school to adult

Language Level
Intermediate to advanced

INTELLIGENCES DEVELOPED	OBJECTIVES

Linguistic

Bodily/kinesthetic

Interpersonal

Intrapersonal

Logical/mathematical

Visual/spatial

To improve listening skills

To develop logical thinking skills

To give students an opportunity to think about what they want and like in clothing

To give students an opportunity to work together

Materials Needed
- Clothing catalogs
- Colored construction paper
- Glue
- Scissors
- Board or flipchart

1 Divide students into groups. Give each group a clothing catalog. Working together, students must find an "outfit" (a model wearing clothing) for each person in their group.

2 Once each student has an outfit, he/she should cut it out and glue it on a piece of colored construction paper.

3 On a separate piece of paper, each student then writes a description of their outfit in such a way that someone listening to the description could identify the outfit from its picture.

4 Assign each student a letter (A, B, C, etc.). Each student labels his/her outfit picture and description with the assigned letter. This will allow you to match the pictures and descriptions (i.e., the picture marked A is matched to its description that is also marked A). Walk around the room, making sure that this is done correctly.

5 Collect all of the pictures and descriptions. Tape 10 of the pictures on the board. Keep the matching descriptions in hand.

6 Ask each student to get out a new piece of paper and write numbers 1 through 10 on it. Read the descriptions as if you were a commentator in a fashion show. Ask students to listen to the descriptions and match them to the pictures on the board (i.e., if the first description you read describes outfit C, students write C next to the number 1 on their papers).

7 After you have gone through the first 10 pictures, select 10 more. Work through the process until all pictures and descriptions have been used.

8 Follow up with a large group sharing that focuses on some or all of the following questions:

Which outfit was your favorite?

Which was your least favorite?

Which outfit do you think would be the most expensive? The least expensive?

Which outfit would you most like to buy?

Which outfit do you think is the most fashionable?

Holiday Scramble 2.6

INTELLIGENCES DEVELOPED	OBJECTIVES	

Linguistic

Interpersonal

Visual/spatial

To familiarize students with some of the major holidays in the United States

To provide visual reinforcement of important words and concepts related to holidays and customs

To give students an opportunity to work together

Age Group
Middle school

Language Level
Intermediate

Materials Needed
- One copy of handouts 2.6A and 2.6B for each pair of students
- Answer key 2.6

1 Ask students to find a partner. Give each pair one copy of handouts 2.6A and 2.6B. Go over the directions verbally with students before they begin.

2 While students are working independently in their groups, walk around the classroom checking work and interacting one-on-one with students.

3 When all students have finished their work, do a large group checking and sharing of answers.

2.7 In a Word

Age Group
Grades 1 and 2

Language Level
Beginning

INTELLIGENCES DEVELOPED	OBJECTIVES
Linguistic	To reinforce language development through movement
Bodily/kinesthetic	To improve listening skills
Interpersonal	To introduce students to children's literature
Visual/spatial	To give students an opportunity to work together

Materials Needed
- A storybook that has word or phrase repetition
- Index cards or strips of paper
- Colored markers
- A basket (or some type of container to hold the index cards)
- Tape
- Board or flipchart

1 This activity works best with a small group of students (maximum 12). Before class, choose a storybook that students like. Stories that have repetition of key words and phrases work best.

2 Read the story several times aloud, encouraging student participation on the repeated sections. After the first couple of repetitions, students almost automatically join in.

3 From the story, select words that students know. Using colored markers, write these words on index cards or strips of paper.

Put the cards into a basket. Each student picks a card from the basket, points to letters in the word that he or she recognizes, reads the word (if possible), and tapes the word on the board. If a student cannot read the word, read the word and give it to the student to tape on the board. Words can be repeated. Students have a chance to work with the words, review the words on the board, and see how many they collectively recognize.

4 After students have had a chance to work with all of the words, read the story again. This time have each student listen for his or her word. When a student hears his/her word spoken, the student goes to the board and takes down the card with that word. At the end of the second reading, there should be no cards (words) left on the board.

5 This activity can be repeated many times with different books.

Interactive Writing 2.8

INTELLIGENCES DEVELOPED	OBJECTIVES
Linguistic	To develop written skills
Interpersonal	To foster creative expression
Logical/mathematical	To develop logical thinking skills
	To give students an opportunity to work together

Age Group
Middle school to adult

Language Level
Intermediate to advanced

Materials Needed
- One copy of handout 2.8 for each pair of students
- Scissors

1 Divide students into pairs. Give each pair a problem from handout 2.8.

2 Go over the directions orally to check understanding. Ask students to follow the directions carefully.

3 Give students ample time to respond to the prompts. Walk around as students are working on their dialogs, giving feedback and helping as needed.

4 Allow time for students to present their dialogs to the entire class.

Letter Writing 2.9

INTELLIGENCES DEVELOPED	OBJECTIVES
Linguistic	To improve letter writing skills
Interpersonal	To develop problem-solving skills
Logical/mathematical	To give students an opportunity to work together

Age Group
High school to adult

Language Level
Intermediate to advanced

Materials Needed
- One copy of handout 2.9 for each pair of students
- Scissors

1 Divide students into pairs. Give each pair an activity from handout 2.9. You may also create activities that are more relevant to your class content.

2 Provide students with a sample letter, showing them the format you wish them to follow.

3 Give students ample time to complete the assignment. Walk around as students are working, giving them feedback on content, grammar, and letter structure.

4 Follow up with a large group sharing, giving students a chance to read the letters they have written.

2.10 Memories

Age Group Middle school to adult	

INTELLIGENCES DEVELOPED	OBJECTIVES
Linguistic	To foster creative expression
Intrapersonal	To build self-awareness
Visual/spatial	To help students develop an understanding of the world around them

Age Group
Middle school to adult

Language Level
Intermediate to advanced

Materials Needed
- Meaningful pictures, photographs, or paintings (supplied by students)

1 Ask each student to bring a picture, photo, or painting of personal importance to class.

2 Give each student time to write a short piece about the picture, photo, or painting, explaining why it is important and why it has personal meaning. While students are working, walk around the room answering questions and interacting one-on-one.

3 After students have had time to finish their written work, conduct a large group sharing. Encourage students to volunteer to present orally and encourage other students to ask questions. Try to see that each student who presents is asked at least two questions.

2.11 Miles to Go

Age Group
Middle school to adult

Language Level
Intermediate to advanced

INTELLIGENCES DEVELOPED	OBJECTIVES
Linguistic	To develop skills in using timelines and graphs
Interpersonal	To develop basic mathematical skills
Logical/mathematical	To provide meaningful practice using language related to timelines, graphs, and charts
Visual/spatial	To give students an opportunity to work together

Materials Needed
- One copy of handouts 2.11A and 2.11B for each pair of students
- Answer key 2.11

1 Ask students to find a partner. Give each pair handouts 2.11A and 2.11B.

2 Have each pair read the directions, study the information on the flights chart, and answer the questions.

3 Conduct a large group sharing in which you check for correct answers. Ask students to explain how they arrived at their answers.

Missing Letters 2.12

INTELLIGENCES DEVELOPED	OBJECTIVES

Linguistic

Bodily/kinesthetic

Visual/spatial

To develop and improve literacy skills

To familiarize students with the letters of the alphabet

Age Group
Grades K and 1
Language Level
Beginning

Materials Needed
• Colored paper
• Scissors
• Colored markers

1 Before class, cut colored paper into one-inch strips. On some of the strips write the first names of the students in the class. On other strips write the names with some of the letters missing. Leave other strips completely blank.

2 Give each student the strip of colored paper with his/her name written on it. Ask students to stand up one at a time, say their names, and show their strips of paper.

3 Give each student the strip of colored paper displaying his/her name with letters missing. Ask students to look at the first strip, identify the missing letter(s) in the second strip, and write the missing letters in the blank spaces. Walk around the room as students work independently. Try to help students spell their names.

4 Once all students have finished with the task, ask for three or four volunteers to spell their names for the class and to identify which letters are missing. Stand close to the volunteering students so that you can help them with the spelling if needed.

5 Using the blank strips of colored paper, have all students write their first names and place them on a bulletin board or poster.

6 The activity can be extended over three or four class periods with several students volunteering to spell their names each day.

2.13 Numbered Words

Age Group
Grade 5 to middle school

Language Level
Intermediate

INTELLIGENCES DEVELOPED	OBJECTIVES
Linguistic	To develop new vocabulary
Interpersonal	To give students meaningful practice in counting and working with numbers
Logical/mathematical	To give students an opportunity to work together

Materials Needed
- Several copies of handout 2.13
- Scissors
- Colored markers
- A paper bag (or some type of container to hold the paper circles)

1 Before class, make copies of handout 2.13. Cut out the circles. Write numbers from two to eight randomly on the front of each circle. Put all circles in a paper bag.

2 Divide students into groups.

3 Call on a student to choose a circle from the paper bag.

4 Each group brainstorms a list of words with the total number of letters in each word equal to the number on the circle. Tell groups that they are working under a time limit; tell them when they are out of time.

5 The task is to get as many words as possible on the list. The process continues until all numbers have been used.

6 Example:

7 Once all circles have been drawn, groups should alphabetize their lists.

8 Conduct a large group sharing. Ask students if they know all of the words generated by all of the groups. If they do not, ask the group that generated the new word to explain it.

The Prize 2.14

INTELLIGENCES DEVELOPED	OBJECTIVES

Linguistic

Intrapersonal

To get students to reflect on their needs and wants

Age Group
Middle school to adult

Language Level
Intermediate

Materials Needed
• Writing paper

1 Ask students to work individually on this activity. Tell students to imagine that it is the holiday season in either the United States or Canada. The local stores in the area where the students live have a drawing for $350 to which the local merchants have all contributed. Tell students that they have just won the prize and to consider what they would choose to buy and why.

2 Students write down their answers.

3 Students share their answers with the class.

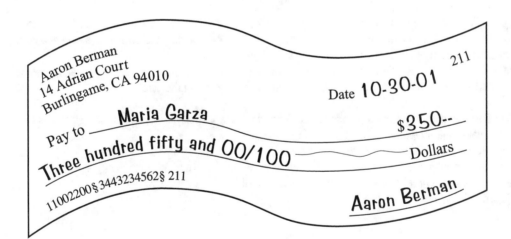

Aaron Berman
14 Adrian Court
Burlingame, CA 94010

Date 10-30-01   211

Pay to ___Maria Garza_____ $350--

Three hundred fifty and 00/100 ~~~~~~~ Dollars

11002200§3443234562§ 211

Aaron Berman

2.15 Scrolled Stories

Age Group
Grade 5 to middle school

Language Level
Intermediate

INTELLIGENCES DEVELOPED	OBJECTIVES
Linguistic	To foster creative expression
Bodily/kinesthetic	To develop coordination
Interpersonal	To develop an awareness of the print environment
Logical/mathematical	To develop logical thinking skills
Visual/spatial	To develop sequencing skills
	To give students an opportunity to work together

Materials Needed
- One copy of handout 2.15A, 2.15B, 2.15C, or 2.15D for each group
- Catalogs, magazines, and/or newspapers
- Long sheets of butcher paper
- Glue
- Scissors
- Colored markers

1 Collect all supplies and place them on a central table.

2 Divide students into small groups. Have each group choose one person who will be responsible for collecting supplies. In order to encourage students to share, enforce the rule that supplies not in use (e.g., glue, scissors, and catalogs) must be returned to the central table.

3 Give each group one of the handouts. Each handout contains a list of words. Students must work together to create an original story in which they use each word on their handout list. Have students think about who will be in the story, where it will take place, and what will happen.

4 Once groups have agreed on a story and written it out, direct them to illustrate the story on long sheets of butcher paper. The activity works best if students divide the paper into frames and illustrate each frame. They can illustrate the frames by finding pictures in magazines, catalogs, and newspapers; drawing original pictures; or doing both.

5 When the story has been completely illustrated, students should roll up the illustrated frames, starting with the end of the story. This forms a "story scroll."

6 Demonstrate how students can retell their story by unrolling the scroll one frame at a time.

7 In their groups, students practice retelling their stories using the scrolls.

8 Finally, groups present their stories to the entire class.

Sentence Autobiographies   2.16

INTELLIGENCES DEVELOPED	OBJECTIVES

Linguistic

Intrapersonal

Logical/mathematical

To give students time to reflect on their lives and what is important to them

To give students an opportunity to learn about each other

To develop sequencing skills

Age Group
Middle school to adult

Language Level
Intermediate

Materials Needed
• Short excerpts from autobiographies
• Writing paper

1 Before class, select short excerpts from several autobiographies. Choose people your students are likely to know (i.e., celebrities). You may have to adapt the selections so that the language is easy and simple.

5 Ask students to think about their own lives and identify some events that have been important. Write students' ideas on the board.

6 Invite students to write sentence autobiographies. Have each student begin the task by listing five important events that have occurred in his/her life. The events should be put in chronological order, beginning with the event most distant to the present moment. Walk around the room, giving students individual attention.

2 Help students understand the term "autobiography." Contrast it with "biography."

3 Read the excerpts out loud.

4 Ask students to recall important events and ideas in the selections that you read. Write students' answers on the board.

7 When all students have finished, conduct a large group sharing for students who would like to volunteer to read their sentence autobiographies aloud.

2.17 Shopping Mall

Age Group
Middle to high school

Language Level
Intermediate

INTELLIGENCES DEVELOPED

Linguistic

Interpersonal

Intrapersonal

Logical/mathematical

OBJECTIVES

To give students an opportunity to learn more about themselves

To develop logical thinking skills

To give students an opportunity to work together

Materials Needed
• Writing paper

1 Divide students into small groups using your favorite technique (see activity 6.5 for suggestions).

2 Have students imagine that they are on a shopping trip at the local mall. Ask each group to generate a list of 10 items that they would like to buy. They must all agree on this list. The maximum they can spend is $500.

3 Ask students to write why it is they want to purchase each item.

4 Once students have had a chance to create their lists, conduct a large group sharing. Have the class decide whether they think the amount of money assigned to each item is too much money, too little, or just right.

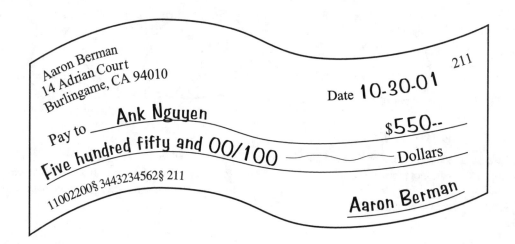

Shopping Patterns 2.18

INTELLIGENCES DEVELOPED	OBJECTIVES

Linguistic

Interpersonal

Logical/mathematical

To improve question-forming abilities

To provide an opportunity for students to interact with native speakers

To develop problem-solving skills

To give students practice in collecting and analyzing data

To give students an opportunity to work together

Age Group
High school to adult

Language Level
Intermediate to advanced

Materials Needed
• Writing paper

1 Tell students that they are going to participate in a short research project. The research project will involve a local store.

2 Divide students into small groups. Have each group choose one store on which they agree to focus. It could be a convenience store, gas station, grocery store, department store, clothing boutique, etc. It must be a real store in their community.

3 Once each group has chosen a store, they write the name of their store on the board so that other groups will know their selection.

4 Each group writes a list of questions that they may ask interested shoppers in the store. The questions could focus on a variety of areas. For example, one area of focus might be what shoppers like or dislike about the store. Other possibilities include why shoppers chose the store, how often they shop there, what they most commonly buy, and when they do their shopping. Walk around, offering feedback and support.

5 Once each group has written ten questions, conduct a large group sharing. Ask each group to identify the store they will use for their research and to read two of the questions they are going to ask.

6 Instruct groups to conduct their own research projects outside of class. They should go to the store, ask to speak with the store manager, introduce themselves, explain the purpose of their research, and ask for permission to collect the data. Each group should set a target of 20 shoppers in their selected store to interview.

7 Students collect the data, analyze the data, and make a presentation to the class based on their results.

2.19 Spelling Maze

Age Group
Grades 2 and 3

Language Level
Beginning

INTELLIGENCES DEVELOPED	OBJECTIVES
Linguistic	To develop coordination
Bodily/kinesthetic	To develop social and team-building skills
Interpersonal	To improve spelling abilities
Visual/spatial	To see patterns and to use visual cues to solve problems
	To give students an opportunity to work together

Materials Needed
• Large alphabet letter cards (all lowercase)
• Spelling word cards
• A paper bag (or some type of container to hold the cards)

1 If you do not have pre-made alphabet letter cards and/or spelling word cards, create them. The alphabet letter cards should be the size of a piece of writing paper or larger. The spelling word cards should be a size suitable for drawing from a paper bag. It's a good idea to laminate the cards so that you can use them again and again.

2 Place the spelling word cards in a paper bag. Select alphabet letter cards that match the letters in the spelling words. You can use two or three of some letters and none of others (if they aren't in the spelling words). Scatter the alphabet cards face-up randomly on the floor. Make sure they are spaced apart from each other.

3 Divide students into teams. Two students volunteer, one from each team.

4 One volunteer steps forward and chooses a word from the paper bag. The other volunteer (from the same team) spells out the word by stepping from alphabet letter card to alphabet letter card on the floor. The student must step on the cards in the order that the word is spelled. When a student spells and steps correctly, the team gets a point. Team members may help the student who is spelling.

5 This activity continues for a specified timeframe or until one team has achieved a certain number of points.

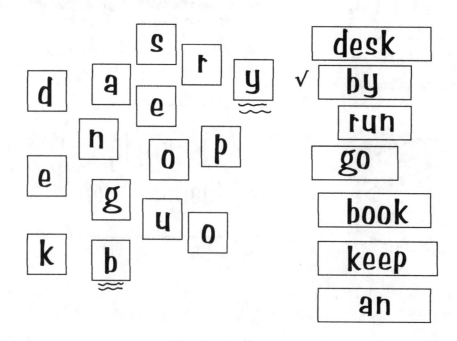

Storytelling 2.20

Age Group
Grade 3 to middle school

Language Level
Intermediate to advanced

INTELLIGENCES DEVELOPED	OBJECTIVES
Linguistic	To foster creative expression
Interpersonal	To develop vocabulary
Visual/spatial	To give students an opportunity to work together

Materials Needed
- One copy of handout 2.20 for each student
- Pictures of people participating in various activities
- Colored construction paper
- Glue
- Writing paper

1 Before class, find pictures of people participating in various activities. Mount each picture on colored construction paper. Make sure you have a picture for every pair or small group of students in your class.

2 Give each student one copy of handout 2.20. Explain that many stories contain each of the elements in the handout.

3 Divide students into pairs or small groups. Give each group a picture. Explain that the picture will serve as a springboard for creating a story.

4 Ask students to think of a story and complete the story map (handout 2.20).

5 Once students have completed the story map, instruct them to write out the story.

6 Finished stories can be entered into a word processing program, printed, and displayed on a bulletin board alongside the pictures.

Student Quizzes 2.21

Age Group
Middle to high school

Language Level
Intermediate to advanced

INTELLIGENCES DEVELOPED	OBJECTIVES
Linguistic	To develop language skills specific to the materials chosen
Interpersonal	To help students develop skills in selecting main ideas from written texts
Logical/mathematical	To help students develop skills in writing questions
	To give students an opportunity to work together

Materials Needed
- One copy of handout 2.21 for each student
- Copies of selected readings or chapters from students' textbooks

1 Divide students into small groups. Give each student in the group a copy of the selected reading or chapter.

2 Students imagine that they are teachers. Their job is to make up quizzes on the reading/chapter for their students. Encourage students to use as many different types of questions as they can—true/false, multiple choice, short answer, matching, fill-in-the-blank, essay, etc. While students are working on their questions, walk around giving groups personal attention.

3 Once students have finished their quizzes, they exchange the quizzes with another group.

4 Students take each other's quizzes.

5 Give each student handout 2.21 and have students work in their groups to complete the form.

2.22 Valuing Diversity

Age Group
High school to adult

Language Level
Intermediate to advanced

INTELLIGENCES DEVELOPED	OBJECTIVES
Linguistic	To develop an appreciation of other cultures
Interpersonal	To learn more about one's own culture
Intrapersonal	To develop vocabulary for talking about culture and diversity
	To give students an opportunity to work together

Materials Needed
• One copy of handout 2.22 for each student

1 Give each student one copy of handout 2.22. Ask students to complete Side A of the diagram on their own.

2 Have students find a partner. Their partner must come from a different cultural and/or linguistic background.

3 In pairs, have students complete Side B of the handout.

4 Students compare Sides A and B and write down the similarities where the circles overlap. The following topics can be covered and written in the blank spaces: food, types of clothing, holiday customs or traditions, ways of behaving, and/or features of the educational system.

2.23 Who's Smart?

Age Group
Middle to high school

Language Level
High beginning to intermediate

INTELLIGENCES DEVELOPED	OBJECTIVES
Linguistic	To help students recognize the different ways in which people can be intelligent
Interpersonal	To help students learn more about themselves
Intrapersonal	To give students an opportunity to work together

Materials Needed
• One copy of handout 2.23 for each group of students
• Board or flipchart

1 Conduct a class discussion on the different ways in which people can be intelligent. Write students' ideas on the board as they say them. Make two lists—one list for the eight intelligences identified by Gardner and another to include student-generated ideas about the different ways of being smart. If students do not suggest all eight, add the last one or two.

2 Have students form small groups. Ask each group to choose a secretary.

3 Give the secretary a copy of handout 2.23. The group's task is to think of two people who represent each intelligence—two people with highly developed intelligences in the particular area of focus. These people could be their friends, family, or celebrities. Choose one of the intelligences as an example and get a few ideas from students. Write the ideas on the board. Give students about 15 minutes to complete the task.

4 Follow up with a large group sharing.

Word Pictures 2.24

Age Group
Grade 5 to high school

Language Level
High beginning to
intermediate

INTELLIGENCES DEVELOPED	OBJECTIVES
Linguistic	To develop vocabulary
Interpersonal	To develop skills in using a dictionary

Materials Needed
• Pictures of words that are difficult to understand
• Colored construction paper
• Glue
• Scissors
• Dictionaries

1 Before class, find pictures of objects that often need to be illustrated in dictionaries to get the meaning across. Mount the pictures on colored construction paper. Beneath each picture, write six or seven different words for the object shown. Only one of the words is correct.

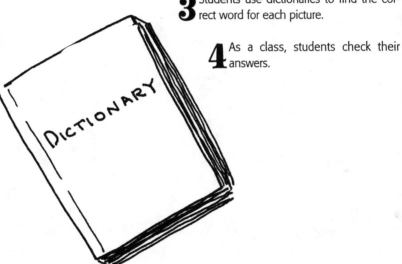

2 If students are working individually, each student must be given a picture sheet. If students are working in groups, give each group a picture sheet.

3 Students use dictionaries to find the correct word for each picture.

4 As a class, students check their answers.

Words

DIRECTIONS

The words below are associated with different holidays in the United States. Place the words in the "Holiday Scramble Grid" (handout 2.6B) according to the correct month for the holiday.

Once you have finished, check your answers with another pair of students.

baby

black cats

brightly-wrapped packages

bunny rabbit

cards saying *Be Mine*

Chinese New Year

chocolate candy in red, heart-shaped boxes

Christian holiday

Christmas

Columbus Day

confetti

day for sweethearts

day to stop working

decorated evergreen trees

dreidel

Easter

eggs in a basket

family dinners

fasting

fireworks

flags

flowers in cemeteries

ghosts

green

green river

human dragon

Independence Day in the U.S.

Irish

Halloween

Hanukkah

kinara

Kwanzaa

Labor Day

leprechauns

Memorial Day

menorah

New Year

old, white-haired man

parade in Chicago

parades

pilgrims

Presidents' Day

pumpkins

Ramadan

reindeer

remembering family members who have died

Santa Claus

St. Patrick's Day

Thanksgiving

Times Square in New York

turkey and dressing

Valentine's Day

Veterans' Day

witches

zawadi

January	February
March	April
May	June
July	August
September	October
November	December

Interactive Writing

Problems

DIRECTIONS

There are four problems below. Make a copy of this page and select the problems that are most appropriate for your students. Cut along the dotted lines and give a problem to each pair of students. You may give different problems to different pairs.

Problem #1

Directions: Read the problem below. Write a dialog that helps you practice in advance the kind of conversation that you need to have in order to solve the problem.

You wish to return a bright green sweater that someone gave you for your birthday. You know where the sweater was purchased, but you do not have a sales receipt. Write a dialog that you might use with the store clerk about this problem.

Problem #2

Directions: Read the problem below. Write a dialog that helps you practice in advance the kind of conversation that you need to have in order to solve the problem.

You have been traveling by air. Your first flight was delayed and you have now missed the connecting flight to your final destination. You need to talk to the airline agent to get on another flight in order to get to your destination. Write a dialog that you might use with the airline agent.

Problem #3

Directions: Read the problem below. Write a dialog that helps you practice in advance the kind of conversation that you need to have in order to solve the problem.

You are buying groceries. You notice the store clerk rings up one of the sale items at the regular price. Write a dialog that you might have with a store clerk who doesn't believe the item is on sale.

Problem #4

Directions: Read the problem below. Write a dialog that helps you practice in advance the kind of conversation that you need to have in order to solve the problem.

You have just received the final exam back from your teacher. There are two questions that you thought you answered correctly, but your teacher has marked your answers wrong. Write a dialog that you might use with your teacher to talk about this issue.

DIRECTIONS TO THE TEACHER

There are six letter-writing activities below. Make a copy of this page and select the activities that are most appropriate for your students. Cut along the dotted lines and give a problem to each pair of students. You may give different activities to different pairs.

Activity #1

You want to make a career in fashion sales. Write a letter to the manager of a clothing store in your area. Ask the manager if you could be considered for a summer internship. Give the manager important information about yourself.

Activity #2

You are a talented artist. You and some of your classmates who are also artists would like to hold an exhibit of your work for the community. You believe the community should be more appreciative of the art teachers in your school and think that a student art show would help raise awareness. Write a letter to several places in your community (a café, library, youth center, etc.) asking them to consider letting you hold an art exhibit in their space. Explain that you are all students with no money and that the money you make from the exhibit would be used to pay school tuition and expenses.

Activity #3

You have an idea for promoting sales at the shopping mall in your town. You believe that you and your friends could organize a fashion show featuring all the great clothes for going back to school. This is a project you would really enjoy. Write a letter explaining your idea and requesting an appointment to meet with the shopping mall manager. Be certain to mention the fact that this project will bring much needed business to the shops in the mall.

Activity #4

Your school band is trying to raise money in order to travel to a competition. Think of something you could sell. Then write a letter to the manager of a local shopping mall or store asking for permission to sell your product to raise money for your band.

Activity #5

Write a letter to your grandmother who lives in a different state. Tell her about school, your friends, and the activities in which you are involved.

Activity #6

Your town has a community center with a large central room that can be used for meetings and other functions. The use of the room is free for projects that support the community. Your club wants to sponsor a Christmas party for all children who need help at Christmas. Write a letter to the town council requesting permission to use the community center for your project. Be certain to explain how the event will help the children and why you should not be charged a fee to use the room.

Multiple Intelligences and Language Learning © 2005 Alta Book Center Publishers, San Francisco, California

Miles to Go

Flights Chart

Airline and Flight Number	Departure City and Time of Departure	Arrival City and Time of Arrival
United 271	Los Angeles 07:30	Salt Lake City 10:00
United 242	Los Angeles 08:05	New York City, La Guardia 16:30
United 374	Los Angeles 07:45	Seattle 09:45
United 744	Los Angeles 10:15	Cincinnati 17:45
United 745	Los Angeles 09:00	Denver 12:15
United 763	Los Angeles 09:15	Seattle 11:15
United 809	Los Angeles 08:35	New York City, JFK 16:15
United 921	Salt Lake City 10:30	Denver 11:45
Delta 1090	Salt Lake City 10:40	Atlanta 16:30
Delta 1135	Salt Lake City 11:05	Atlanta 15:55
Delta 1141	Salt Lake City 10:50	Chicago 14:50
Delta 1153	Salt Lake City 11:00	Denver 12:15
Delta 1245	Salt Lake City 07:45	Los Angeles 08:50
Delta 1261	Los Angeles 07:00	Denver 10:10
Delta 1290	Salt Lake City 19:30	Denver 20:45
Delta 1340	Salt Lake City 11:30	Cincinnati 17:00
American 2114	Salt Lake City 09:30	Denver 10:45
American 2145	Seattle 09:00	Salt Lake City 12:25
American 2160	Seattle 07:00	New York, JFK 15:20
American 2185	Denver 13:45	New York, JFK 20:15
American 2218	Salt Lake City 11:30	Miami 18:45
American 2240	Salt Lake City 09:50	Chicago 13:25
American 2340	Salt Lake City 14:00	Denver 15:15
Northwest 27	Denver 13:45	New York, La Guardia 20:15
Northwest 38	Denver 18:45	Dallas 20:45
Northwest 49	Los Angeles 09:00	Honolulu, Hawaii 13:15

DIRECTIONS

You are planning some travel for your business in the next few months. You will be traveling from Los Angeles to Salt Lake City, Denver, New York, Seattle, Miami, Cincinnati, Dallas, and quite possibly Honolulu. Your travel agent has given you a print out of some of the regularly scheduled flights for various airlines to these destinations. Study the flight schedule and answer the following questions. Work with a partner. After you have answered all of the questions, check your answers with the rest of the class.

1 You have a meeting to attend in Salt Lake City. You need about four hours to conduct your business. You do not wish to stay overnight in Salt Lake City because you have to attend another meeting in Denver early the next day. You are hoping to fly to Denver on the same day you fly to Salt Lake City, preferably later in the afternoon or early evening. Which flights might you use?

2 If you decide to depart for New York City from Los Angeles, what are your choices for flights?

3 If you fly to Seattle first, can you get to New York from there? What if you go to Denver first? If you can get to New York from either Seattle or Denver, which flights might you use?

4 What are your choices of flights for getting to Denver from Los Angeles?

5 If you want to get to Miami, which flight will you have to take from Los Angeles? In what city will you make a connection? How long will you have to wait between flights?

6 If Los Angeles is two hours ahead of Hawaii, what will be the actual flying time from Los Angeles to Honolulu on Northwest Flight 49?

7 Which flight(s) can you take in order to get from Los Angeles to Cincinnati? Will you need to use different airlines? Do you have an option?

8 If New York City is three hours ahead of Los Angeles, what will the actual flying time be on United Flight 242 from Los Angeles to New York City?

9 Seattle and Los Angeles are in the same time zone. Is the flight from Seattle to New York on American 2160 longer or shorter than United Flight 242?

10 What are the different options available for getting to Denver from Los Angeles?

11 Which flight(s) will you need to take in order to get to Dallas from Los Angeles?

12 How many flights on each airline are available for a trip from Los Angeles to Salt Lake City? Is it possible to take a flight in the afternoon? If so, which flight(s)?

13 United 271 is fully booked. What is the next available flight from Los Angeles to Salt Lake City?

14 You are in Denver and need to get to Dallas. Which flight(s) can you take?

Multiple Intelligences and Language Learning © 2005 Alta Book Center Publishers, San Francisco, California
www.altaesl.com Permission granted to photocopy for one teacher's classroom use only.

Circle Patterns

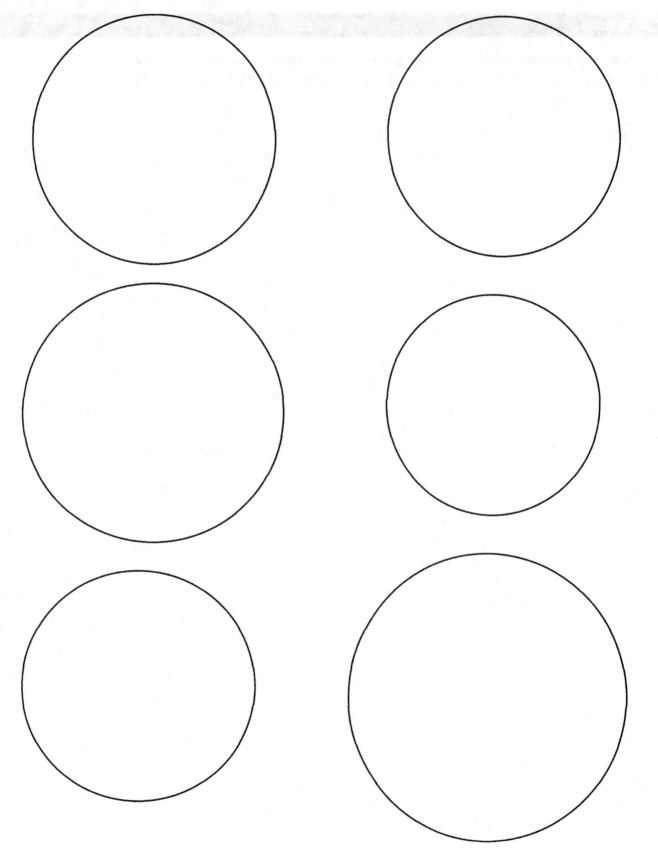

DIRECTIONS

Work with your group. Write an original story using all of the words below. After you have written your story, illustrate it on a long sheet of paper. You may use pictures from catalogs, magazines, or newspapers. You may also draw your own pictures.

fence	garden	cats	chase	gate
neighbor	dog	police officer	angry	newspaper

Scrolled Stories

Word List

Multiple Intelligences and Language Learning © 2005 Alta Book Center Publishers, San Francisco, California
www.altaesl.com Permission granted to photocopy for one teacher's classroom use only.

DIRECTIONS

Work with your group. Write an original story using all of the words below. After you have written your story, illustrate it on a long sheet of paper. You may use pictures from catalogs, magazines, or newspapers. You may also draw your own pictures.

job	part-time	insurance	payments	expensive
money	motorcycle	bank	work	difficult

DIRECTIONS

Work with your group. Write an original story using all of the words below. After you have written your story, illustrate it on a long sheet of paper. You may use pictures from catalogs, magazines, or newspapers. You may also draw your own pictures.

| bicycle | car | smash | toys | teenage brother |
| tricycle | driveway | move | father | cry |

Scrolled Stories

Word List

DIRECTIONS

Work with your group. Write an original story using all of the words below. After you have written your story, illustrate it on a long sheet of paper. You may use pictures from catalogs, magazines, or newspapers. You may also draw your own pictures.

| dance | old shoes | late | flat tire | worried |
| boyfriend | new dress | date | excited | parents |

Location:

Main characters:

The problem:

Event #1:

Event #2: (optional)

Event #3: (optional)

Solution:

Ending:

Theme or message:

Multiple Intelligences and Language Learning © 2005 Alta Book Center Publishers, San Francisco, California

Student Quizzes

Quiz Evaluation Form

Work with the members in your group to evaluate the quiz you have just taken. You must agree on the answers in your group.

1 The questions on the quiz focused on the main ideas of the reading.

___ agree completely   ___ agree somewhat   ___ do not agree

If you do not agree, which questions do not focus on main ideas?

2 The questions were too easy.

___ agree completely   ___ agree somewhat   ___ do not agree

3 The questions were too difficult.

___ agree completely   ___ agree somewhat   ___ do not agree

4 There were a variety of question types.

___ agree completely   ___ agree somewhat   ___ do not agree

5 What question types were used?

DIRECTIONS

Make a list of six traditional foods from your cultural background. Write the list in Side A of the Venn Diagram.

Find a partner who is from another cultural background. Interview your partner and write six of his/her traditional foods in Side B of the Venn Diagram.

Discuss the two lists and write any similarities in the space where the circles overlap.

After you and your partner complete the activity, work together to write a short essay about the similarities and differences between your two cultures.

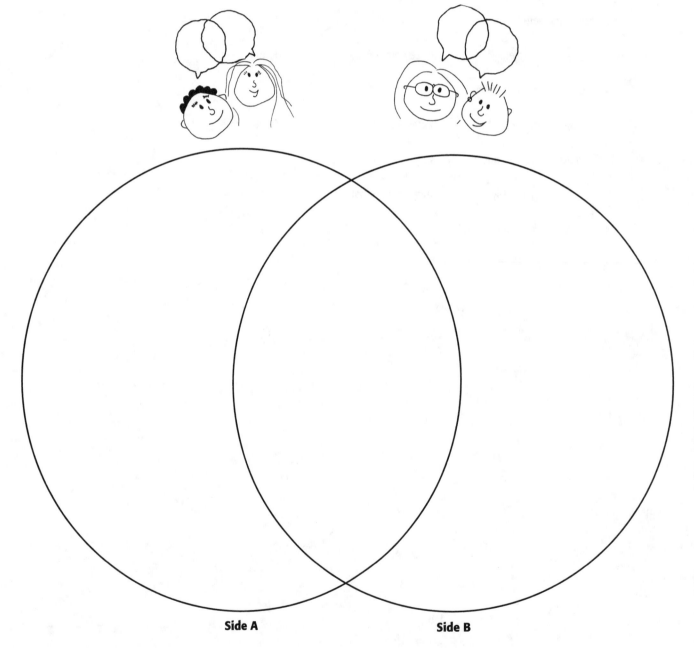

Side A   Side B

Multiple Intelligences and Language Learning © 2005 Alta Book Center Publishers, San Francisco, California

Who's Smart?

List

With your group, brainstorm a list of people who have well-developed intelligences in each of the areas listed below. The people you choose do not have to be famous, but each person in your group must agree on the choices.

 Bodily/kinesthetic intelligence

1.

2.

 Logical/mathematical intelligence

1.

2.

 Interpersonal intelligence

1.

2.

 Musical intelligence

1.

2.

 Intrapersonal intelligence

1.

2.

 Naturalist intelligence

1.

2.

 Linguistic intelligence

1.

2.

Visual/spatial intelligence

1.

2.

Logical/Mathematical Intelligence

*"As far as the laws of mathematics refer to reality,
they are not certain; and as far as they are
certain, they do not refer to reality."*

— Albert Einstein (1879–1955)

Unit 3 Photocopiable Handouts 79

**The activities in this
unit help students
develop their
logical/mathematical
intelligence by:**

solving problems

finding patterns

completing brain teasers

asking "why" questions

conducting experiments

learning about how
things work

thinking about and
working with numbers

categorizing and sorting

3.1 Across and Down

Age Group
Grade 4 to middle school

Language Level
Beginning to intermediate

INTELLIGENCES DEVELOPED	OBJECTIVES

Logical/mathematical

Linguistic

Visual/spatial

To develop basic mathematical skills

To give students meaningful practice in working with numbers under 50

To develop an awareness of visual patterns

Materials Needed
• One copy of handout 3.1A or 3.1B for each student
• One overhead transparency of the selected handout
• Plain white paper
• Answer key 3.1A or 3.1B
• Overhead projector

1 Give each student a copy of handout 3.1A or 3.1B, depending on students' level and age group. Go over the directions using an overhead transparency of the handout.

2 Students work individually to complete the chart. They then solve the equations on a separate piece of paper. Walk around the room, checking answers and helping students who are having difficulty.

3 Follow up with a large group answer-checking session. Focus on the development of students' language skills for talking about the problem and the solution.

Counting Colored Number Strips 3.2

INTELLIGENCES DEVELOPED	OBJECTIVES
Logical/mathematical	To give students meaningful practice in working with numbers
Bodily/kinesthetic	To develop basic computational skills
Interpersonal	To develop colors vocabulary
Linguistic	To develop finger dexterity and muscle coordination
Visual/spatial	To give students an opportunity to work together

Age Group
Grades K to 2

Language Level
Beginning

Materials Needed
• One 2" x 11" strip of colored paper for each student
• One hole punch for each student or small group

1 Before class, cut one strip of colored paper for each student. The colors should vary. Write a number from 1–10 on each strip.

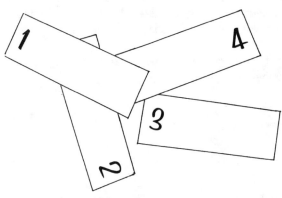

2 Give a strip to each student. As you hand each strip out, say the number that appears on it.

3 Ask for a volunteer to hand out the paper punches—one for each student. (You may also divide students into small groups if you have an aide or a parent to help you, or if you have a very small class. In this case, you need one hole punch for each group and students will need to share.)

4 Using the hole punches, students make holes in the paper corresponding to the number written on the strip. The holes can be any place on the strip and/or in any configuration. Instruct students to count out loud as they make each hole. Tell them to say the numbers in the language being studied, encouraging them by repeating the numbers as you hear them.

5 After students have finished punching the appropriate number of holes in their strips of paper, ask them to stand in their numbered groups (i.e., all 5's stand together). A good way to handle this is to write the numbers on the board or post them around the room. Then ask students to stand in front of their numbers. If you have a large class, do numbers 1–5 first, followed by 6–10.

6 First, each student says the color of his/her paper. Then, together the group counts the holes. As they count, they point to the holes they punched in their individual papers. If you work with young children, know that the number 1 written on a strip presents as much of a challenge as the number 10, but in a slightly different way. With the number 10, children must use the hole punch many different times and count correctly; with the number 1, children must resist the temptation to make more than one punch in the paper.

3.3 Data Graphs

Age Group
Grade 4 to middle school

Language Level
Beginning to intermediate

INTELLIGENCES DEVELOPED	OBJECTIVES
Logical/mathematical	To develop basic mathematical skills
Interpersonal	To give students meaningful practice in working with numbers
Linguistic	To give students an opportunity to work together
Visual/spatial	

Version One

Materials Needed
• Plain white paper
• Rulers
• Colored markers
• Board or flipchart

1 Ask students to tell you their favorite sports. List the first six you are given on the board.

2 Of the six sports listed, have students vote for their favorite sport. Students share their preference by a show of hands. Ask some students to count the number of hands for each of the six sports.

3 Give a piece of plain white paper, a ruler, and colored markers to each student. Ask students to study the information on the board and make a bar graph. They graph the sports along the horizontal axis and the number of students along the vertical axis. They should make a vertical bar for each sport and mark each bar with a different color.

4 After students have made their graphs, conduct a large group sharing. Focus on the numbers. Give students an opportunity to talk about the graphs (e.g., the green bar represents basketball; 17 people voted for it; it is the most popular sport).

5 If you have a bulletin board, create a collage of all the bar graphs.

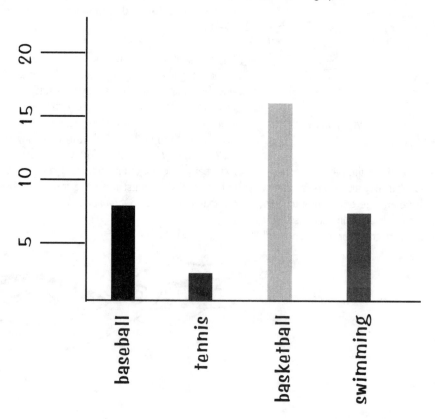

Data Graphs (continued) 3.3

Version Two

Materials Needed
(in addition to Version One materials)
• A variety of wrapped candies
• A bag
• Tape

1 Put a variety of wrapped candies in a bag. Ask students to take a piece (or several pieces). They may eat the candy, but they need to save the wrappers.

2 Draw a bar graph on the board. The number of bars on the graph should be equal to the number of different kinds of candy.

3 Tell students to tape the wrappers from their candies on the bar graph. All wrappers of the same type belong on the same bar. Let students decide which candies belong where. Encourage students to place them neatly and consecutively.

4 When all candy wrappers have been placed on a bar, ask students to count the wrappers and create their own bar graphs. Give a piece of plain white paper, a ruler, and colored markers to each student. They graph the different candy types along the horizontal axis and the number of each candy along the vertical axis. They should make a vertical bar for each candy and mark each bar with a different color.

5 After all bar graphs have been completed, ask students general questions about their graphs:

How many students chose the _____ candy?

Which candy does the _____ bar represent?

Which is the most popular candy? Least popular?

Which is the second most popular candy?

How many students in total chose the two most popular candies?

3.4 Easy Subtraction

Age Group
Grade 3 to middle school

Language Level
Beginning to low intermediate

INTELLIGENCES DEVELOPED

Logical/mathematical

Interpersonal

Linguistic

Visual/spatial

OBJECTIVES

To give students practice in working with numbers under 100

To develop computational skills in subtraction

To build and improve vocabulary related to subtraction

Materials Needed
- One copy of handout 3.4 for each student
- Answer key 3.4
- Board or flipchart

1 Give each student a copy of handout 3.4. Ask students to solve the problems individually. While students are working on the problems, walk around the classroom checking answers. Help those who are having trouble and jot down the names of students with correct answers so that you may call on them during the large group discussion (this technique cuts down on the possibility of embarrassing students who are having difficulty).

2 Put the following cues/useful words and phrases on the board for students:

The problem is _____.

Beginning on the right, _____.

On the left, _____.

So, _____.

Take away

Minus

Subtract

Total

Equals

3 Ask students to check their answers with a partner.

4 Write each problem on the board. Ask for volunteers to come to the board, read the problems, and give the correct answers. Ask students to read the problems in the following way: "The first problem is eighteen minus seventeen. Beginning on the right, eight minus seven is one. On the left, one minus one is zero. So, eighteen minus seventeen is one."

5 Help students write a rule for subtracting two-digit numbers. Give examples of mathematical rules as guidance.

Easy to Figure 3.5

INTELLIGENCES DEVELOPED	OBJECTIVES
Logical/mathematical	To build basic math vocabulary
Interpersonal	To develop basic mathematical skills
Linguistic	To develop an awareness of the print environment
Visual/spatial	To reinforce language development with visual cues
	To give students an opportunity to work together

Age Group
Grade 5 to middle school

Language Level
Beginning to intermediate

Materials Needed
- One copy of handouts 3.5A, 3.5B, and 3.5C or 3.5D for each group of students
- Answer key 3.5C and 3.5D
- Scissors
- Paper bags (or some type of containers to hold paper pieces)

1 Divide students into small groups. Give one copy of handouts 3.5A, 3.5B, and 3.5C or 3.5D to each group. Have students cut handouts 3.5A and 3.5B into rectangle-sized pieces as marked. (Note: Laminating the pieces is very useful and allows you to use the pieces over and over again.)

2 Tell students to separate the pieces into two groups: the words and money pieces in one pile, and the picture pieces in another.

3 Give each group a paper bag. Tell students to place the word and money pieces in the paper bag. Students then take turns drawing pieces from the bag, reading the words, and quoting the prices. Other students in the group must then find the corresponding pictures.

4 Once all the words and pictures have been put into pairs, students try to put the pieces into categories (e.g., food, clothing, household objects, tools, and furniture).

5 Finally, instruct students to answer the questions on handout 3.5C or 3.5D.

6 Do a large group sharing and follow-up to check answers.

3.6 Grocery Store Math

Age Group
High school to adult

Language Level
Intermediate to advanced

INTELLIGENCES DEVELOPED	OBJECTIVES
Logical/mathematical	To give students meaningful practice in working with numbers
Bodily/kinesthetic	To develop basic computational skills
Interpersonal	To develop vocabulary for talking about money
Linguistic	To develop vocabulary for talking about groceries, including containers for grocery items
Visual/spatial	To provide tactile/kinesthetic reinforcement of the concepts
	To give students an opportunity to work together

Materials Needed
- Samples of empty food packages (e.g., box, bottle, tube, carton)
- One copy of handout 3.6 for each student (alternatively, see "Creating Your Own Handout" below)
- Answer key 3.6

Creating Your Own Handouts

Though a handout has been provided for this activity, it works best if you make your own and include visuals. To do this, find a grocery store shopping advertisement in a newspaper (if you are working in a situation where you don't have ready access to newspapers in the language being taught, use pictures of food items from a magazine or the Internet). Identify 10–15 items from the ad for the grocery list. These should be items that come in packaging of various sorts. Cut out the pictures, paste them on a blank piece of paper, and write the words underneath, along with pricing information in the currency with which your students are familiar. Then create a "shopping list" chart using handout 3.6 as a guideline.

---

1 Explain to students that they are "going shopping" during the class period. Introduce examples of various empty food containers. Write the phrases they will be using in the activity on the board (i.e., box of rice, tube of toothpaste).

2 Divide students into small groups. Give each group one copy of handout 3.6 (or your own handout if you've created one following the guidelines above) and ask each group to designate a secretary to record the group's answers.

3 Allocate 20–30 minutes for groups to complete the shopping list chart, including totaling amounts in the columns and answering the question that follows.

4 Follow up with a large group discussion and checking of answers.

Extension

On a separate piece of paper, students make a chart with five columns—the first with the regular price, the second with the sale price, the third with the total amount of the product needed, and the fourth column with the total spent. They leave the fifth column blank, leave a space at the bottom of the chart for totals, and leave the amounts blank. Students then use the chart to help them answer the following questions in their groups (answers should be written in the fifth column):

How much money would you save if you bought 10 lbs. of hamburger at the sale price?

How much money would you save if you bought a jar of strawberry jam at the sale price?

How much would you save by buying seven heads of lettuce at the sale price?

How much money would you save over the regular price of lettuce?

If you bought all of the items you've now written on the chart on sale, how much money would you save?

How Much Money Can I Make? 3.7

INTELLIGENCES DEVELOPED	OBJECTIVES
Logical/mathematical	To develop basic mathematical skills
Interpersonal	To develop problem-solving skills
Linguistic	To give students an opportunity to work together

Age Group
High school

Language Level
Intermediate

Materials Needed
- One copy of handout 3.7 for each student or group
- Answer key 3.7

1 Divide students into groups. Give each student one copy of handout 3.7.

2 Read through the problem together. Focus on any vocabulary that might be difficult (e.g., *flat fee*). Introduce the vocabulary to students in a manner that is consistent with your own personal style for vocabulary instruction.

3 Have each group appoint a secretary to record answers.

4 Encourage each student to compute the amounts for each day. The entire group must agree on a final answer.

5 Conduct a large group sharing once all groups have finished.

3.8 Missing Pieces

Age Group
Middle school to adult

Language Level
Intermediate

INTELLIGENCES DEVELOPED	OBJECTIVES
Logical/mathematical	To develop problem-solving skills
Interpersonal	To give students meaningful practice in working with numbers
Linguistic	To give students an opportunity to work together

Materials Needed
• Writing paper
• Answer key 3.8

1 Make sure each student has a piece of writing paper. Ask students to take notes as you read *Problem #1* below. Instruct students to write down the numbers they hear and any other information they believe might be important.

2 Read the problem slowly. After the first reading, ask students to share their notes with a partner.

3 Read the problem again.

4 Read the questions that come after the problem. Ask students to say and/or write down their answers.

5 Do a large group sharing and follow-up to check answers (see answer key).

6 Repeat the process with *Problem #2*.

Problem #1

Philip Carter is 18 years old. He has just passed a driver's training course and has received his driver's license. He has been saving his money for four years so that he can buy a car. At age 15, he delivered newspapers and saved $250. At age 16, he worked for a summer in a gas station and saved $450. During this past year, he has been working at the public library and has earned $850. The car Philip wants costs $4,850. Philip intends to ask his parents to help him buy the car. Philip's dad has said that he will help Philip pay for the car if Philip can save at least 75% of the total cost of the car. How much does Philip need to save in order to buy the car? Does he have enough? If yes, how much over the amount needed does he have? If no, how much more does he need to save?

Questions

1. What numbers have you written down?

2. Of these numbers, which ones are not necessary to solve the problem?

3. How many numbers are important?

4. Which ones are they?

5. What is the first step in solving Problem #1? Next step(s)?

6. How much money does Philip have to save in order for his father to help him?

7. How did you get the answer to #6?

8. How much money has Philip saved? Does he have enough?

Problem #2

Philip does not yet have enough money for a car. He still has his job at the library. If he makes $6 per hour, works 15 hours a week, and saves 50% of what he makes, how long will it take Philip to earn the money to buy his car?

Mystery Products 3.9

INTELLIGENCES DEVELOPED	OBJECTIVES
Logical/mathematical	To develop basic mathematical skills
Interpersonal	To give students meaningful practice in working with numbers
Linguistic	To develop logical thinking skills
Visual/spatial	To develop sensitivity to the print environment
	To give students an opportunity to work together

Age Group
Grade 4 to middle school

Language Level
Intermediate

Materials Needed
- One copy of handout 3.9 for each student or the information written on the board/an overhead transparency
- Answer key 3.9

1 Divide students into pairs or small groups. Give each student one copy of handout 3.9.

2 Explain the directions orally and provide examples of the problems on the board or overhead projector (e.g., 284 x 84 and/or 32 x 68).

3 Give students 15–20 minutes to work through the task. In order to help students describe the task and the decisions they make, introduce a specific way of talking about the problems. For example, in Set A, if a student has written 284 x 84, the equation should be read "two hundred eighty-four multiplied by eighty-four."

4 In a large group discussion, ask students to explain how they arrived at the different sets of problems. See the answer key for the largest and smallest products.

3.10 Next in Line

Age Group
Grade 4 to middle school

Language Level
Beginning to intermediate

INTELLIGENCES DEVELOPED	OBJECTIVES
Logical/mathematical	To see logical relationships between numbers
Bodily/kinesthetic	To improve counting skills
Interpersonal	To reinforce language development through movement
Linguistic	To give students an opportunity to work together

Materials Needed
• One copy of handout 3.10 for each student

1 Give a copy of handout 3.10 to each student. Ask each student to write the first three or four numbers of a number sequence (e.g., 1, 2, 3 . . .) on each strip and leave the remaining spaces blank:

2	4	6			

50	55	60			

2 After students have completed the handout, have them walk around the room talking to each other and guessing each other's sequences. The task for other students in the class is to figure out what comes next in the sequence and then finish the sequence by writing the appropriate numbers in the remaining empty boxes. Note that some students will write simple sequences while others will write more challenging ones. If you are doing this activity with beginning-level students, teach them the following useful phrases:

What's next?

Can you tell me what's next?

Do you give up?

I give up.

Tell me what comes next, please.

3 Conduct a final large group sharing, giving all students an opportunity to share their sequences.

Numbered Messages 3.11

INTELLIGENCES DEVELOPED	OBJECTIVES

Logical/mathematical

Interpersonal

Linguistic

Visual/spatial

To develop basic mathematical skills

To develop logical thinking skills

To give students meaningful practice in working with numbers

To give students practice in working with the alphabet

To develop an awareness of patterns in language

To give students an opportunity to work together

Age Group
Grade 5 to adult

Language Level
Beginning to intermediate

Materials Needed
• Copies of handouts 3.11A or 311.B
• Writing paper
• Scissors
• Board or flipchart

1 Divide students into small groups. Explain to students that they are going to take the message they are given and encode it for another group. In order to encode a message, each letter of the alphabet is assigned a number. For example, if all letters of the alphabet were given a consecutive number beginning with the letter A, you could code the message, "Meet me at ten," in the following way: 13, 5, 5, 20, 13, 5, 1, 20, 20, 5, 14. Explain how to do this by writing examples on the board. It is important that all students understand how to do this; students who are unclear on the concept of coding will not be able to participate in the remaining tasks.

2 Cut apart the messages from handout 3.11A or 3.11B (3.11A is most appropriate for beginning-level students, grade 5 and up; 3.11B is most appropriate for intermediate-level students, high school and above). Give each group a message.

3 Each group encodes the message they were given. They should write the new encoded message on a blank piece of writing paper.

4 After each group has encoded their message, the groups exchange messages.

5 Ask the second group to decode the messages (i.e., assign letters to each number to form a message).

6 Students write their messages on the board.

7 Finally, students make up their own messages, encode them, and exchange coded messages for deciphering.

8 Follow up with a large group discussion.

3.12 Odd Addition

Age Group
Grade 4 to middle school

Language Level
Intermediate

INTELLIGENCES DEVELOPED	OBJECTIVES
Logical/mathematical	To give students meaningful practice in working with numbers
Linguistic	To develop basic computational skills
Visual/spatial	

Materials Needed
• One copy of handout 3.12 for each student
• One overhead transparency of handout 3.12 (optional)
• Answer key 3.12

1 Give one copy of handout 3.12 to each student. Read the directions on the handout out loud. For beginning-level students, explain the directions using an overhead transparency; on the transparency, circle the odd numbers in the first line, total the numbers at the end of the line, and write the answer.

2 Students complete the handout individually.

3 When students are finished, they share their answers with a partner.

4 Conduct a large group checking of answers. As you call on students, ask them to read aloud all the numbers in the line and then tell you which numbers they circled. You may also use an overhead transparency for checking answers.

Problem Solving for Adults 3.13

INTELLIGENCES DEVELOPED	OBJECTIVES
Logical/mathematical	To develop logical thinking skills
Interpersonal	To develop problem-solving skills
Intrapersonal	To give students an opportunity to learn about themselves
Linguistic	To give students an opportunity to work together

Age Group
High school to adult

Language Level
Intermediate to advanced

Materials Needed

• One copy of handout 3.13A, 3.13.B, 3.13C, 3.13D, 3.13E, 3.13.F, 3.13G, or 3.13H and one copy of handout 3.13I for each student or group

1 Divide students into small groups of three or four. Give each student a handout (3.13A, 3.13.B, 3.13C, 3.13D, 3.13E, 3.13.F, 3.13G, or 3.13H) and one copy of the accompanying worksheet (3.13I). Be certain that all students within a group have the same problem as well as a copy of handout 3.13I. You may use different problems with different groups, bearing the interests of the group members in mind.

2 Ask students to read the problem and follow the steps outlined on the handout. Each group should appoint a "leader" to make certain that everyone understands the problem and participates in the discussion, a "task-master" to keep the group focused, and a "note-taker" to record the decisions of the group.

3 Once groups have completed the task, they each choose a spokesperson and follow up with a large group discussion.

Problem Solving for Children 3.14

INTELLIGENCES	OBJECTIVES
	To develop problem-solving skills
Logical/mathematical	To give students an opportunity to learn about themselves
Interpersonal	To give students an opportunity to work together
Intrapersonal	
Linguistic	

Age Group
Grades 2 to 5

Language Level
High beginning to intermediate

Materials Needed

• One copy of handout 3.14A, 3.14B, 3.14C, 3.14D, or 3.14E for each student
• One overhead transparency of the selected handout
• Overhead projector

1 Give each student a handout (3.14A, 3.14B, 3.14C, 3.14D, or 3.14E). Make a transparency of the handout and put it on the overhead projector.

2 Read the problem out loud. Ask students to tell you some possible solutions to the problem. Write their solutions on the board.

3 Ask students to write possible solutions on their own handouts.

4 After you have generated four or five solutions, ask students to choose the one they think is best and tell you why they chose it.

5 Once students understand the procedure, give them another problem to solve together in small groups.

3.15 Purchase Power

Age Group
Middle school to adult

Language Level
Intermediate to advanced

INTELLIGENCES DEVELOPED	OBJECTIVES
Logical/mathematical	To develop problem-solving skills
Interpersonal	To improve listening skills
Linguistic	To give students meaningful practice in working with numbers
Visual/spatial	To develop sensitivity to the print environment

Materials Needed
• One copy of handout 3.15 for each student
• Answer key 3.15

1 Begin this activity by having students work individually. Give each student a copy of handout 3.15.

2 See the questions following these instructions. Ask students to listen as you read each question. After you read each question, give students time to answer. While students are working individually, walk around the room checking answers and helping students who are having difficulty. Note the names of students who have correct answers so that you can ask for their participation later.

3 After you have asked each of the questions, instruct students to share their responses in small groups.

4 Conduct a large group sharing of answers.

5 For more practice, see activity 3.17.

Questions

1. My four friends and I want to go to the movies on Friday. We are all age 18 and over. How much will it cost us in total?

2. How much will it cost my family—mother, father, two sisters, a brother, and me—to go to the symphony?

3. Which is more expensive for an adult to attend, the ballet or the symphony? What's the difference?

4. How much will it cost me to buy eight raffle tickets?

5. My three friends and I want to buy six raffle tickets among us. How much will we each have to pay?

6. How much will it cost my family to get into the amusement park? We are two seniors, seven adults, and five children.

7. There are nine lectures in the dance lecture series. If I buy tickets for all the lectures, I save $7.00 off the regular price. How much will it cost me? What percentage of the total amount will I save?

8. What number is on the raffle ticket that isn't on the other tickets? Why is this number necessary?

9. What information appears on the ballet, symphony, and dance lecture series tickets, but not on the movie ticket?

10. What do you think "#10–7" means on the dance lecture series ticket?

11. How much would it cost to take 10 children to the movies for my daughter's birthday?

12. What other events can you think of that require tickets for entry?

13. What is a "string quartet"?

14. Which tickets do not have dates on them and why?

Recipes for Math 3.16

Age Group
Grade 5 to middle school

Language Level
Intermediate

INTELLIGENCES DEVELOPED

Logical/mathematical

Bodily/kinesthetic

Interpersonal

Linguistic

OBJECTIVES

To give students practice in working with numbers

To improve basic mathematical skills

To develop vocabulary for talking about food and cooking

To reinforce language development through movement

To give students an opportunity to work together

Materials Needed

- One copy of handout 3.16A or 3.16B for each student
- Items for the "no-bake" recipe if you decide to do the follow-up activity

1 Select the recipe you'd like to use (either handout 3.16A, Brownies, or 3.16B, Cookies). Give students a copy of the corresponding handout.

2 Have students work through the tasks individually.

3 Instruct them to find a partner and check their work.

4 Repeat using the other handout if you feel students need more practice.

Follow-up Activity

Note: Your school may have specific policies concerning cooking in classrooms. Be certain to check with your administrator to make sure this activity is in keeping with school regulations.

1 Following these instructions you will find the recipe for "no-bake" cookies. Make sure you have a small hot plate and the ingredients listed in the recipe. First, write the recipe on the board.

2 Ask students to make a list of everything that you will need to make the cookies. Collect all of the ingredients on a central table according to students' instructions.

3 Have students rewrite the recipe, making only half the original quantity.

4 Now tell students that they are going to actually make the cookies. Choose two students to stand at the table and follow directions. Choose four students to take turns giving the directions, including timing the cooking. Supervise carefully during the cooking process, especially when students are using the hot plate.

Here's what's cookin' _No-Bake Cookies_ **Makes** _4 dozen_

In a small pan combine

2 cups sugar
3 tablespoons cocoa
1/2 cup butter
1/2 cup milk

Bring ingredients to a boil and boil two minutes.

Add 1/2 cup peanut butter and 3 cups uncooked rolled oats. Stir well.

Drop by teaspoonfuls on waxed paper.

Cool for 15 minutes before eating.

3.17 Ten Times

Age Group
Grade 5 to middle school

Language Level
Beginning

INTELLIGENCES DEVELOPED

Logical/mathematical

Linguistic

OBJECTIVES

To develop problem-solving skills

To develop basic computational skills

To give students meaningful practice in working with numbers

Materials Needed
- One copy of handout 3.15 (originally used for activity 3.15) for each student
- Answer key 3.17

1 Begin this activity by having students work individually. Give each student a copy of handout 3.15.

2 See the questions following these instructions. Ask students to listen as you read each question. After you read each question, give students time to answer.

While students are working individually, walk around the room checking answers and helping students who are having difficulty. Note the names of students who have correct answers so that you can ask for their participation later.

3 After you have asked each of the questions, instruct students to share their responses in small groups.

4 Conduct a large group sharing of answers.

Questions

1. How much will ten tickets cost for the string quartet?

2. How much more will ten tickets to the ballet performance cost than 10 tickets to the symphony orchestra?

3. The entire senior class of 100 students at Nelson Avenue High School wants to go to McDee's Amusement Park for their graduation party. How much will it cost them?

4. How much will 10 raffle tickets cost? 100?

5. How much more will it cost for 10 adults to go to McDee's Amusement Park than 10 senior citizens?

6. I and nine other adults are going to the movies on Friday. How much will it cost? My 65-year-old mother is also going along with nine other senior citizens. How much more will I have to pay than she will?

7. You have been working with multiplying powers of 10. What general principle did you use to help you in multiplying by 10? By 100?

The Yard Sale 3.18

INTELLIGENCES DEVELOPED	OBJECTIVES
Logical/mathematical	To develop basic mathematical and computational skills
Interpersonal	To develop vocabulary for talking about money and household items
Linguistic	To give students an opportunity to work together

Age Group
High school to adult

Language Level
Intermediate

Materials Needed
- One copy of handout 3.18 for each student
- Answer key 3.18

1 Explain the phrase "yard sale" to students who may not be familiar with it. For example: *Yard sales are very popular in American suburban neighborhoods where homes have lawns facing the street. Homes in the suburbs in the United States are not generally surrounded by high fences with locking gates as they are in many countries. Therefore, items to be sold can be placed in the front yard on tables or racks, and can be easily viewed from the street by those who pass by. Oftentimes, neighbors will join together to hold one large yard sale with many items.*

2 Divide students into groups. Give each student a copy of the handout (You could also make an overhead transparency of the handout or write the inventory and questions on the board; both options are alternatives to photocopying.)

3 Appoint a "leader" in the group to read the questions aloud and a "note-taker" to record the answers. Instruct students to work together to solve the problems.

4 Conduct a large group sharing to check answers.

3.19 What's Inside?

Age Group
Grade 4 to adult

Language Level
Intermediate to advanced

INTELLIGENCES DEVELOPED	OBJECTIVES
Logical/mathematical	To develop logical thinking skills
Interpersonal	To develop problem-solving skills
Linguistic	To give students an opportunity to work together
Visual/spatial	

Materials Needed
• One copy of handout 3.19 for each group
• Four boxes
• A black marker
• Four small, common household items to fit in the boxes
• Tape

1 Before class, select four small boxes for the activity and label them A, B, C, and D. (If you have a large class, you may want to use five to seven boxes.) Place a small, common household item in each box (e.g., toothbrush, salt shaker, bar of soap, fork, sponge, keys). Tape the boxes shut.

2 Divide students into groups. Give each group one copy of handout 3.19 and one box. Explain to students that their task is to guess the item in each box using the "Guessing Grid" (handout 3.19) for guidance.

Emphasize that the boxes cannot be opened. Ask each group to choose a secretary to record the group's answers.

3 Set a time limit for working with each box; ring a bell or blow a whistle when it's time for the groups to start and conclude their investigations.

4 When students have completed the examination of one box, have groups exchange boxes and repeat Step 3.

5 When each group has examined all of the boxes, stop the activity and conduct a large group sharing. Use the handout as a springboard to discussion. Write each group's guesses on the board.

6 Finally, ask for student volunteers to open the boxes. Check to see which groups guessed correctly.

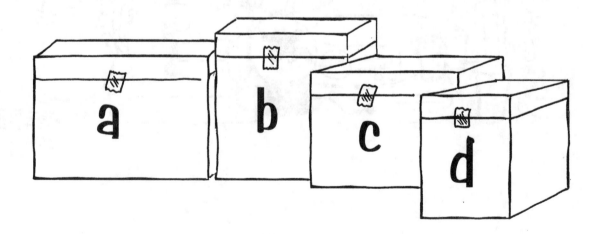

Your Change 3.20

INTELLIGENCES DEVELOPED	**OBJECTIVES**

Logical/mathematical

Interpersonal

Linguistic

To familiarize students with U.S. currency (see note below)

To develop basic computational skills

To develop logical thinking skills

To give students an opportunity to work together

Age Group
Grade 4 to adult

Language Level
Intermediate

Materials Needed
• One copy of handout 3.20 for each group
• Paper coins and bills (see Step 1)

Note: Teachers in countries other than the United States may want to use this activity to familiarize students with the currency of the United States or they may develop a similar handout introducing the monetary system of the students' native country.

1 To make your own paper money, tape pennies, nickels, dimes, and quarters as well as one, five, ten, and twenty-dollar bills on pieces of paper and make several copies. Then have students cut out the paper money and organize it into piles on a central table (with six or seven students working, this takes a very short time).

2 Divide students into groups. Ask each group to get paper coins and bills from the table.

3 Give a copy of handout 3.20 to each group. Once the groups have the materials, explain to students that they need to work through the tasks on the handout, using the paper money to determine the answers. Use Task 1 on the handout as an example and work through it with the entire class. Be certain to demonstrate how to make and count change.

Example
In Task 1, pick up one penny, one dime, and two quarters. Then count the change for $5.00 in the following way: $4.39 (add the penny), $4.40 (add the dime), $4.50 (add the first quarter), $4.75, (add the last quarter), $5.00.

4 Give students time to work through the tasks and conclude with a large group sharing. Use the follow-up questions as a springboard to discussion.

In what jobs do you see people counting change?

Why do you think that counting change is important? For the business? For the customers?

DIRECTIONS

1 Count the number of striped squares and plain squares in each row. Fill in the numbers in the last box of each corresponding row (S = striped, P = plain).

2 Count the number of striped squares and plain squares for each column. Fill in the numbers in the last box of each corresponding column.

3 Complete the two equations for each row and column as follows:

Rows: For the first equation, add the striped and plain squares together. For the second equation, subtract the plain squares from the striped squares.

Example
The top row across (Row 1) has four striped squares and two plain squares.
Equations: $4 + 2 = 6$ and $4 - 2 = 2$.

Columns: For the first equation, add the striped and plain squares together. For the second equation, multiply the plain squares by the striped squares.

Example
The far left column (Column 1) has one striped square and four plain squares.
Equations: $1 + 4 = 5$ and $4 \times 1 = 4$.

4 Be prepared to share your answers with the entire class.

	Column 1	Column 2	Column 3	Column 4	Column 5	Column 6	
Row 1			▨	▨	▨	▨	S= P=
Row 2		▨		▨			S= P=
Row 3							S= P=
Row 4	▨	▨				▨	S= P=
Row 5						▨	S= P=
	S= P=	S= P=	S= P=	S= P=	S= P=	S= P=	

Multiple Intelligences and Language Learning © 2005 Alta Book Center Publishers, San Francisco, California
www.altaesl.com Permission granted to photocopy for one teacher's classroom use only

Across and Down

Grid 2/Intermediate Level

DIRECTIONS

1 Count the number of striped rectangles and plain rectangles in each row. Fill in the numbers in the last box of each corresponding row (S = striped, P = plain).

2 Count the number of striped rectangles and plain rectangles for each column. Fill in the numbers in the last box of each corresponding column.

3 Complete the two equations for each row and column as follows:

Rows: For the first equation, subtract the striped rectangles from the plain rectangles. For the second equation, multiply the plain rectangles by the striped rectangles.

Example
The top row across (Row 1) has four plain rectangles and six striped rectangles.
Equations: 4 – 6 = -2 and 4 x 6 = 24.

Columns: For the first equation, add the plain and striped rectangles together. For the second equation, multiply the plain rectangles by the striped rectangles.

Example
The far left column (Column 1) has eight plain rectangles and five striped rectangles.
Equations: 8 + 5 = 13 and 8 x 5 = 40.

4 Be prepared to share your answers with the entire class.

	Col 1	Col 2	Col 3	Col 4	Col 5	Col 6	Col 7	Col 8	Col 9	Col 10	
Row 1											S= P=
Row 2											S= P=
Row 3											S= P=
Row 4											S= P=
Row 5											S= P=
Row 6											S= P=
Row 7											S= P=
Row 8											S= P=
Row 9											S= P=
Row 10											S= P=
Row 11											S= P=
Row 12											S= P=
Row 13											S= P=
	S= P=	S= P=	S= P=	S= P=	S= P=	S= P=	S= P=	S= P=	S= P=	S= P=	

1 Find the answers to each of the two-digit subtraction problems below. Write your answers in the space provided.

2 Check your answers with a partner. Be prepared to write your answers on the board.

3 Study the problems and write a rule for subtracting two-digit numbers.

First Row	18 -17	34 -14	10 -10	68 -33	50 -20
Second Row	15 -13	16 -11	17 -6	66 -22	40 -27
Third Row	27 -12	70 -17	60 -16	45 -31	45 -14

Rule: _____

_____

_____

Multiple Intelligences and Language Learning © 2005 Alta Book Center Publishers, San Francisco, California

Words and Money Sheet

apples $1.89	bowl $7.00	corn 40¢	fork $4.00	jacket $69.00
pans $79.99	pots $99.00	shoes $85.00	sofa $499.00	television $150.00
chair $349.00	bread $3.49	cup $4.00	glass $2.00	knife $4.00
pants $49.50	radio $25.00	shorts $25.00	spatula $7.98	toothbrush $2.29
bananas 79¢	carrots 69¢	dishes $32.00	grapes $3.99	lamp $125.00
peas $2.99	scarf $15.00	skirt $36.00	spoon $3.50	towels $14.99
bed $348.00	chest of drawers $159.00	dress $65.00	hairbrush $5.99	milk $2.70
pineapple $4.99	screwdriver $7.00	soap 99¢	stool $39.99	wastebasket $12.00
book $13.95	computer $1200.00	dresser $279.00	hat $28.00	pajamas $42.00
potatoes 89¢	shirt $38.00	socks $2.89	table $350.00	yogurt 79¢

3.5C Handout

DIRECTIONS

Work together. Take turns reading the questions in your group. Choose a secretary to record your answers.

1 How much is the sofa?

2 How much is the dresser?

3 Which item is cheaper?

4 How much do the pots, dishes, glass, and knife cost in total?

3.5D Handout

DIRECTIONS

Work together. Take turns reading the questions in your group. Choose a secretary to record your answers.

1 How much more does the sofa cost than the table?

2 What's the cheapest item? Most expensive?

3 How much money would it take to buy all of the food items?
Clothing items?
Kitchen items?
Furniture?

4 If someone gave you $300 to spend on any of the items, what would you buy? (You can buy more than one item as long as the total cost does not go over $300.)

5 Work individually. If someone gave you $200 to spend on any of the items, what would you buy? Write down each item and the cost. Share your list with your group.

Multiple Intelligences and Language Learning © 2005 Alta Book Center Publishers, San Francisco, California

Grocery Store Math
Shopping List

Grocery Item	Amount Needed	Regular Price	Total Regular Price	Sale Price	Total Spent	Total Saved
Hamburger	2 lbs.	99¢ per lb.		89¢ per lb.		
Rice	2 boxes	$1.29 per box		$1.25 per box		
Pasta	1 package	79¢ per package		75¢ per package		
Shampoo	1 bottle	$3.79 per bottle		$3.56 per bottle		
Tomatoes	2 cans	59¢ per can		4 cans/$1.00		
Lettuce	2 heads	$1.49 per head		99¢ per head		
Carrots	1 bag	79¢ per bag		75¢ per bag		
Tuna Fish	3 small cans	89¢ per can		75¢ per can		
Chicken Soup	2 large cans	`$1.79 per can		$1.69 per can		
Olive Oil	1 bottle	$3.69 per bottle		$3.49 per bottle		
Toothpaste	1 tube	$2.79		$2.59		
Strawberry Jam	1 jar	$2.59		$2.37		
Frozen Peas	1 bag	$1.29		$1.19		
Crackers	2 boxes	$2.39 per box		$2.19 per box		
					GRAND TOTAL SAVED	

Do you think shopping for grocery items that are on sale is a good idea? Why? Why not?

3.7 Handout

How Much Money Can I Make?

Read through the following problem and then discuss the solution with your group. You should be able to explain how you arrived at your answer.

Problem

A neighbor has offered you a 17-day job painting his house during the summer. He's offered to either pay you either a flat fee of $600 or 1¢ for the first day with the fee doubling each day thereafter. Which offer will make you more money? Be prepared to explain your answer and computations to the entire class.

Multiple Intelligences and Language Learning © 2005 Alta Book Center Publishers, San Francisco, California
www.altaesl.com Permission granted to photocopy for one teacher's classroom use only.

Mystery Products

DIRECTIONS

Place the following numbers in each of the boxes below in random order: 2, 3, 4, 6, 8. Use these numbers to create multiplication problems. Do not use a number more than once in any one problem and do not repeat the problems. To clarify, you can use the digit 8 in several combinations (68 x 238, 834 x 8 etc.) but you cannot repeat the exact numbers (for example, 68 x 68 or 8 x 8 cannot be used). Not all numbers need to be used.

1 Solve the problems. Record the product (the answer) of each set.

2 What arrangement will result in the largest product?

3 What arrangement will give you the smallest product?

4 Explain your reasoning for selecting the position of the numbers.

Set A	Set B	Set C	Set D	Set E
Set F	Set G	Set H	Set I	Set J

The largest product =

The smallest product =

Numbered Messages

Beginning Level

Message A
Please take the papers off the table.

Message E
What's your answer?

Message B
The elevator is around the corner.

Message F
I left my key on the desk.

Message C
Where is the restaurant?

Message G
May I help you?

Message D
Do you need help with your bags?

Numbered Messages

Intermediate Level

Message A
Do you know what Planet Hollywood is and where it is located?

Message D
He was able to register for all of the classes he wanted to take this semester.

Message B
Some people from my hometown are working on the new road in front of the school.

Message E
The northbound bus will leave the university in five minutes.

Message C
Just what Tom wants to do now is a mystery.

Message F
Can you think of a way to make it work?

DIRECTIONS

Circle the odd numbers in each row. Then add the odd numbers in the row and record your answer in the space provided.

Row 1:   1   2   3   4   5   6   7   8   =   _____

Row 2:   14   17   21   11   12   13   2   3   =   _____

Row 3:   4   5   7   8   9   6   3   1   =   _____

Row 4:   21   3   22   4   24   25   2   5   =   _____

Row 5:   5   10   15   20   1   3   5   6   =   _____

Row 6:   18   20   22   23   21   7   11   3   =   _____

Row 7:   17   7   6   16   8   18   9   19   =   _____

Row 8:   3   33   21   23   4   6   9   10   =   _____

Row 9:   9   28   29   15   17   19   7   3   =   _____

Row 10:   2   4   6   7   3   17   29   20   =   _____

Problem Solving for Adults

Problem 1: Where's My Bike?

Read through the problem carefully. Follow each step. Choose a note-taker in your group to record the answers.

Problem

You and your family live in an apartment complex where there are many young families with children. Your little girl, Jennifer, just received a new bike for her birthday. Last week when your daughter went to get her new bike, she found that it was missing. You searched the immediate area with no luck. You also posted signs in the laundry room and in the entrances to each building in the complex. No one responded. One night when you were doing laundry, you saw a young girl about your daughter's age come into the laundry to get a drink from the soda machine. She was riding a bike just like your daughter's, including the padded seat cover you had made for it. You asked the little girl about the bike. She said she got it for her birthday about a week ago. You found out where the little girl lives and visited her parents the next day. They claimed they bought the bike, but got upset when you asked them to show you a receipt. You know that the family has little or no money (you don't have much either!), and you know the little girl loves her bike (your little girl does, too!). You are certain that the bike belongs to your little girl. What should you do?

Steps to solving the problem:

1 Use the chart on handout 3.13I to help you.

2 Identify the problem. Write it down in your own words.

3 With your group, think of two different ways to solve the problem (i.e., two different solutions). Write down each solution.

4 Write down one strength and one weakness of each solution.

5 Finally, make a recommendation for one final solution from your group.

6 Choose someone from your group to be the spokesperson during the large group sharing.

DIRECTIONS

Read through the problem carefully. Follow each step. Choose a note-taker in your group to record the answers.

Problem

Your best girlfriend has just told you about and shown you pictures of her new boyfriend. His name is Derek. Although she has only been dating him for a few short weeks, she says that she is in love with him and plans to marry him. She tells you that Derek feels the same way about her. Although you think the romance has happened a bit too quickly and you wish she would take more time before making up her mind about marriage, you are happy for her. At a party you meet a young man named Derek who looks like the Derek in the pictures your girlfriend showed you. At the same time you are introduced to Derek you are also introduced to his fiancé, Tessa! Could this be a coincidence? Is this Derek the same young man who is dating your best friend? What should you do?

Steps to solving the problem:

1 Use the chart on handout 3.13I to help you.

2 Identify the problem. Write it down in your own words.

3 With your group, think of two different ways to solve the problem (i.e., two different solutions). Write down each solution.

4 Write down one strength and one weakness of each solution.

5 Finally, make a recommendation for one final solution from your group.

6 Choose someone from your group to be the spokesperson during the large group sharing.

DIRECTIONS

Read through the problem carefully. Follow each step. Choose a note-taker in your group to record the answers.

Problem

You are having a large party at your home for a group of old friends as well as some new acquaintances. These new friends have brought along three additional guests whom you have not met before. Sometime during the evening, you go upstairs to get some photos taken on your vacation. Before coming out of the study, you run into a man you have not met. You assume he is one of the people who came with your new friends. The man says he is looking for the bathroom. At the time you think this is somewhat strange because you pointed out the guest bath downstairs earlier in the evening and even posted a couple of signs. But the man is nice and apologetic, so you don't give it another thought.

Two days after the party, you lose your car keys and end up having to get your spare keys. When you go to retrieve the spare keys from your study, you find that they are missing. These keys include keys to your car, house, safety deposit box, office, storage unit, and workshop. Since you have been keeping spare keys in the same secret place for years, you are concerned. You finally find your car keys, but the spare keys never turn up. You remember the strange man at your party who had been in your study. Suddenly, you begin to feel very frightened. Could this person have taken your keys? Who was this man? What should you do?

Steps to solving the problem:

1 Use the chart on handout 3.13I to help you.

2 Identify the problem. Write it down in your own words.

3 With your group, think of two different ways to solve the problem (i.e., two different solutions). Write down each solution.

4 Write down one strength and one weakness of each solution.

5 Finally, make a recommendation for one final solution from your group.

6 Choose someone from your group to be the spokesperson during the large group sharing.

3.13D Handout

Problem Solving for Adults
Problem 4: The Party Dilemma

Read through the problem carefully. Follow each step. Choose a note-taker in your group to record the answers.

Problem

On New Year's Eve, you and your spouse give a party. The party begins at 10 pm with drinks and hors d'oeuvres. Dinner is at 11 pm; dessert and champagne are served just before midnight. Non-alcoholic beverages are in abundance because a number of your friends do not drink alcohol. The party continues until about 2 am with more drinking and dancing. Most of your guests have either appointed a designated driver (i.e., a person who will drive and, therefore, not drink), do not drink, came by taxi, or live within walking distance. Since you have not been drinking, you volunteer to drive anyone home who has been drinking and may need a ride. One of your best friends is about to leave the party. He has obviously been drinking and should not drive, but he heads off toward his car. You know he is going to try to drive home. Driving will be dangerous for him as well as for others. What should you do?

Steps to solving the problem:

1 Use the chart on handout 3.13I to help you.

2 Identify the problem. Write it down in your own words.

3 With your group, think of two different ways to solve the problem (i.e., two different solutions). Write down each solution.

4 Write down one strength and one weakness of each solution.

5 Finally, make a recommendation for one final solution from your group.

6 Choose someone from your group to be the spokesperson during the large group sharing.

Problem Solving for Adults

Problem 5: Little White Lies

Handout 3.13E

DIRECTIONS

Read through the problem carefully. Follow each step. Choose a note-taker in your group to record the answers.

Problem

Your parents have gone on a short trip. You are left in charge of the house and plan to have your two best friends stay the night with you. You have just learned to drive a car and have passed your driving test, but your parents have forbidden you to use the second car while they are away. Your friends have made arrangements for one of their parents to bring them to your house. After your parents leave, one of your friends calls to say that she cannot come now because her father had unexpected business and has taken the car. She wonders if it would be possible for you to come and pick them up. You have your license, your parents have left the car and the car keys, and it's only a 15-minute drive across town on streets you know very well. You can't imagine how boring the night would be without your friends, and you don't want to stay in the house alone. You could pick up your friends and return without your parents ever knowing. What should you do?

Steps to solving the problem:

1 Use the chart on handout 3.13I to help you.

2 Identify the problem. Write it down in your own words.

3 With your group, think of two different ways to solve the problem (i.e., two different solutions). Write down each solution.

4 Write down one strength and one weakness of each solution.

5 Finally, make a recommendation for one final solution from your group.

6 Choose someone from your group to be the spokesperson during the large group sharing.

3.13F Handout

Problem Solving for Adults
Problem 6: The Confession

DIRECTIONS

Read through the problem. Follow each step. Choose a note-taker in your group to record the answers.

Problem

You and your spouse have just bought a new house in a neighborhood with many young children. It's a great house and it will be a great home for the family you plan to have someday. Families with small children live on either side of you and bikes, toys, etc., often end up in your driveway. You have spoken to the neighbors many times about the problem of toys in the driveway, but nothing seems to change. In order to avoid a mishap, you have developed the habit of checking behind the car before you back up.

Today you leave for work a little late. You jump in the car and quickly back out of the driveway without checking to see if the way is clear. As a result, you accidentally run over a small bicycle and bend the rear wheel. The bicycle belongs to the little girl who lives next door. You feel bad about the incident, but also believe that this is a good lesson for your neighbors. You have told them a million times to keep their children's toys out of your driveway. You throw the bicycle in the neighbors' driveway, and, in frustration, head to work without saying anything to anyone. You think about the accident all day, and the more you think about it the angrier you become. You decide to confront your neighbors when you get home. When you return from work, the little neighbor girl is standing in her driveway. She greets you as you get out of your car, telling you that some mean person smashed her new bicycle. She begins to cry. She says her mother and father told her that she can't get another one. You know you are right about this issue; if toys are left in your driveway, they are bound to get damaged. But you also feel sorry for the little girl. What should you do?

Steps to solving the problem:

1 Use the chart on handout 3.13I to help you.

2 Identify the problem. Write it down in your own words.

3 With your group, think of two different ways to solve the problem (i.e., two different solutions). Write down each solution.

4 Write down one strength and one weakness of each solution.

5 Finally, make a recommendation for one final solution from your group.

6 Choose someone from your group to be the spokesperson during the large group sharing.

Problem Solving for Adults
Problem 7: Holiday Gifts

Handout 3.13G

DIRECTIONS

Read through the problem. Follow each step. Choose a note-taker in your group to record the answers.

Problem

During the holidays, your family usually does a gift exchange. You are given the name of someone in the family and someone is given your name. This year, your older sister has your name. She says that she has a very special gift for you and is sure you are going to love it. Even though your family has a $100 limit on gifts, your sister tells you that she has spent a bit more on your gift because she wants you to have it so much. Your entire family is present when you open your sister's gift. You are very surprised: it is a piece of art—a painting of your favorite place. But in all honesty, you hate it. The colors are wrong and it's too large for the space she has in mind, the front entry of your house. Your sister is frequently in and out of your home, so she would know if you didn't hang the picture. What should you do?

Steps to solving the problem:

1 Use the chart on handout 3.13I to help you.

2 Identify the problem. Write it down in your own words.

3 With your group, think of two different ways to solve the problem (i.e., two different solutions). Write down each solution.

4 Write down one strength and one weakness of each solution.

5 Finally, make a recommendation for one final solution from your group.

6 Choose someone from your group to be the spokesperson during the large group sharing.

3.13H Handout

Problem Solving for Adults
Problem 8: Which Job Should I Take?

Multiple Intelligences and Language Learning © 2005 Alta Book Center Publishers, San Francisco, California
www.altaesl.com Permission granted to photocopy for one teacher's classroom use only.

DIRECTIONS

Read through the problem. Follow each step. Choose a note-taker in your group to record the answers.

Problem

You have just finished your program of study and are about to graduate from university with a degree in business management. Your father is very excited about your upcoming graduation. It has been his dream for many years for the two of you to work together in the family company. He has offered you a competitive salary and the position of vice president. It sounds like the perfect arrangement. The only problem is that you have no interest in your father's business. Last week, a small company offered you a job. The company is new and the salary is much lower than what your father would pay you, but it is work you are very interested in doing. While there is every possibility the company will grow and be successful, there are no guarantees; you could be without a job in a year if the company folded. But if you turn down the job with your father, his pride would never allow him to offer it to you again. What should you do?

Steps to solving the problem:

1 Use the chart on handout 3.13I to help you.

2 Identify the problem. Write it down in your own words.

3 With your group, think of two different ways to solve the problem (i.e., two different solutions). Write down each solution.

4 Write down one strength and one weakness of each solution.

5 Finally, make a recommendation for one final solution from your group.

6 Choose someone from your group to be the spokesperson during the large group sharing.

Problem Solving Worksheet

Student Name(s)_____

Name of Problem			
Explain the Problem			
Solution 1		Weakness:	Strength:
Solution 2		Weakness:	Strength:
Final Recommendation			

Problem Solving for Children
Problem 1

Your friend feels sad. Name two things you can do to help your friend feel better.

Multiple Intelligences and Language Learning © 2005 Alta Book Center Publishers, San Francisco, California
www.altaesl.com Permission granted to photocopy for one teacher's classroom use only.

Problem Solving for Children

Problem 2

Your friend lost some money. Name two things you might do to help your friend find the money.

A new student joins your class at school. Name two things you can do to help the student feel at home.

Problem Solving for Children

Problem 4

Someone took your bike from the playground bike rack. Name three things you can do to help get the bike back.

You missed the bus for school and both of your parents have already left for work. Name three ways you can get to school.

Multiple Intelligences and Language Learning © 2005 Alta Book Center Publishers, San Francisco, California
www.altaesl.com Permission granted to photocopy for one teacher's classroom use only.

Tickets

Below are seven different types of tickets. **Read the information printed on the tickets as you listen to the teacher's questions.** Use the information on the tickets to determine your answers.

The Cinematic Movie Theater

ADMIT ONE.

Adults	$9.50
Senior Citizens	$6.00
Children Under 12	$6.00

The University Club Presents
The Carter String Quartet
March 26 & 27
Admit One General Admission
All Seats $10.00

SECTION DD
ROW 20 SEAT A

The Nutcracker

December 12-27
The City Ballet
at the Capitol Theater

ADULT $40.00

The Rockies Symphony Orchestra
at Kingsburg Hall
October 12-13
Main Floor Seating
Row G Seat 105
$8.50

McDee's Amusement Park
Adults $12
Seniors $7   Admit One
Children $6

Number 160580   **Raffle Ticket** $5.00   Number 160580

The World Dance Lecture Series

February 26
All seats reserved
Seat #10-7
$4.00

DIRECTIONS

Imagine that you are making brownies for a large party. In order to have enough brownies for your guests, you will need to triple the recipe in your cookbook. The original recipe is given on the left-hand side of the page. Write the tripled recipe that you will need to follow on the right-hand side.

Brownies

1/2 cup butter (1 stick)

1/4 cup cocoa

1/2 cup sugar

2 eggs

1/2 teaspoon salt

1/2 teaspoon baking powder

1 cup flour

1/3 cup nuts

Melt butter and cocoa in a small pan. Beat eggs and sugar together. Add melted butter and cocoa mixture. Mix baking powder and salt with flour. Add flour mixture. Fold in nuts. Scrape mixture into a greased and floured pan. Bake 20 minutes at 350 degrees. Do not over-bake.

Brownies—Tripled Recipe

_____ cup(s) butter

_____ cup(s) cocoa

_____ cup(s) sugar

_____ egg(s)

_____ teaspoon(s) salt

_____ teaspoon(s) baking powder

_____ cup(s) flour

_____ cup(s) nuts

Melt butter and cocoa in a small pan. Beat eggs and sugar together. Add melted butter and cocoa mixture. Mix baking powder and salt with flour. Add flour mixture. Fold in nuts. Scrape mixture into a greased and floured pan. Bake 20 minutes at 350 degrees. Do not over-bake.

Multiple Intelligences and Language Learning © 2005 Alta Book Center Publishers, San Francisco, California

Recipes for Math

Cookies

DIRECTIONS

You are holding a meeting at your house for a small group of people. You want to offer tea, coffee, juice, and something sweet. You have decided to make cookies from the chocolate chip cookie recipe your mother gave you. The recipe, however, is too large. You have decided to cut the recipe in half. The original recipe is on the left-hand side on the page. Write the halved recipe that you will need to follow on the right-hand side.

Chocolate Chip Cookies

2/3 cup butter

1/2 cup white sugar

2/3 cup brown sugar

2 eggs

2 teaspoons vanilla

2 1/4 cups flour

1 teaspoon baking soda

1/2 teaspoon salt

1 1/2 cups chocolate chips

3/4 cup chopped walnuts

Beat butter and sugar together. Add vanilla and eggs. Sift all dry ingredients together and add to the butter and egg mixture. Mix thoroughly. Add chocolate chips and nuts. Take a heaping tablespoon of dough and roll it into a ball. Place each ball 2" apart on a greaseless cookie sheet. Bake for 8–10 minutes at 375 degrees. Remove cookie sheet from oven and place cookies on a rack to cool.

Chocolate Chip Cookies—Halved Recipe

_____ cup(s) butter

_____ cup(s) white sugar

_____ cup(s) brown sugar

_____ egg(s)

_____ teaspoon(s) vanilla

_____ cup(s) flour

_____ teaspoon(s) baking soda

_____ teaspoon(s) salt

_____ cup(s) chocolate chips

_____ cup(s) chopped walnuts

Beat butter and sugar together. Add vanilla and eggs. Sift all dry ingredients together and add to the butter and egg mixture. Mix thoroughly. Add chocolate chips and nuts. Take a heaping tablespoon of dough and roll it into a ball. Place each ball 2" apart on a greaseless cookie sheet. Bake for 8–10 minutes at 375 degrees. Remove cookie sheet from oven and place cookies on a rack to cool.

DIRECTIONS

Work with your group to solve the following problem. Choose a note-taker to record your answers.

Your family wants to take a vacation and has made a budget of $1,400. In order to raise the money for this vacation, the family has decided to have a yard sale. Different family members are selling the following items:

Mother

2 twin beds at $75 each

bicycle $70

6 pairs of jeans (size 8) at $5 each

70 paperback books at $1 each

20 plastic glasses at 50¢ each

Father

skis and poles $125

motorcycle (Honda 175cc) $275

hiking boots $50

lamp $50

10 assorted kitchen plates at $1 each

Oldest Brother

rollerblades $60

cassette player $30

10 shirts at $2 each

10 pairs of pants at $2 each

Middle Brother

small bicycle $40

20 assorted toys at $2 each

5 pairs of shoes at $4 per pair

Youngest Brother

CD player and CDs $20

20 assorted toys at $2 each

Sister

15 pairs of shoes at $2 per pair

15 pants and shorts at $2 each

10 skirts at $2 each

Other Items for Sale

crib and mattress $45

stroller $15

table $40

2 outdoor chairs $20 for the pair

2 lounge chairs $80 for the pair

small sofa $85

1 How much would the family make if they sold everything? Would it be enough for their vacation?

2 If all the items sold, how much would each family member contribute?

3 What is the most expensive item being sold? Who is selling it?

4 If the family didn't sell the table, outdoor chairs, and motorcycle, would they still have enough money for the vacation? How short would they be or how much extra would they have?

Multiple Intelligences and Language Learning © 2005 Alta Book Center Publishers, San Francisco, California
www.altaesl.com   Permission granted to photocopy for one teacher's classroom use only.

What's Inside?

Guessing Grid

DIRECTIONS

1 Complete the chart below for the box you have.

2 Guess as a group what the box contains.

3 After you guess, pass the box on to another group.

4 After all groups have guessed what is in all boxes, open the boxes.

Box Number	Size	Smell	Shape	Weight	Sounds like	Guess: what is it?
Box 1						
Box 2						
Box 3						
Box 4						
Box 5						
Box 6						

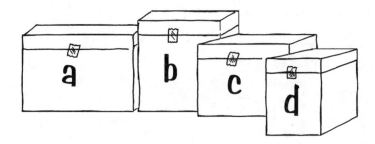

Task 1

You go to the grocery store to buy milk, bananas, and bread. The total bill is $4.39. You give the clerk a five-dollar bill. Role-play this exchange with a partner. Make correct change.

Task 2

You go to the bookstore to buy a book for your sister's birthday. The book costs $15.29. You give the clerk a twenty-dollar bill. Role-play this exchange with a partner. Count out the correct change.

Task 3

Two movie tickets cost $12.50. You give the ticket vendor a ten-dollar bill and a five-dollar bill. Role-play this exchange with a partner. Count out the correct change.

Task 4

You pay for your hotel room with cash. The invoice is for $89.00. You give the cashier a $100 bill. Role-play this exchange with a partner. Count out the correct change.

Task 5

You must pay to park your car at the airport. The cost is $5.00 per day with a maximum of $20.00 a week. Your car has been parked at the airport for 10 days. You give the ticket attendant three twenty-dollar bills. Role-play this exchange with a partner. Count out the correct change.

Multiple Intelligences and Language Learning © 2005 Alta Book Center Publishers, San Francisco, California www.altaesl.com. Permission granted to photocopy for one teacher's classroom use only.

Visual/Spatial Intelligence

*"I found I could say things with color and shapes
that I couldn't say in any other way—
things I had no words for."*

— Georgia O'Keeffe (1887–1986)

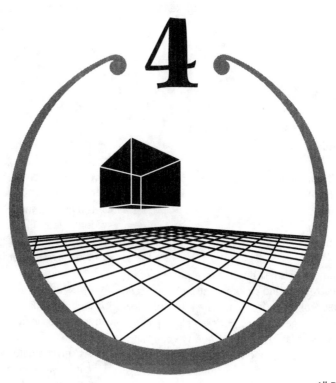

The activities in this unit help students develop their visual/spatial intelligence by:

developing a good sense of direction

locating objects on maps

remembering visual details

working with mazes

recognizing visual patterns

paying attention to spatial relationships

responding to color and form

Unit 4 Photocopiable Handouts   137

4.1 All Boxed Up

Age Group
Middle school to adult

Language Level
Beginning

INTELLIGENCES DEVELOPED	OBJECTIVES

Visual/spatial

Linguistic

Logical/mathematical

To develop vocabulary

To make logical connections from visual cues

Materials Needed
- Small boxes
- Small pictures representing categories (e.g., food, house, classroom)
- Vocabulary cards
- Scissors
- Board or flipchart

1 Collect a number of small boxes. Cut a paper slot in the top of each one. Find pictures that represent certain categories of words that are useful for beginning-level language students. For example: a picture of a woman (for words like *girl, she, her, woman*, and *female*), food (for words about food), a house (for household items), and a classroom (for school items). Tape a picture to each box (make sure categories are not duplicated).

2 Give each student a handful of vocabulary cards; words may be repeated on the cards, but the words should not be repeated within each student's individual stack. The words should fit within one of the categories.

3 Students must look at each card, understand the word, determine the category to which the word belongs based on the pictures, and drop the card in the appropriate box.

4 Once all of the cards have been placed in their respective boxes, check to see that they are correct. Have two students come to the front of the classroom. Instruct the first student to open the box, take out the cards, and give them to the second student. The second student reads the words out loud. Together the class decides if each card is properly placed. A third student can then tape the cards to the board.

5 Ask students to copy the words on the board into their notebooks, choose five words from the list, and use the words in five original sentences.

6 As an alternate activity, ask students to select five cards, work with a small group, and write a short story or a group of connected sentences using the words on the five selected cards.

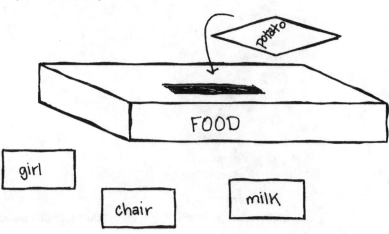

Calendar Daze 4.2

INTELLIGENCES DEVELOPED	OBJECTIVES
Visual/spatial	To develop basic mathematical skills
Interpersonal	To give students meaningful practice in working with numbers
Linguistic	To give students an opportunity to work together
Logical/mathematical	

Age Group
Grade 3 to middle school

Language Level
Beginning to intermediate

Materials Needed
- Old calendars
- Scissors
- Plain white paper
- Glue

1 Divide students into small groups. Give each group several old calendars.

2 Have each group cut out five columns of numbers under the days of the week on various months (i.e., all the numbers under Monday in March) and glue the columns onto one piece of plain white paper.

3 Now ask students to work individually within their groups. Each student should add up the numbers in each column and record his/her answers on a separate sheet of paper. Students should then compare answers within their groups and discuss any differences that may arise.

4 Finally, each group switches papers with another group and students repeat Step 3.

5 Have students repeat Steps 3 and 4 with at least two other groups.

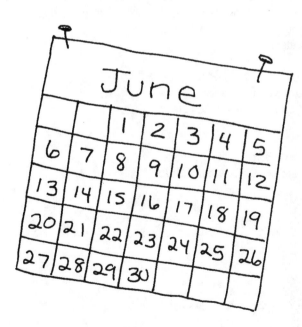

4.3 Can You Believe Your Eyes?

Age Group
High school to adult

Language Level
Intermediate to advanced

INTELLIGENCES DEVELOPED	OBJECTIVES
Visual/spatial	To foster creative expression
Linguistic	To give students practice in completing visual images and seeing patterns

Materials Needed
- One overhead transparency of each of the images on handout 4.3A (for Version One)
- One copy of handout 4.3A for each group of students (for Version Two)
- One overhead transparency or copies of handout 4.3B
- Overhead projector (for Version One)
- Board or flipchart

Version One

1 Place the transparency of Image 1 (handout 4.3A) on the overhead projector.

2 Ask students to tell you what they see and record their answers on the board. If students have sufficient vocabulary, ask them to show you on the transparency where different parts of the picture appear. For example, a student might say, "It looks like a man." You might respond, "Can you show me on the transparency where the man is located?"

3 Place the transparency of Image 2 (handout 4.3A) on the overhead projector. Get feedback from students. Find out if they have changed their minds about what they see.

4 Once all ideas have been recorded, show a transparency of handout 4.3B to reveal the actual picture to students.

Version Two

1 If you do not have an overhead projector, divide students into groups and give one copy of Image 1 (handout 4.3A) to each group.

2 Ask students to discuss what they see. Walk around the room, offering help and encouragement.

3 Give one copy of Image 2 (handout 4.3A) to each group. Ask students to discuss what they see. Have they changed their minds?

4 Conduct a large group discussion, recording ideas on the board and having students show their respective groups what they see.

5 Once all ideas have been recorded, give each group a copy of handout 4.3B to reveal the actual picture.

Events in History 4.4

INTELLIGENCES DEVELOPED	OBJECTIVES

Visual/spatial

Interpersonal

Linguistic

To develop knowledge about historical events

To develop visual awareness for layout and patterns in newspapers

To introduce the structure of short newspaper articles

To give students an opportunity to work together

Age Group
High school to adult

Language Level
Intermediate to advanced

Materials Needed
- Newspapers or news magazines (depending on your choice in Step 1)
- Writing paper
- Computers (if computers aren't available, you'll need scissors, glue, and plain white paper for each group of students)

1 Do one of the following, depending on your curriculum:

a Select a representative year from a time period that you have been studying. Have students make a list of five important events that happened during that year.

b Have students select a year at random. Ask them to leaf through old newspapers or news magazines from that year and choose five important events. This will usually require that you have access to a library.

c Have students focus on events from the past year. In this case, bring newspapers and magazines that you have on hand to class and have students select five important events.

2 After students have identified five events, ask them to write headlines for articles covering those incidents.

3 Students then write short articles for each event. The articles should answer the following questions: What is the event? When did it happen? What happened? Who was involved? Why was the event important?

4 Finally, tell students they are going to create the front page of their own newspaper. In groups, students first study and discuss the front pages of several newspapers. Ask each group to select four principles related to visual form to follow in constructing their own front pages. For example, each article has a heading or title, titles are centered over articles, the print size for titles varies, the largest print size is on the front page, under the newspaper title there is a double line with the date and day of the week, all pictures have captions, etc. Have students write down the principles.

5 Conduct a large group sharing with the entire class. Then have students create their front pages. Access to computers is very helpful; if you don't have computers, students can cut and paste by hand.

6 After all of the front pages have been completed, give each group an opportunity to talk about their "newspaper," the events they identified, and why the group thought the events were important.

7 If you have your own classroom, create a bulletin board featuring all of the front pages.

4.5 **Food Pyramids**

Age Group
Middle school to adult

Language Level
Intermediate to advanced

INTELLIGENCES DEVELOPED	OBJECTIVES
Visual/spatial	To teach important content on food and nutrition
Interpersonal	To develop food vocabulary
Linguistic	To give students an opportunity to work together
Logical/mathematical	

Materials Needed
- One copy of handout 4.5 for each student
- Magazines and/or newspapers
- Plain white paper
- Glue
- Scissors

1 Assemble all materials in piles on a central table and label each pile with a name card. When students are finished with the various items they are using, instruct them to return the materials to the correct piles (i.e., scissors are returned to the pile labeled "scissors," etc.).

2 Give each student a copy of handout 4.5. Draw the pyramid on the board or use an overhead transparency to review the various food categories that form the pyramid (traditionally, categories are as follows, from top to bottom: *Sugar and Fat, Dairy, Protein, Fruit, Vegetables,* and *Carbohydrates).*

3 Ask students to find food pictures in magazines and/or newspapers, cut them out, and glue them in the appropriate pyramid categories on their handout.

4 Follow up with a large group sharing of the different pyramids that students have created. What other food pyramids have students seen? Include the importance of healthy eating in the class discussion.

It Looks Like . . . 4.6

INTELLIGENCES DEVELOPED	OBJECTIVES
Visual/spatial	To develop colors and shapes vocabulary
Bodily/kinesthetic	To foster creative expression
Linguistic	To communicate about the location of items
Logical/mathematical	

Materials Needed
- One copy of handout 4.6
- Colored paper
- Scissors
- Plain white paper
- Glue

1 Make shapes out of colored paper using the patterns on handout 4.6 as a guide. Some of the shapes may be standard (i.e., squares, circles, ellipses) while others may be irregular. You'll need to make five shapes for every student.

2 Place all materials on a central table. Ask each student to choose five colored shapes. Each student glues his/her shapes to a piece of plain white paper in any arrangement he/she chooses.

3 Once students are finished, conduct a large group sharing. Call on students individually to talk about their pictures. For example, "I have a green cylinder in the top left corner and a red triangle in the center." Encourage students to talk about what unusual shapes resemble. Older children in grades 3 and 4 may be able to do a small group sharing once they have had a chance to share for a few minutes in a larger group. If small group sharing is not possible, the individual sharing can be extended over two or three days with five or six students sharing their pictures each day.

4 If you have your own classroom, create a bulletin board with the picture shapes.

4.7 Learning Gameboard

Age Group
Grades 3 to 5

Language Level
Intermediate

INTELLIGENCES DEVELOPED	OBJECTIVES
Visual/spatial	To reinforce content
Interpersonal	To give students an opportunity to work together
Linguistic	

Materials Needed
- One copy of handout 4.7A for each group of students
- Several copies of handout 4.7B for each group of students
- Colored markers
- Scissors
- One die
- Playing pieces (i.e., small buttons of various colors)

1 Divide students into groups. Give a copy of handout 4.7A, one die, and playing pieces to each group. You might want to enlarge the handout to create a bigger gameboard and more playing space.

2 Give colored markers to each group. Have students mark each square of the gameboard with a different color.

3 Give each group several copies of handout 4.7B. Tell students that they are going to make gameboard cards using the patterns on the handout. Students first cut out the blank cards, then divide the cards within their group. Each student should have one to three cards.

4 Ask students to write a simple task they could ask another student to do on each card (i.e., "spell the word truck" or "count to 20 by even numbers"). Walk around the room, checking what students have written and collecting cards. Once all of the cards have been collected, place a pile of cards on the spot marked "Gameboard Cards" on each group's gameboard.

5 Use one group to model the procedure for playing the game. Choose a student to go first by throwing the die. The student can move ahead on the board only after drawing a card and performing the task on the card to the satisfaction of the other members of the group. If the question or request on the card is not answered or performed adequately, the student cannot move ahead.

6 In groups, students play the game! The goal of the game is to be the first to reach the end of the gameboard.

Map Reading 4.8

Age Group
High school to adult

Language Level
Intermediate to advanced

INTELLIGENCES DEVELOPED	OBJECTIVES

Visual/spatial

Interpersonal

Linguistic

To develop map reading skills

To develop knowledge about different countries in the world and national borders

To give students an opportunity to work together

Materials Needed
- One copy of handout 4.8 for each pair or group of students
- World maps or atlases
- Answer key 4.8

1 Give each pair or group of students a world map or atlas and a copy of handout 4.8 (you may also write the handout questions on the board or make a transparency and use an overhead projector).

2 Ask students to answer as many questions as they can without the reference. Then allow them to use the map/atlas to finish.

3 Once students have answered all the questions, have them write 14 additional questions about world geography. Check student-generated questions for clarity.

4 Have pairs/groups exchange papers and answer each others' questions. Check answers.

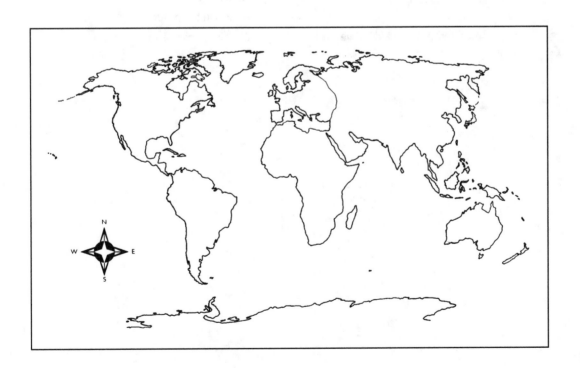

4.9 Match Me Up

Age Group
Grades 2 to 4

Language Level

Beginning

INTELLIGENCES DEVELOPED	OBJECTIVES

Visual/spatial

Interpersonal

Linguistic

Logical/mathematical

To reinforce language development with visual cues

To see logical relationships

To give students an opportunity to work together

Materials Needed
• Magazines
• Colored construction paper
• Scissors
• Glue

1 To carry out this activity, you will need word and picture cards. To create your own cards, first cut out interesting images from magazines. The pictures should have a central focus—food, fashion, sports, etc. Glue each picture onto colored construction paper. Have the mounted pictures laminated if possible (good pictures are hard to find, so do what you can to keep them in nice condition!). On separate sheets of construction paper of a similar size, write the corresponding vocabulary.

2 Mix up the word and picture cards. Give each student a card.

3 Have students hold their cards against their bodies so no one sees their word or picture. Ask students to find a corresponding word or picture, depending on the card they have. For example, Student 1 has a picture. She begins by asking Student 2, "Do you have a picture or a word?" Student 2 answers, "I have a word." Student 1 asks, "What is the word?" Student 2 says the word. If students believe their word and picture match, they stand together and stop searching. This questioning technique must be taught to beginning-level students in advance. If this is the first time students are doing the activity, it is helpful to write the following questions on the board:

Do you have a picture or a word?

What is the word?

What is in the picture?

What is it a picture of?

Measuring and Graphing 4.10

INTELLIGENCES DEVELOPED	OBJECTIVES
Visual/spatial	To give students meaningful practice in working with numbers
Interpersonal	To give students practice in measuring and graphing information
Linguistic	To develop vocabulary for talking about shapes and numbers
Logical/mathematical	To give students an opportunity to work together

Materials Needed
- One copy of handout 4.10 for each student
- Rulers
- Plain white paper

1 This activity is an excellent follow-up to a lesson on bar graphs (see activity 3.3). It can also be used to introduce the concept. If you use this activity as part of an introductory lesson, draw some sample figures on the board (i.e., a square and a rectangle). Have students measure the figures and then show them how to graph their findings (see the directions on handout 4.10).

2 Once students understand the concept, give a copy of handout 4.10, a plain white sheet of paper, and a ruler to each student. Ask students to work individually within groups to measure the figures and create graphs.

3 Once all students in a group have completed their individual graphs, ask them to appoint a note-taker to record the answers to the questions on handout 4.10.

4 When groups have finished, conduct a large group sharing. Collect one answer sheet from each group.

4.11 Memory Pictures

Age Group
Middle school to adult

Language Level
All (the conversation involved can be beginning to advanced)

INTELLIGENCES DEVELOPED	OBJECTIVES
Visual/spatial	To reinforce language development with visual cues
Interpersonal	To develop personal strategies for recalling information
Intrapersonal	To give students an opportunity to work together
Linguistic	

Materials Needed
- One copy of a picture containing many items for each group
- Board or flipchart

1 Divide students into small groups. Give each group a copy of the same picture. Ask students to put the picture face down. The picture should remain face down until all groups have received the picture.

2 When all groups are ready, ask them to turn over their picture and study it. Tell them to try to get a good mental image of everything they see in the picture. Give them one minute. When the minute is up, tell the groups to turn over the picture again.

3 Give each group five minutes to recall items from the picture. Have students work individually at first. After five minutes, ask them to share their individual lists with the group, adding things they may have forgotten.
4 Allow groups to look at the picture again, adding items they may have missed altogether.

5 Conduct a large group sharing. Ask one student to list 10 things on the board and another student to add 10 more without repeating items. Continue in this manner until no more items can be listed.

7 Finally, students explain the mnemonics they used to help them remember the items. List the techniques on the board.

Family Gift Boxes 4.12

INTELLIGENCES DEVELOPED	OBJECTIVES	**Age Group**

Visual/spatial

Bodily/kinesthetic

Linguistic

To develop finger dexterity

To foster creative expression

To give students practice in expressing gratitude

Age Group
Grades 3 to 5

Language Level
Beginning

Materials Needed
• One copy of handout 4.12 for each student
• Colored markers
• Scissors
• Glue or tape
• Writing paper

1 Give one copy of handout 4.12 to each student. Ask students to color and decorate the pattern on the handout.

2 Show students how to cut the pattern out, fold it along the lines, and tape or glue it in place to form a "gift box." Keep the top of the box open.

3 Once the boxes have been assembled, students write a brief note to someone in their family using the sample below. You might want to write this sample on the board for students to copy. Students will need to understand what the letter says in order to supply the appropriate information.

4 Finally, tell students to place the letters in the gift boxes and tape them shut. Each student should then give his/her box to the recipient of the letter inside.

Dear _____,

This gift box is a thank you gift for you. I want to thank you for _____, and _____.

Love,

[student signs his/her name]

4.13 Preference Clocks

Age Group
Grades 3 to 5

Language Level
Beginning

INTELLIGENCES DEVELOPED

Visual/spatial

Interpersonal

Linguistic

Logical/mathematical

OBJECTIVES

To give meaningful practice in telling time and adding and subtracting numbers

To develop vocabulary for talking about numbers and time

To develop problem-solving skills

To give students an opportunity to work together

Materials Needed
- One copy of handout 4.13 for each student or group
- File folders
- Glue
- Scissors
- Hole punch
- Brads
- Board or flipchart

1 Before class, follow the instructions on handout 4.13 to create a clock for each student or group of students.

2 Students must already have a basic understanding of telling time to do this activity. Give each student (or group) a clock. Write these questions on the board:

What time is your favorite time to . . .

get up?

go to bed?

eat breakfast?

eat lunch?

eat dinner?

watch a movie?

study?

3 Tell students to first answer the questions individually. Then have each student share his/her answers in a group. All students should record the responses of fellow group members.

4 After students answer the first set of questions, ask them to answer the following:

What is the range of times people in this class prefer to . . .

go to bed?

eat breakfast?

eat lunch?

eat dinner?

watch a movie?

study?

What's the earliest time at which someone prefers to eat breakfast? The latest?

What's the time difference?

5 Conduct a large group sharing. Students should use their clocks when giving answers. One student can read the answer, while another moves the hands of the clock (e.g., "Our group prefers to get up between 6:00 am and 9:00 am.").

Puppets 4.14

INTELLIGENCES DEVELOPED

Visual/spatial

Bodily/kinesthetic

Interpersonal

Linguistic

OBJECTIVES

To foster creative expression

To give students an opportunity to use manipulatives

To give students an opportunity to work together

Materials Needed
- One copy of handout 4.14 for each student
- Colored markers
- Scissors
- Paper bags
- Yarn
- Glue

1 Assemble all materials in piles on a central table and label each pile with a name card. When students are finished with the various items they are using, instruct them to return the materials to the correct piles (i.e., scissors are returned to the pile labeled "scissors," etc.).

2 Show students a model of the puppet they will be making. If you have not done this activity with your classes before, you will need to make a couple of samples by following these steps (using a copy of handout 4.14):

Color the hat, ears, feet, and arm patterns.

Cut out the patterns.

Get a paper bag.

Add yarn for hair. Glue the hat, ears, arms, and feet on the bag.

Draw a face on the front of the bag.

Give your puppet a name. Write it at the bottom.

3 Students create their puppets following the same steps.

4 When students have completed their puppets, tell them to bring their puppets to life by placing their hands in the bags. Students then interact with their puppets through the following dialogs, role-plays, and other activities.

Dialog 1

A. What is your name?

B. My name is

_____.

A. What do you like to do?

B. I like to _____.

Dialog 2

A. What's your name?

B. I'm _____. What's yours?

A. I'm _____. What are you doing after school?

B. I'm _____. What about you?

A. I'm _____. Do you want to come?

B. Thanks, I do.

Role-Play

Imagine that you and your friend are planning a party. Decide when it will be, where, what time, whom to invite, and what to do. Use your puppets as the characters in the role-play.

Other Activities

Line up five or six puppets in a row. Ask one student to mentally choose one of the puppets and describe it to the rest of the class. The class members listen to the description and then guess which puppet is being described.

Make a bulletin board with the puppets. Choose one puppet from the board and describe it to the class. Ask students to identify which one you are describing.

Make a bulletin board with the puppets. Select three puppets and ask students to talk about the differences.

4.15 Ringing Bells

	INTELLIGENCES DEVELOPED	OBJECTIVES

Age Group
Grades 2 to 5

Language Level
Beginning

INTELLIGENCES DEVELOPED

Visual/spatial

Bodily/kinesthetic

Interpersonal

Linguistic

OBJECTIVES

To develop vocabulary

To develop finger dexterity

To foster creative expression

To give students an opportunity to work together

Materials Needed
- Copies of handout 4.15
- Colored construction paper
- Glue
- Scissors
- Ribbons
- Buttons
- Glitter
- Colored markers

1 Give each student a pattern for the bell, tree, or ball from handout 4.15. Have students trace the pattern on a colored sheet of construction paper.

2 Assemble all decorating materials in piles on a central table and label each pile with a name card. When students are finished with the various items they are using, instruct them to return the materials to the correct piles (i.e., scissors are returned to the pile labeled "scissors," etc.).

3 Students decorate their pattern.

4 When each student finishes, he/she writes a brief description of his/her item.

5 Select two of the same items that are decorated differently and ask the class to identify the differences and similarities. Refer to the vocabulary lists below.

Nouns	Verbs	Adjectives
ball	to cut out	blue
bell	to paste	brown
colored paper		green
glitter		orange
glue		pink
ribbon		purple
scissors		red
tree		yellow

Rooms in My House 4.16

Age Group
Grade 5 to middle school

Language Level
Intermediate

INTELLIGENCES DEVELOPED

Visual/spatial

Bodily/kinesthetic

Interpersonal

Linguistic

Logical/mathematical

OBJECTIVES

To develop vocabulary for talking about common household items

To develop a sense of the logical relationships between household items and the rooms they usually belong in

To give students an opportunity to work together

Materials Needed
- One copy of handout 4.16A for each student
- One copy of handouts 4.16B and 4.16C for each pair of students
- Colored markers
- Scissors
- File folders

1 Ask students to work in pairs. Give each student a copy of handout 4.16A. Give Student A in each pair a copy of handout 4.16B. Give Student B in each pair a copy of handout 4.16C.

2 Pairs decide on a color for each room on handout 4.16A. Using colored markers, they color their floor plans. The floor plans of both students should look exactly alike.

3 Next, ask students to cut apart the words and pictures on handouts 4.16B and 4.16C; Student A should have all the words, while Student B has all the pictures.

4 Ask pairs to sit either back-to-back or side-by-side with a file folder between them so that they do not see each other's floor plans and words or pictures.

5 Student A then reads a word to Student B and Student B finds the corresponding picture.

6 Student A puts the word in the room in which he/she thinks it belongs on his/her floor plan, and Student B does the same with the picture for his/her floor plan.

7 Pairs repeat Steps 5 and 6 until all the words and pictures have been placed.

8 Ask pairs to compare their floor plans, checking to see if they have the same answers. When partners' answers are different, encourage them to converse and find out why.

9 Follow up with a large group sharing and discussion.

4.17 Scrambled Up

Age Group
Middle school to adult

Language Level
All (varies depending on the complexity of the sentences chosen)

INTELLIGENCES DEVELOPED

Visual/spatial

Interpersonal

Linguistic

Logical/mathematical

OBJECTIVES

To develop vocabulary

To improve spelling

To develop logical thinking skills

To recognize patterns in combinations of letters

To give students an opportunity to work together

Materials Needed
- Handout 4.17
- One copy of a worksheet based on handout 4.17 for each student
- Answer key 4.17

1 Using handout 4.17 as a guideline, create a worksheet of scrambled sentences that address content being studied in your class. The sentences should be related as in the sample handout (this sample could be used with a lesson on mammals).

2 Group students into pairs. Give each pair a copy of the handout. Ask students to decipher the scrambled words in the sentences and write their answers on the lines provided. Walk around, identifying and helping students who are having trouble.

3 Follow up with a large group sharing to check answers.

Self-Service 4.18

INTELLIGENCES DEVELOPED	OBJECTIVES
Visual/spatial	To give students practice in working with images and shapes
Bodily/kinesthetic	To foster creative expression
Interpersonal	To give students practice in seeing patterns
Linguistic	To reinforce language development through movement
Logical/mathematical	To give students an opportunity to work together

Age Group
Grade 5 to middle school

Language Level
Intermediate

Materials Needed
- Copies of handout 4.18A (see Step 2)
- Colored paper
- Scissors
- Copies of handouts 4.18B, 4.18C, 4.18D, and 4.18E (the combined total copies should equal the number of students in your class)
- Glue
- Plain white paper
- Rulers

1 Divide students into groups of four.

2 Make copies of handout 4.18A on four different colors of paper: green, blue, red, and yellow. Each group of students should have four copies of the handout; one in each of the colors.

3 Have groups cut out the figures on their copies and place the figures in piles according to shape and color. Put all materials on a central table.

4 Ask each student to choose a second handout (4.18B, 4.18C, 4.18D, or 4.18E) and select shapes from the central table according to his/her handout's directions. Students glue the selected shapes onto pieces of plain white paper.

5 Give each student a ruler. Each student works individually to answer the questions on his/her handout.

6 After students have answered the questions, ask them to form groups according to their handout's letter (i.e., all students with handout 4.18B should work together). Students check their answers in these groups.

7 Finally, conduct a large group sharing.

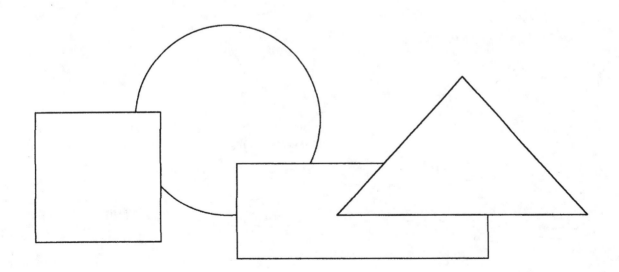

4.19 Semantic Mapping

Age Group
Grade 3 to adult

Language Level
Intermediate to advanced

INTELLIGENCES DEVELOPED

Visual/spatial

Linguistic

Logical/mathematical

OBJECTIVES

To draw upon student knowledge

To create connections between images and content

To develop logical thinking skills

Materials Needed
• Board or flipchart

1 Semantic mapping can be used as a pre-reading or pre-listening activity for almost any academic content. It is an excellent warm-up activity for group discussion as well. To begin the activity, write the content area on which you want to focus in the middle of the board and circle it. For example, "mammals."

2 Ask students to tell you what they already know about mammals or perhaps what comes to mind when you say the word "mammals." Students might give examples of mammals (e.g., cats, dogs, bats, whales), features of mammals (e.g., mammary glands, young born alive), or habitats (e.g., land, water), etc. As students volunteer information, write their contributions on the board and connect them to the topic. Study this example of semantic mapping to clarify your understanding of this organizing principle:

3 Once completed, the semantic maps can be used in a variety of ways:

Students might compare what they will read about the topic with what they thought they knew before reading.

In small groups or pairs, students make lists of what is missing, what is true, or what is false.

Semantic mapping can also be used as a springboard for student discussion in small groups (i.e., "What new information did you learn?") or for short student writing assignments following the mapping activity.

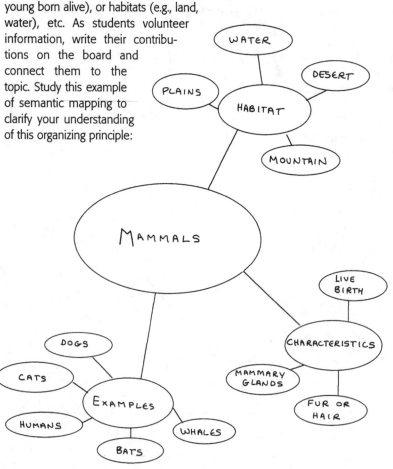

Shared Writing 4.20

INTELLIGENCES DEVELOPED	OBJECTIVES
Visual/spatial	To foster creative expression
Interpersonal	To make logical connections between ideas
Linguistic	To give students an opportunity to work together

Age Group
High school to adult

Language Level
Intermediate to advanced

Materials Needed
- One magazine picture of a person for each student
- Scissors
- Glue
- Colored construction paper
- Stapler
- Plain white paper

1 Find interesting pictures of people in magazines, cut them out, and mount them on pieces of colored construction paper. Each picture should focus on one person.

2 Staple a blank piece of white paper to the back of each picture.

3 Ask students to get into groups of four or five; group sizes should be as uniform as is possible.

4 Give each student a picture. Ask students to look carefully at their pictures, but not to show them to anyone else.

5 Read questions #1 listed below. Instruct students to write the answer to the questions on the blank piece of paper attached to their pictures.

6 When students have finished, ask them to pass their picture (with the answers to questions #1 on the back) to the person on their right.

7 Ask students to evaluate the picture and read what the previous student has written. Read questions #2 and have students answer them.

8 The pictures and answers circulate in this way until all questions have been read and answered. On the final pass, students should receive the picture they started with.

9 Follow up with a large group sharing. This activity is an excellent way for students to develop writing fluency. Once students realize that the story will be shared and that they are responsible for only a part of the writing, they become focused on the message and relaxed in their composition.

Sample questions for groups of four or five

1. What is this person's name? How old is he/she? Where does he/she live?

2. Where does this person work? Does this person like his/her job?

3. Tell me about this person's family. Is this person married? Does he/she have children? Parents?

4. What does this person like to do in his/her free time? What are his/her hobbies?

5. What is something that this person loves to do? Hates to do?

4.21 Spelling Puzzles

Age Group
Grade 3 to middle school

Language Level
Intermediate to advanced

INTELLIGENCES DEVELOPED	OBJECTIVES
Visual/spatial	To develop vocabulary
Linguistic	To improve listening skills
Logical/mathematical	To improve spelling
	To foster creative expression
	To see patterns in written language

Materials Needed
- Handout 4.21
- One worksheet based on handout 4.21 for each student
- Colored markers
- Answer key 4.21

1 Using handout 4.21 and its corresponding dictation as a guide, prepare a worksheet of vocabulary words with missing letters. You can use the sample; remember, however, that a worksheet that includes the specific words with which students have been working is going to be more effective than a general list.

2 Dictate the letters in the words in random order. Students listen and write the letters down as they hear them.

> **Dictation**
> 1. doar
> 2. reeng
> 3. nair
> 4. ysk
> 5. grof
> 6. dhan
> 7. gof

3 After the letters in the words have been dictated, students unscramble the words using the letters provided and blank spaces to guide them.

4 Once the missing letters have been added and students identify the word, they use colored markers to create a quick sketch of the item spelled.

Visual Names 4.22

INTELLIGENCES DEVELOPED	OBJECTIVES

Visual/spatial

Linguistic

To foster creative expression

To give students meaningful practice in using the letters of the alphabet

To give students practice in writing their names

To see visual patterns and relationships

Age Group
Grade 1 to middle school

Language Level
All

Materials Needed
- Plain white paper
- Colored markers

1 Give each student a piece of plain white paper. Explain to students that they are going to create a series of several folds in the paper. They must listen to your directions carefully and crease the fold lines several times so that the lines become more visible when the paper is unfolded.

2 Next, ask each student to write his/her first name or nickname in the squares, repeating the name continuously until all squares are full. For example, Mary Ann would write:

3 Ask students to assign a color and/or design to each letter of their name (i.e., "m" is yellow, "a" is green, "r" is striped, etc.). Instruct students to color/design each box according to the letter's assigned color/design. When students finish, they will have their own unique visual representation of their names.

4 As a follow-up activity, ask students to describe the visual representation of their name either orally or in writing. For example, at the beginning level, students might simply describe the colors they have chosen. At a more advanced level, students might give a more detailed description: "The letter 'a' is colored blue with black spots. It is in the middle of the red striped squares and the black squares. These three designs dominate the pattern because they are the bolder, darker colors."

5 If you teach in a classroom where you can create a bulletin board, make an interesting "quilt" design with all the names.

Directions

1. Hold your piece of paper.
2. First fold the paper in half lengthwise.
3. Fold it in half again.
4. Fold it in half again.
5. Open the paper. There should be eight columns.
6. Fold the paper in half widthwise.
7. Fold it in half again.
8. Fold it in half again.
9. Open the paper. There should be 64 squares in total.

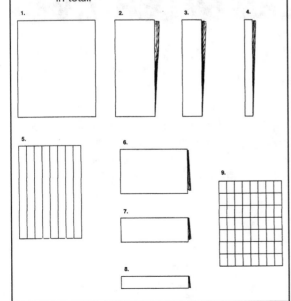

4.23 Weaving

Age Group
Grades 3 to 5

Language Level
Beginning

INTELLIGENCES DEVELOPED

Visual/spatial

Bodily/kinesthetic

OBJECTIVES

To foster creative expression

To develop vocabulary for describing patterns and colors

To introduce students to the concept of weaving

To provide tactile stimulation for learners

Materials Needed
- Scissors
- Colored paper
- Box (or some type of container to hold paper strips)
- Swatches of woven fabric
- One copy of handouts 4.23A and 4.23B for each student
- Glue

1 Cut several sheets of different colored paper into strips approximately 3/4" by 8 1/2". Mix up the colors and put them all in a box. Place the box, scissors, and glue on a central table.

2 Show examples of woven fabric to students. Explain to them that they are going to make woven designs using paper.

3 Give each student one copy of handouts 4.23A and 4.23B. Go over the instructions for steps 1-3 on handout 4.23A. Show students how to fold their papers in half and where and how far to cut.

4 When all students have successfully finished cutting their papers, have them choose eight or nine strips from the box and go over steps 4-8 with them, modeling how the weaving works.

5 When finished, each student will have their own unique woven creation. If you teach in a classroom where you can create a bulletin board, make an interesting "quilt" design with all the woven pieces.

4.24 Word Mazes

Age Group
Middle school to adult

Language Level
All (depending on the words being used)

INTELLIGENCES DEVELOPED

Visual/spatial

Linguistic

OBJECTIVES

To reinforce vocabulary

To reinforce letters, the alphabet, and letter combinations

To help students see visual patterns

Materials Needed
- One copy of handout 4.24A, 4.24B, 4.24C, 4.24D, 4.24E, 4.24F, or 4.24G for each student or pair
- Answer key 4.24A, 4.24B, 4.24C, 4.24D, 4.24E, 4.24F, or 4.24G

1 Give one copy of the selected handout to each student or pair of students. Ask students to work through the vocabulary list, finding each word in the maze, circling it, and checking it off the list. Show students how words may be horizontal, vertical, diagonal, backwards, or forwards.

2 Once students have found all of the words, conduct a large group sharing. Ask students to describe where they found the words (i.e., in handout 4.24A, the word "markers" is at the beginning of the last row).

DIRECTIONS TO THE TEACHER

Make overhead transparencies or copies of the images.ake overhead transparencies or copies of the images.

Image 1

- -

Image 2

Can You Believe Your Eyes?

Image 3

DIRECTIONS TO THE TEACHER

Show this image after students have completed the activity. Make an overhead transparency or copies of it.

Image 3

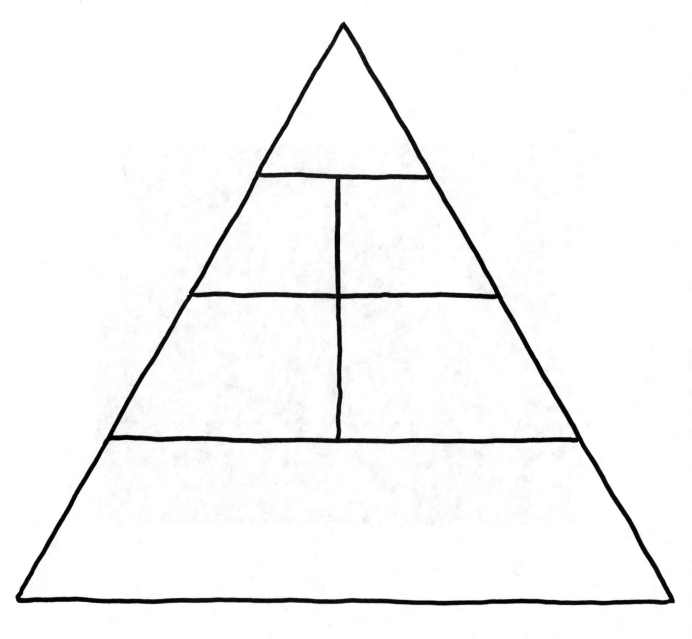

It Looks Like . . .
Patterns

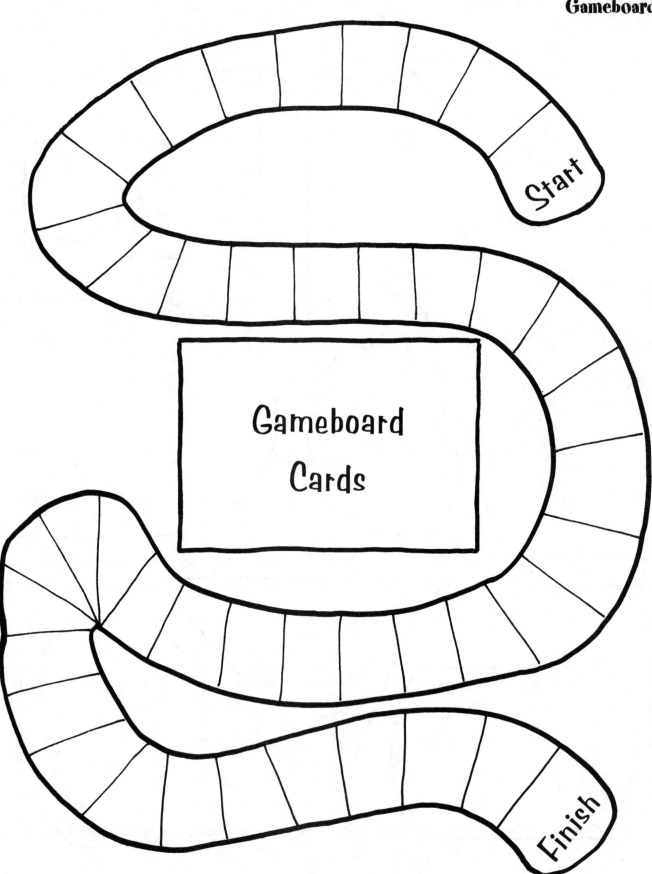

Start

Gameboard

Cards

Finish

Learning Gameboard
Gameboard Cards

1 What countries border France?

2 What countries border the United States?

3 Where is Peru? What countries border Peru?

4 Which country is farther north, Argentina or South Africa? How do you know?

5 What is to the west of the United States? To the east?

6 What countries surround Switzerland?

7 How many main islands make up Japan?

8 In what country is the city of Mumbai? Where is that country located?

9 Where is Rio de Janeiro? Buenos Aires?

10 Which city is farther south, Miami, Florida or Florence, Italy? How do you know?

11 What countries in North Africa border the Mediterranean?

12 What countries share a border with Jordan?

13 In what country is Toronto? In what part of that country is it located?

14 Which city is farther north, Beijing or Taipei?

Measuring and Graphing

Squares and Rectangles

DIRECTIONS

1 Look at the squares and rectangles below. Measure the length and width of each figure and write the measurements on this handout.

2 On a separate piece of paper, make two bar graphs. Use 1/2 of the paper for each graph. Graph the widths on one graph and the lengths on the other. Place the letters identifying the figures across the bottom and the measurements along the left-hand side. Label and color each bar on the graph and make a key.

3 When you are finished, answer the following questions:

Which figure has the shortest width? Length?

Which figure has the longest width? Length?

Which figure is closest to being a square?

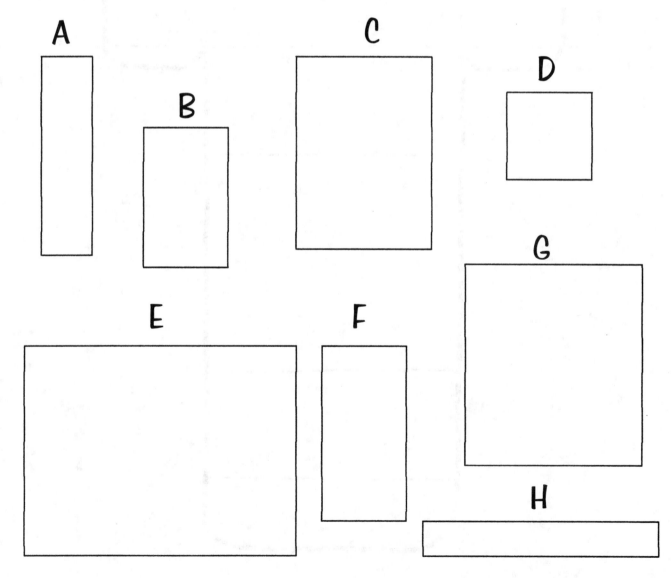

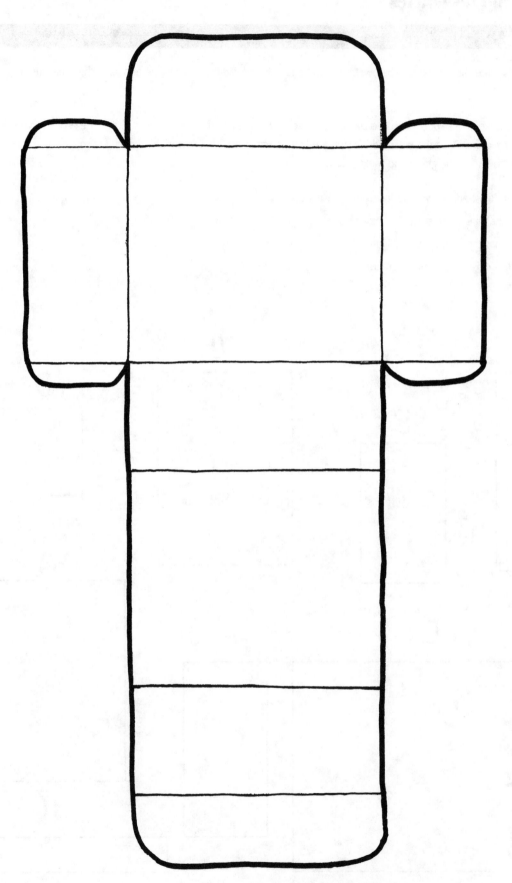

Preference Clocks

Patterns

DIRECTIONS FOR THE TEACHER

1 Cut a file folder in half. Mount a copy of this page onto the file folder using glue.

2 Cut out the clock and the clock hands.

3 Punch a hole in the flat end of each clock hand and the center of the clock.

4 Insert a small brad so that it goes through the clock hands and the clock. Fasten the brad on the back side of the clock. The clock hands should move easily.

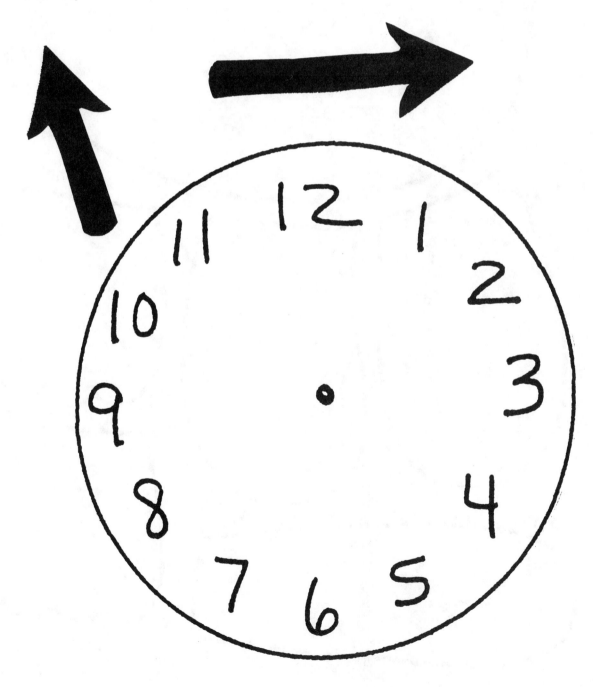

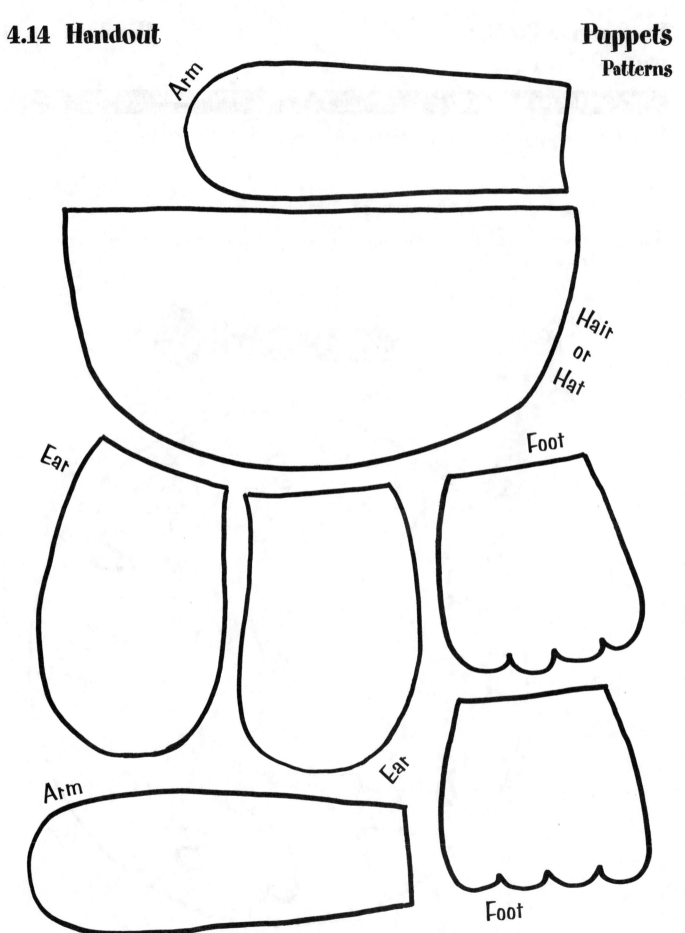

Arm

Hair
or
Hat

Ear

Foot

Ear

Arm

Foot

Patterns

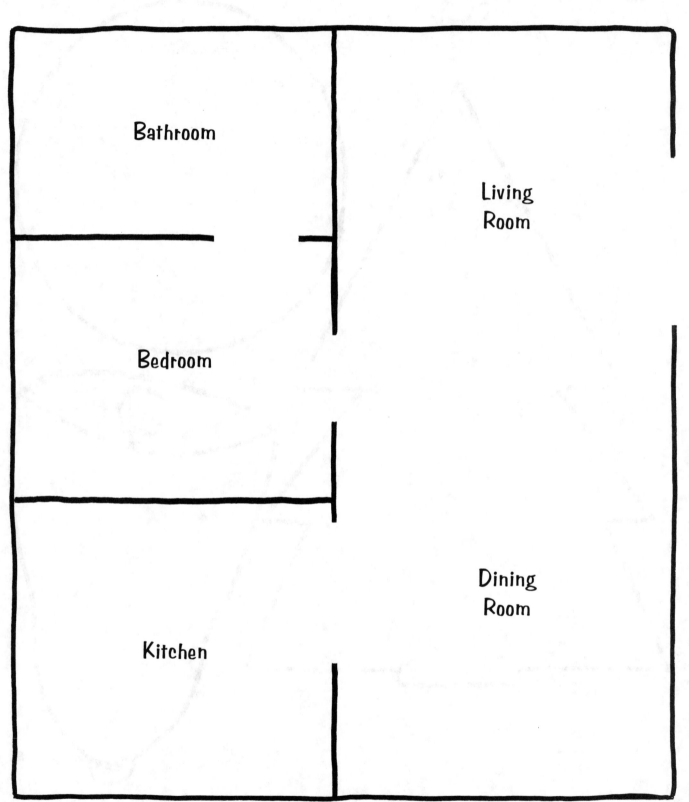

Words

coffee table	end tables	hairbrush	dresser with mirror	chest with three drawers
dining table	queen-sized bed	chest with six drawers	twin beds	wastebasket
sofa	pictures	pots	pans	computer
stools	chairs	television	refrigerator	stove
bookcase	radio	toothbrush	soap	comb
towels	dishes	silverware	sewing machine	armchair

Multiple Intelligences and Language Learning © 2005 Alta Book Center Publishers, San Francisco, California

Sentences

Multiple Intelligences and Language Learning © 2005 Alta Book Center Publishers, San Francisco, California
www.altaesl.com Permission granted to photocopy for one teacher's classroom use only.

DIRECTIONS

Work with a partner to unscramble the sentences below. Rewrite the sentences on the lines provided.

1 amamlsm evah raih.

_____

2 toms amamlsm ear norb aliev.

_____

3 leswha ear esa amamlsm.

_____

4 leswha ear losa het gestlar amamlsm.

_____

5 meso amamlsm kiel melsac veil ni het serted.

_____

6 gynou amamlsm ear def kilm romf rieth thersom.

_____

7 tacs nda gods ear amamlsm.

_____

8 manhus ear losa amamlsm.

_____

4.18A Handout

DIRECTIONS TO THE TEACHER

This page should be copied in four colors—green, blue, red, and yellow.

Multiple Intelligences and Language Learning © 2005 Alta Book Center Publishers, San Francisco, California

Tasks

1 Take these items from the central table:

> green circle
>
> blue rectangle
>
> red square
>
> yellow triangle

2 Glue each figure on a sheet of white paper. Then answer the following questions:

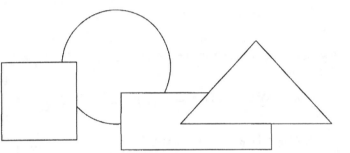

1. What is the diameter of the circle? _____

2. What is the area of the rectangle? _____

3. What is the area of the square? _____

4. What is the area of the triangle? _____

Tasks

1 Take these items from the central table:

> yellow circle
>
> green rectangle
>
> blue square
>
> red triangle

2 Glue each figure on a sheet of white paper. Then answer the following questions:

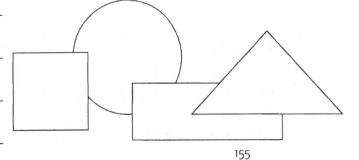

1. What is the diameter of the circle? _____

2. What is the area of the rectangle? _____

3. What is the area of the square? _____

4. What is the area of the triangle? _____

4.18D Handout

DIRECTIONS

1 Take these items from the central table:

    red circle

    yellow rectangle

    green square

    blue triangle

2 Glue each figure on a sheet of white paper. Then answer the following questions:

1. What is the diameter of the circle? _____

2. What is the area of the rectangle? _____

3. What is the area of the square? _____

4. What is the area of the triangle? _____

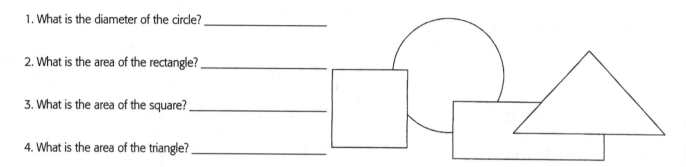

4.18E Handout

DIRECTIONS

1 Take these items from the central table:

    blue circle

    red rectangle

    yellow square

    green triangle

2 Glue each figure on a sheet of white paper. Then answer the following questions:

1. What is the diameter of the circle? _____

2. What is the area of the rectangle? _____

3. What is the area of the square? _____

4. What is the area of the triangle? _____

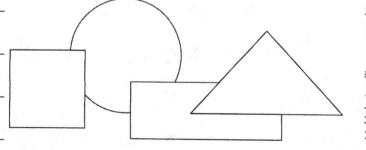

156

Sample

1 Listen as your teacher "spells" the words for you. The letters in the words will be given in random order. Write down each word's letters in Part A.

2 After you have written down all of the letters in the dictation, look at the section of the handout labeled Part B. Study the letters you wrote in Part A. Use this information to help you complete Part B and identify the word.

3 Once you know the word, use colored markers to draw a picture of the word anywhere on your paper. Give the picture a number to match the written word in the list.

Part A

1.

2.

3.

4.

5.

6.

7.

Part B

1. _____ O A _____

2. _____ _____ E E _____

3. _____ A I _____

4. _____ _____ Y

5. _____ _____ O _____

6. _____ A _____ _____

7. _____ O _____

DIRECTIONS

1 This is your weaving sheet.

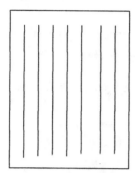

2 Fold your weaving sheet in half.

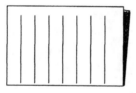

3 Cut along the lines. Cut from the folded edge. Careful! Don't cut farther than the line!

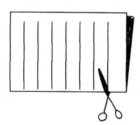

4 Choose eight or nine strips from the teacher's box. Choose the colors you like.

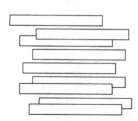

5 Weave one colored strip through your paper. Go over and under.

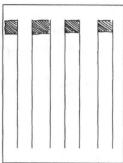

6 Continue weaving strips through the paper until your weaving is finished.

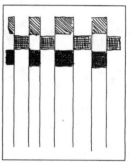

7 Glue down the loose ends. You are finished!

Multiple Intelligences and Language Learning © 2005 Alta Book Center Publishers, San Francisco, California
www.altaesl.com. Permission granted to photocopy for one teacher's classroom use only.

Weaving
Sheet

DIRECTIONS

Find the following words in the word maze below. Words may be horizontal, vertical, diagonal, backwards, or forwards. Check off each word in the list as you find it.

board	computer	notebooks	ruler
book	desk	paper	scissors
chair	eraser	pen	student
chalk	markers	pencil	teacher

```
P E N C I L U I O C O M P U T E R U T S
C A S D F G H C R A S R I U Y T R E W Q
Z H N O T E B O O K S G F D S A R E W Q
Q W A R T Y U M O P L K J T N E D U T S
A S D L G H J P L M N B E R A S E R N B
N O T E K O O U H U Y T P A M E R T T T
C H A Y H G R T H A I R E P O O L K J D
D E S K J Y H E G R F E A W S Q A K J E
Z X C V B N M R K J H G C D S A R E W S
R U L E R G R C H A I R H P O O L K J K
B O O K H A I R G R F E E W S P A P E R
A S D F B L A C K B O A R D X Z P E N B
S C I S S O R S G R F E E S T U D E N T
M A R K E R S T H A I T E A C H E R J D
```

Word Mazes

Animals and Pets

Multiple Intelligences and Language Learning © 2005 Alta Book Center Publishers, San Francisco, California
www.altaesl.com Permission granted to photocopy for one teacher's classroom use only.

DIRECTIONS

Find the following words in the word maze below. Words may be horizontal, vertical, diagonal, backwards, or forwards. Check off each word in the list as you find it.

cats	giraffe	kangaroo	snake
cows	goldfish	lions	tiger
dogs	hamsters	monkey	turtles
elephants	horse	pigs	zebra

```
C A T S C I L T U R T L E S U S E R E G
C A S D F G H C R A S O I U Y T R E L I
Z H N O T T B O R K N G F D S A R E E R
A S D L G H J P E M N B E R A S E R P A
K A N G A R O O H U Y T P I G S R T H F
C H A Y H G R T H A I T E D O G S K A F
D E G O L D F I S H F E U W S Q A K N E
Z X C V B N M R K J H G C R S A R E T S
Z E B R A G R C H A R R H P T O L K S K
H A M P S T E R S R F E E W S L I O N S
A S D F M O N K E Y O A R D X Z E E N B
H O R S E S R S G R F E E S T T I G E R
S N A K E R S T H A I T E A C H C O W S
S D U Y E W T O R K A R E M N G C R B O
```

DIRECTIONS

Find the following words in the word maze below. Words may be horizontal, vertical, diagonal, backwards, or forwards. Check off each word in the list as you find it.

bowl	dish	gratuity	napkin
bread	fish	knife	plate
butter	fork	meat	salad
chicken	fruit	milk	spoon

```
O S D F B L A R K C H I C K E N Z P E N
B O W L U I O C O M M U T E E U T S L G
C A S D F G H C I A E R I U Y T R E W R
Z H N O T E B L O K S A F D S A R E W A
C H I C K E K M O P L K T T N E D U T T
A S D L G H J P L M N B E R A S E N N U
D I S H K O O U H U Y T P L A T E T I I
C H A Y H G R T H A I N K P O O L K J T
D D S K J Y H E G R F A N W S Q A K J Y
Z X C V B N M R K J H P I D S A R E W S
S A L A D G R C H A I K S P O O N K J K
F O R K H A I R R G R I E E W S P A P E
K N I F E L A R K B U T T E R R Z P E N
P L A T E T T I G R F E E S T F R U I T
F I S H H R S T H A I T E A C B R E A D
O S D F B L F U U I T T T E N A P K I N
```

Word Mazes

Clothing

DIRECTIONS

Find the following words in the word maze below. Words may be horizontal, vertical, diagonal, backwards, or forwards. Check off each word in the list as you find it.

belt	hose	shirt	socks
blouse	levis	shoes	sweater
bra	pants	skirt	tie
dress	sandals	slip	t-shirts

```
B E L T L A R S C H I K K E S D P E N B
H O S E U I O A O M M U T E W R T S L L
D A S D F G H N I A E R I U E E R E W O
R H N N T E B D O K S A E D A S R E W U
E H I C K E K A O P L K T T T S D U T S
S S D L G H J L L S K I R T E E N N E E
S H O E S O O S H U Y T P L R T E T I I
C H A Y H G R T H A I N K P O O L K J T
D D S K J Y H E G S F A N W S L E V I S
P A N T S N M R K J H P I D S A R E W S
S A L D D G R C H A I I S P O M N K J K
S O C K S H A P R R S R R E E W S P A P
K N F F E L A R E L U T T T R R K P G N
T T S H I R T S G I F E E S T F I U I T
P I S L I P T T H P I T E A C B R A A D
O S D F B L S R U I T T T E N B T A I N
```

Find the following words in the word maze below. Words may be horizontal, vertical, diagonal, backwards, or forwards. Check off each word in the list as you find it.

bed	dresser	mirror	stove
bookcase	end-table	microwave	table
chair	fridge	rug	television
desk	lamp	sink	toilet

```
M R U G G B L A R K E R H C K E N Z T E
I W W L O I O C O T M U E E E U T S E N
C A S D O G H O I A E R I S Y T R E L D
R H N O K E T B K O K S A F S S U R E T
O H I C C E K M O C L K T T N E G U V A
W S D L A H J P L M A B E R A S R N I B
A I N K S I N K H U Y S P L A R E D S L
V H A Y E G R T H A I N E P E L L K I E
E T O V E Y H E S T O V E S S Q A K O Y
D E S K D N M R K J H P S D S A R E N S
S A L D R T A B L E I E S P Y O N K J K
M I R R O R I R R G R I E L A M P A P E
K N I F L A R K D U T T E R R Z P E N J
P L T T S T F R I D G E E S T F R R I T
F S S H E R S T H A I T E A C B R R A D
C H A I R L F R I I T O I L E T P B E D
```

Word Mazes

Famous People

DIRECTIONS

Find the following words in the word maze below. Words may be horizontal, vertical, diagonal, backwards, or forwards. Check off each word in the list as you find it.

Bill Clinton	John Kennedy	Georgia O'Keeffe
Salvador Dali	Martin Luther King	Britney Spears
Charles DeGaulle	Madonna	R.L. Stein
Michael Jordan	Marilyn Monroe	

```
B S A L V A D O R D A L I A L I Z P E J
I O I L U I O C O M M U T E E U T S L O
L A C D F G H C I A E R I U Y T R E W H
L M A R T I N L U T H E R K I N G E W N
C H A C K E K M O P L K T T N E D U T K
L S M I C H A E L J O R D A N S E N N E
I C H A R L E S D E G A U L L E E T I N
N N J M Y H G R T H A I N K P O O L K N
T D O M A R I L Y N M O N R O E A K M E
O X R V B C M R K J H P I D S A R E A D
N A D R L S T E I N I K S P O N N K D Y
F O A K H A I J R G R I E E W S P A O E
K N N F E L R A G G A J K C I M Z P N N
P L A T E T T I G G F E E S T F R U N T
B R I T N E Y S P E A R S S C B R R A D
G E O R G I A O K E E F F E E N A P K I
```

4.24G Handout

Word Mazes
World Languages

DIRECTIONS

Find the following words in the word maze below. Words may be horizontal, vertical, diagonal, backwards, or forwards. Check off each word in the list as you find it.

Arabic	French	Indonesian	Portuguese
Chinese	German	Japanese	Spanish
English	Hungarian	Navajo	Thai

```
P S D J A P A N E S E I C K E N Z I E H
O O W L U I O C O M M U T E E U T N L U
R A S D F R E N C H E N A V A J O D W N
T H N O T E B L O K S A F D S A R O W G
U H I C K E K M O P L K T T N E D N T A
G S D L G H J P L M N B E H A S E E N R
U I S H K O O U H U Y T P L A T E S I I
E H A Y H C H I N E S E E P O I L I J A
S D S K J Y H E N G F A N W S Q A A J N
E X C V B N M E K J H P I A S A R N W S
E N G L I S H N H A I K S R O O N K J K
D O R K H A I G R G R I E A W S P A P E
K N I E E L A L K B U T T B R R Z P E N
P L A T P T T I G R F E E I T F R U I T
F I S G E R M A N Y T T E C C B R E A D
O S D F B L F H U I S P A N I S H K I N
```

Multiple Intelligences and Language Learning © 2005 Alta Book Center Publishers, San Francisco, California
www.altaesl.com Permission granted to photocopy for one teacher's classroom use only.

Bodily/Kinesthetic Intelligence

"Tell me, I forget. Show me, I remember.
Involve me, I understand."
— Chinese Proverb

The activities in this unit help students develop their bodily/kinesthetic intelligence by:

conducting experiments

participating in role-plays

making crafts

following exercise routines

using manipulatives

following commands

playing games

5.1 The Cat Game

Age Group
Grades 3 to 5

Language Level
Intermediate

INTELLIGENCES DEVELOPED
Bodily/kinesthetic
Interpersonal
Linguistic
Visual/spatial

OBJECTIVES
To reinforce language development with visual cues
To reinforce language development with manipulatives
To give students an opportunity to evaluate their own learning
To give students an opportunity to work together

Materials Needed
- Copies of handouts 5.1A and 5.1B (make copies equivalent to half of your students)
- Envelopes
- Scissors

Version One

1 Before class, cut apart the sentences on each copy of handout 5.1A. Cut the pictures apart on each copy of handout 5.1B.

2 Give sentences to half of the students and pictures to the other half (one picture or sentence to each student). Tell students to keep their sentence or picture concealed from their classmates. (One way to do this is to hold the sentence/picture so that it is facing you and/or flat against your body.)

3 Ask students with sentences to find the matching pictures and vice versa. Matched pairs should then stand together and stop mingling. Here are some useful phrases that you may wish to review with students:

Do you have a sentence or a picture?

Great! I'm looking for a sentence.

Too bad. I need a sentence.

What is your sentence?

What's your picture about?

We're a match!

Version Two

1 Cut apart the sentences on each copy of handout 5.1A. Cut the pictures apart on each copy of handout 5.1B. For each handout copy place the sentences in one envelope and the pictures in another envelope. Mark the envelopes.

2 Have students work in pairs. Give Partner A an envelope of sentences and Partner B an envelope of pictures.

3 Partner B places all pictures face up on top of his/her desk. Partner A reads a sentence to Partner B. Partner B finds the picture that the sentence describes.

4 Once all the pictures have been matched to sentences, ask students to change roles.

Class Moves 5.2

INTELLIGENCES DEVELOPED	OBJECTIVES	Age Group

Bodily/kinesthetic

Intrapersonal

Linguistic

To reinforce language development through movement

To build self-esteem

Age Group
All

Language Level
Beginning

Materials Needed
• None

1 Before beginning the activity, make certain that students have enough room to move without bumping into each other. Review the commands (e.g., raise, shake, put, stand, jump, turn, hop, bend, straighten).

2 Dictate the sequences following these instructions. Students should respond with the appropriate action. Repeat each sequence three times. Demonstrate the actions the first and second times the commands are given. On the third time, only demonstrate the actions if students appear stuck.

Sequence 1
Stand up.
Raise your left arm above your head.
Raise your right arm above your head.
Shake your hands.
Shake them again.
Turn around twice.
Put your arms at your sides.
Bend your knees.
Straighten.
Bend your knees again.
Straighten.
Bend your knees again.
Raise your arms above your head.
Put your arms down.
Straighten.

Sequence 2
Raise your left arm to the side.
Shake your left arm.
Put it down at your side.
Raise your right arm to the side.
Shake your right arm.
Put it down at your side.
Raise both arms to the sides.
Raise your arms above your head.

Put them down at your sides.
Stand on your toes.
Return to the soles of your feet.
Jump in place twice.
Turn around.
Turn around again.
Jump in place twice.
Turn around.

Sequence 3
Bend to the left.
Straighten.
Bend to the right.
Straighten.
Bend forward.
Straighten.
Bend back.
Straighten.
Stand on your left foot.
Hop in place.
Put your right foot down.
Stand on your right foot.
Hop in place.
Put your left foot down.
Hop in place three times on both feet.
Bend to the left.
Straighten.
Bend to the left again.
Straighten.
Bend to the right.
Straighten.
Bend to the right again.
Straighten.
Bend forward.
Straighten.
Bend back.
Bend right.
Straighten.
Turn around.
Smile.
Wave goodbye.

5.3 Classroom Shopping

Age Group
Grade 3 to adult

Language Level
Intermediate to advanced

INTELLIGENCES DEVELOPED

Bodily/kinesthetic

Interpersonal

Linguistic

Logical/mathematical

OBJECTIVES

To familiarize students with the cost of items

To develop basic mathematical skills

To give students an opportunity to work together

Materials Needed
- A variety of household items (toothbrush, alarm clock, spatula, etc.)
- Empty product containers (dishwashing detergent bottle, cereal box, egg carton, etc.)
- Laundry basket (or large container to hold items)
- Price tag labels
- Coins
- Paper bills (e.g., $1, $5, $10 in the United States)

Version One: Grades 3–5

1 Before class, collect a variety of small household items and empty product containers. Place them in a large laundry basket. Label each item with a price tag. Place the basket, coins, and bills on a central table.

2 Call on a student to choose an item from the basket and tell you what it is. Write the name of the item on the board.

3 Ask the student to read the price of the item. Write the price on the board next to the item's name.

4 Finally, ask the student to count out the item's cost from the coins and bills on the table.

5 Work with five or six students each day, repeating Steps 1–5 until all students have had a turn.

Version Two: Middle School, High School, and Adult

1 Before class, collect a variety of small household items and empty product containers. Place them in a large laundry basket. Label each item with a price tag. Place the basket, coins, and bills on a central table.

2 Have students work in pairs. Ask them to select five items from the basket write down the name and price of each item, and total the prices. Students return the items to the basket when finished.

3 Ask each pair to present their list of five items to the class. One partner reads the list while the other locates the items in the basket and records the names and prices on the board. The entire class then totals the prices.

Coins and Coupons 5.4

INTELLIGENCES DEVELOPED	OBJECTIVES

Bodily/kinesthetic

Interpersonal

Linguistic

Logical/mathematical

To familiarize students with U.S. currency (see note below)

To develop basic mathematical skills

To give students an opportunity to work together

Age Group
Grade 4 to adult

Language Level
Beginning

Materials Needed
- Real or paper coins
- Newspapers and/or magazines
- Scissors
- Paper bags

Note: Teachers in countries other than the United States may want to use this activity to familiarize students with the currency of the United States or they may develop a similar activity introducing the monetary system of the students' native country.

1 Before class, gather a collection of coins and place them in small piles (refer to activity 3.20 for instructions on making your own paper money). Make sure that each pile contains pennies, nickels, dimes, and quarters. Then clip coupons from newspapers and/or magazines. Divide the coupons into small paper bags.

2 Place students in small groups using your favorite technique (see activity 6.5 for suggestions). Give each group a pile of change and a paper bag of coupons.

3 Ask one person in each group to select a coupon from the bag. That person then chooses another group member to sort money from the pile of change to equal the amount on the coupon. The student sorting the money counts it out loud.

4 When the student is finished sorting and counting, the group decides whether the amount is correct. If the group agrees that the amount is correct, the change goes back into the pile and the next person in the circle chooses a coupon from the bag. If the amount is not correct, students work together to correct it.

5 The process continues until all of the coupons have been used; coins are used over and over again.

5.5 The Foot Game

Age Group
Middle to high school

Language Level
Intermediate

INTELLIGENCES DEVELOPED	OBJECTIVES
Bodily/kinesthetic	To develop vocabulary
Interpersonal	To reinforce language development through movement
Linguistic	To give students an opportunity to work together
Logical/mathematical	
Visual/spatial	

Materials Needed
• Colored chalk or tempera paint
• Playground or outside area

1 Before beginning the game, ask students to propose a number of categories to represent vocabulary content they have been studying. Common categories include food, clothing, transportation, countries, animals, parts of the body, desserts, fruit, colors, and furniture.

2 Using chalk or tempera paint, draw a circle on the playground blacktop. The circle should measure five feet in diameter. Divide the circle into eight different triangular pieces like a pizza. Number each "slice" as shown below.

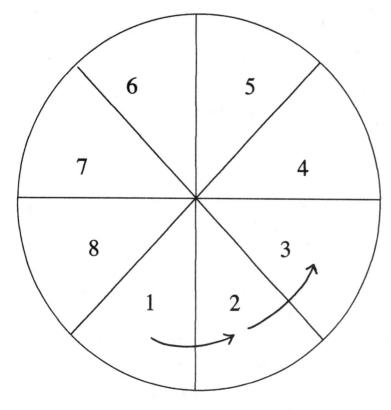

3 Teach students the footwork. Begin by standing with the left foot on #1 and the right foot on #2. Hop on the left foot. Then jump right one slice, landing with the left foot on #2 and the right foot on #3. Jump with both feet. Continue in this way around the circle. Have each student practice the footwork before you teach the verbal portion of the game. Give students ample time to practice.

4 Divide students into teams. The game begins by having one student choose a category (see Step 1). That student gives the first word in that category as he/she jumps with two feet and then does the above-described footwork around the circle. The next student begins with the word from the first student, adds another word, and does the footwork around the circle. Words are spoken each time students land on two feet.

5 The last student to go must remember all eight words and say them each time he/she lands on two feet. If a student misses one of the words in the category being played, the other team wins the point and gets to choose the next category.

Note: This game works well with teams, but can be played without.

Group Chain 5.6

INTELLIGENCES DEVELOPED	OBJECTIVES
Bodily/kinesthetic	To foster a sense of community and belonging
Interpersonal	To build self-esteem
Intrapersonal	To reinforce language development with visual cues
Linguistic	To reinforce language development through movement
Visual/spatial	To give students an opportunity to work together

Age Group
Grades 2 to 4

Language Level
Beginning

Materials Needed
- Strips of paper in different colors (yellow, blue, red, green, etc.)
- Glue
- Markers

1 Give each student a strip of yellow paper. Tell them that yellow strips represent students in the class. Have each student write his or her first name on the strip. Then ask students to form a chain. Glue the first strip in a circle and join it to the second strip, as in this illustration:

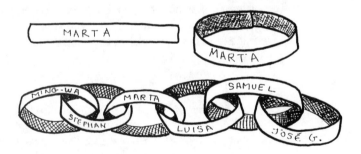

2 Ask students to suggest other categories for forming chains:

    red = girls

    green = boys

    blue = students who walk to school

    pink = students wearing white

3 As students generate ways of forming groups, have identified group members come to the front of the class and make a chain. Then attach the new chains to the yellow chain via one of the students who belongs to both groups (i.e., using the examples above, a boy who walks to school would attach the blue chain to the green). If there are no students who fit the two category chains that need to be joined, ask students to figure out how to join the chains using other criteria. This exercise is an excellent way to help students recognize what they have in common.

173

5.7 Homemade Ring Toss

Age Group
Grades K to 2

Language Level
Beginning

INTELLIGENCES DEVELOPED	OBJECTIVES

Bodily/kinesthetic

Interpersonal

Linguistic

Logical/mathematical

To reinforce numbers and colors vocabulary

To reinforce language development through movement

To give students an opportunity to work together

Materials Needed
- One piece of 1" thick Styrofoam
- Pencil
- Glue
- Plastic lids in various sizes and colors

1 Before class, make several ring toss platforms. To do so, cut an 8" to 9" (approximately 20.32 cm) square piece of Styrofoam. Cover the pointed end of a pencil in glue and stick it into the center of the foam square. Put more glue all around the pencil to hold it firmly in place. Allow the glue to dry thoroughly. You've made a ring toss platform! Make a ring toss platform for every small group of students. In addition to the ring toss platforms, cut out the centers of circular plastic lids—the more colors and sizes the better. These will be the rings.

2 Teach the following key phrases:

One, two, three. Throw your ring to me.

One and two. The____ [color] ring's for you.

Remember to also review the colors in the target language before beginning play.

3 When students have mastered the necessary vocabulary, divide them into teams and create the following chart on the board:

4 Give each team a ring toss platform and an equal number of rings. One student on each team stands near the ring toss. The other students on the team stand about six to nine feet away in a line. The student near the ring toss says, "One, two, three. Throw your ring to me." The first student in the line takes a ring and says, "One and two. The _____ [color of the ring] ring's for you," and tosses the ring. If the student tossing the ring gets the ring over the pencil, he/she gets to go again. If the student misses, he/she takes the place of the student near the ring toss, who moves to the back of the line. Make certain that the ring toss is close enough to the student throwing that he/she has a good chance of succeeding.

5 When all rings have been thrown, ask students to count the rings around the pencil and the rings on the floor, and record the numbers on the board. The team with the most rings around the pencil wins.

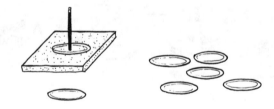

	Team A	Team B	Team C
Rings around the pencil			
Rings on the floor			

How to Make a Piñata 5.8

INTELLIGENCES DEVELOPED	OBJECTIVES

Bodily/kinesthetic

Interpersonal

Linguistic

Visual/spatial

To provide an opportunity for students to participate in a hands-on project

To learn about a cultural custom

To reinforce language development through movement

To reinforce language development with visual cues

To give students an opportunity to work together

Materials Needed

- One copy of handout 5.8 for each group of students
- Water
- Flour or cornstarch
- Paper bowls
- Balloons
- Scraps of newspaper
- Scissors
- String
- Tape
- Brightly colored paint
- Paintbrushes
- Crepe paper
- Bags of candy and/or other prizes
- Glue

Note: It takes portions of three or four class periods to make piñatas, so it is important to plan ahead (the class periods do not need to be scheduled consecutively).

1 Assemble all materials in piles on a central table and label each pile with a name card. When students are finished with the various items they are using, instruct them to return the materials to the correct piles (i.e., scissors are returned to the pile labeled "scissors," etc.).

2 Divide students into small groups. Give each group one copy of handout 5.8 and ask them to work together to figure out how to proceed. Have each group appoint a person to collect the materials. Encourage students to return items to the table when not in use. Walk around, helping students as necessary.

3 When all piñatas are complete, hang them around the room. End with a discussion about the custom of piñatas in Mexico.

Extension: Piñata Party

1 Piñata parties are a fun way to reinforce language learning through physical experience. Before class, fill finished piñatas with candy and suspend them safely in the air. Play some lively Mexican music in the background to set the mood.

2 Explain to students that they are going to take turns hitting the piñata while blindfolded. It is the responsibility of the class to help each student target the piñata since he/she won't be able to see it. Teach students instructions for how to move (i.e., step left, move right, move forward, swing higher, swing lower). The instructions can be written on the board and practiced.

3 Write the numbers 1-6 on small cards and place them in a bag. Ask students to close their eyes, reach in the bag, and choose a number. The number on the card indicates how many swings the student gets at the piñata. One student is then blindfolded, turned around, and given a small "stick" (plastic works best). The other students yell out instructions and count out loud the number of swings. If the student fails to crack the piñata in his/her allotted number of swings, the turn is finished and another student tries.

4 When the piñata is finally broken open, students scramble for the candy, trying to collect as much as they can.

5.9 Introductions

Age Group
Grades K and 1

Language Level
Beginning

INTELLIGENCES DEVELOPED	OBJECTIVES
Bodily/kinesthetic	To develop literacy skills
Intrapersonal	To build self-esteem
Linguistic	To reinforce language development through movement

Materials Needed
• Poster board cut into name card-sized pieces
• Colored markers

1 Before class, create name cards by folding pieces of poster board in half and writing the student's first name on the front. If students share the same first name, include the first letter of their last names. Use colored markers. Each name card should look similar to this:

2 Place the name cards on a table or on the ledge of the board. Call out students' names one at a time. The student whose name is called goes to the board, finds his/her name card, holds it in front of him/her, and says in the target language, "Hello. My name is _____. I like _____."

3 This process is repeated until all of the cards are gone and each student has had a turn.

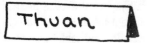

Thuan

José M.

José G.

Laundry Time 5.10

Age Group
Pre-K to grade 2

Language Level
Beginning

INTELLIGENCES DEVELOPED

Bodily/kinesthetic

Linguistic

Visual/spatial

OBJECTIVES

To give students meaningful practice with clothing vocabulary

To develop finger dexterity

To foster creative expression

To reinforce language development with visual cues

Materials Needed
- One copy of handout 5.10
- Colored markers
- Scissors
- Plain white paper
- A piece of yarn or thread for each student
- Glue

1 Give each student a copy of handout 5.10 and colored markers. Review the names of the clothes pictured on the handout and have students color them. As students are working independently, move around the room asking simple questions to review clothing and colors (e.g., What are you coloring? What color is the dress?).

2 When students have finished, pass out scissors and ask students to carefully cut out the clothes.

3 Give each student a piece of plain white paper. Ask students to turn their papers horizontally and draw two trees—one on the left and one on the right.

4 Give each student a piece of yarn or thread. Demonstrate how to glue one end of the yarn to each tree in order to form a "clothesline."

5 Ask students to "hang" their clothes pictures on their clotheslines using a small amount of glue. Have students write their names on the finished artwork.

6 After each student has made a clothesline, use the finished product as a springboard to further language development. Review this vocabulary:

Colors: black, blue, brown, gray, green, orange, purple, red, yellow

Clothing: socks, t-shirt, shorts, shirt, skirt, blouse, sweatshirt, pants, scarf, jacket, pajamas, dress

Locators: next to, beside, in the middle of, between, to the left of, to the right of, on the left, on the right, on the far left, on the far right

Other: clothesline, to hang clothes, to dry clothes

7 Now randomly select one clothesline at a time from students and ask the following questions:

What color is the sweatshirt? Pants? Dress? Socks? Skirt? Blouse? T-shirt?

Where is the jacket hanging (i.e., between the scarf and the shorts)?

8 Next, select two, three, or four clotheslines to look at collectively. Tape them to the board or have students hold them. Give each clothesline a number or use the student's name as a reference. Then ask the following questions:

What color are the skirts? Pants? Pajamas? Socks? Skirts? Blouses? T-shirts?

What difference do you see between clotheslines one and two? One and three? Two and three?

What items (or colors) do clotheslines three and four have in common?

On which clothesline do you see a _____-colored skirt? Shirt? Scarf? Dress? T-shirt?

Where is the dress in clothesline _____? Skirt? Jacket? Blouse? Sweatshirt?

5.11 Measure Me

Age Group
Grade 1 to high school

Language Level
Beginning to intermediate

INTELLIGENCES DEVELOPED	OBJECTIVES

Bodily/kinesthetic

Interpersonal

Linguistic

Logical/mathematical

Visual/spatial

To develop problem-solving skills

To develop vocabulary for measurement

To reinforce language development with visual cues

To give students an opportunity to work together

Materials Needed
- Handouts 5.11A or 5.11B and 5.11C or 5.11D (depending on level) for each student
- Tape or glue
- Colored markers
- Scissors

Version One: For Grades 1 and 2

1 Give each student a copy of handouts 5.11A and 5.11C. Ask students to color the inchworms on handout 5.11A, cut out the inchworm strips, and paste them together to form an inchworm measuring tape.

2 Show students how to use the inchworm measuring tape to measure five specific body parts (wrists, arms, legs, etc.) and record the number of inchworms using handout 5.11C. Put students in same-sex pairs and ask them to help each other measure.

3 Once students have completed the task, give them a chance to make short presentations.

4 Post all finished handouts on a bulletin board.

Version Two: For Grade 3 to Adult

1 Give each student a copy of handouts 5.11B and 5.11D. Ask students to cut out the measuring tape strips on handout 5.11B and paste them together.

2 Show students how to use the measuring tape to measure themselves and complete handout 5.11D. Put students in same-sex pairs so they can help each other if needed.

3 Follow up with a large group discussion.

Murals for Parents 5.12

INTELLIGENCES DEVELOPED	OBJECTIVES
Bodily/kinesthetic	To foster creative expression
Interpersonal	To reinforce language development through movement
Linguistic	To develop vocabulary
Visual/spatial	To give students an opportunity to work together

Age Group
Grades 2 to 5

Language Level
Beginning to intermediate

Materials Needed
- Large sheets of butcher paper (6 feet/2 meters in length)
- Colored markers
- Tape
- Sticky notes

1 Before class, tape large sheets of butcher paper to an available wall or lay them on the floor; it is a good idea to double the paper so the artwork doesn't bleed through. Place colored markers on a central table.

2 Tell students that they are going to create a mural to help their parents understand what goes on in a typical school day. Have students identify four or five daily activities (silent reading, recess, lunch, etc). Write these activities horizontally across the board.

3 Ask each student what activity he/she wants to focus on. Write his/her name under the chosen activity on the board.

4 Divide the students into groups according to the activity they want to focus on. Explain that each group will be responsible for illustrating its particular activity. Station each group in front of a piece of butcher paper and allow them enough time to illustrate their activity using colored markers.

5 When the murals are finished, ask students to label as many items as they can with words in the language being taught. Then ask them to identify items they don't know in the target language and circle them.

6 Ask the class to look at each mural and try to write target-language words beside any circled items. For circled items that remain unlabeled, write the word on a brightly colored "sticky note" and place it beside the item.

7 Have students make lists of words from the mural that they do not know for later vocabulary work.

8 Save the murals to decorate the classroom or for a time when parents visit the school. Students can show the mural to their parents and talk about the activities.

5.13 Numbered Stoplights

Age Group
Grades K to 2

Language Level
Beginning

INTELLIGENCES DEVELOPED

Bodily/kinesthetic

Linguistic

Logical/mathematical

Visual/spatial

OBJECTIVES

To develop language skills with numbers from 1-10

To develop basic mathematical skills

To become familiar with the shapes and colors associated with stoplights

Materials Needed

• Copies of handouts 5.13A on red, yellow, and green paper (see Step 2)
• Four copies of handout 5.13B for each pair of students
• Cardboard or poster board
• Scissors
• Glue

Note: The shape of the stoplight pattern on handout 5.13B is taken from the United States. Adapt it if necessary to conform to the shape of stoplights in the country in which you are teaching.

1 Before class, use handouts 5.13A and 5.13B to create stoplights. Cut out each stoplight and mount it on cardboard or poster board. Cut out the circles and number each one, using numbers 1-10. Create four stoplights for each pair of students: two stoplights with numbered red, yellow, and green circles glued onto them, and two stoplights without the numbered circles.

2 Place all materials on a central table and divide students into pairs. Ask one student from each pair to come to the table to collect two numbered stoplights, two stoplights without numbers, and a stack of numbered, colored circles. Each student should thus have the materials to create a blank stoplight and a numbered stoplight.

3 Instruct students to find the appropriate numbered circles and place them on the stoplight with no numbers in order to make the two stoplights match.

4 When the stoplights match, ask students to read the numbers out loud to each other.

5 Once students have successfully matched the stoplights, ask them to return their materials to the central table and take two more.

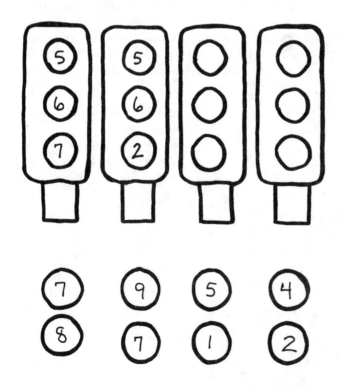

Pocket Charts 5.14

Age Group
Grades K to 2

Language Level
Beginning

INTELLIGENCES DEVELOPED

Bodily/kinesthetic

Interpersonal

Linguistic

Logical/mathematical

Visual/spatial

Materials Needed
- Colored paper
- Tape
- Colored markers
- Magazines and/or newspapers
- Scissors

OBJECTIVES

To develop colors vocabulary

To reinforce language development through movement and the use of manipulatives

To develop skills in categorizing and organizing

To give students an opportunity to work together

1 Before class, make paper pockets in different colors. Steps in making pockets:

a Begin with one piece of colored paper:

b Bring the bottom of the paper up to within one inch of the top to form a pocket:

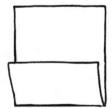

c Tape the sides together and use colored markers to label the pocket with the appropriate color:

2 Using magazines and/or newspapers, find pictures of items in each color. Cut out the pictures and place them in the appropriate pocket. Have students help you. Examples:

Red: apple, potato, radish, tomato, lipstick, valentine, red pepper

Yellow: sun, lemon, banana, grapefruit, cheese, egg yolk, yellow dress, yellow pepper

Green: lettuce, grass, avocado, green door, spinach, lime, green apple

Orange: orange, carrot, pumpkin, orange shirt

3 Divide students into pairs and have each pair choose a pocket. Instruct Student A to select pictures from the pocket and Student B to identify them.

4 Ask finished pairs to return everything to the pocket and move on to a pocket of another color.

5 Once students have had a chance to work with all the pockets, ask them to look in magazines and/or newspapers to find additional pictures for each color. Give them a chance to show the pictures they select to the rest of the class, name the pictures, and place them in the correct pockets.

6 Call on students to review the pictures in the pockets periodically.

7 You may also take pictures from the different pockets, mix them up, and ask students to name the items and return them to the appropriate pocket.

5.15 Matching Shapes

INTELLIGENCES DEVELOPED	OBJECTIVES
Bodily/kinesthetic	To develop number recognition
Interpersonal	To develop skills in sorting and categorizing
Linguistic	To reinforce language development with visual cues
Logical/mathematical	To give students an opportunity to work together
Visual/spatial	

Materials Needed
- Copies of handout 5.15 on different sheets of colored paper
- Scissors

1 Ask students to help you cut out the patterns on handout 5.15 and place them in piles according to color and shape. Check to see that there are two shapes of every color so that students can form matching pairs.

2 Distribute the patterns randomly to students, making sure that each student has one.

3 Instruct students to mingle, find the student who has a pattern that matches theirs (in both shape and color), shake hands, introduce themselves, and say the shape and its color.

4 When all students have found their match, ask them to return their pattern to the central table. Each student then chooses a second pattern and the process begins again.

Puzzle Partners 5.16

INTELLIGENCES DEVELOPED	OBJECTIVES
Bodily/kinesthetic	To reinforce language development with visual cues
Interpersonal	To reinforce language development through movement
Linguistic	To give students an opportunity to work together
Visual/spatial	

Age Group
Grades 2 to 4

Language Level
Intermediate

Materials Needed
- Pictures from magazines
- Glue
- Poster board or file folders
- Scissors
- Paper clips

1 Before class, find interesting magazine images that relate to the content you have been teaching. Glue these pictures on poster board or on one-half of a file folder. On the back of the board or folder, draw lines dividing the picture into pieces to make a puzzle. Vary the number of pieces per puzzle from two to six. Number the pieces:

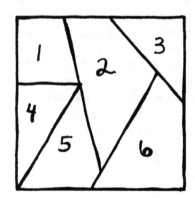

Cut the pieces out and group each puzzle together with a paper clip; attach a small piece of paper indicating how many pieces are in the puzzle. Make a puzzle for each student.

2 When you are ready to begin the activity, mix up all the puzzle pieces. Give one piece to each student. Then ask students to mingle and put the puzzles together. The catch is, students must not show their puzzle pieces to one another. Instead, they may ask each other questions about the images contained on their respective pieces. Teach the following strategies for obtaining information (post these phrases on the board or a chart so that students can refer to the phrases when they are doing the activity):

What's on your puzzle piece?

My puzzle piece is _____.

What colors do you see?

My puzzle piece has _____.

Do you think our puzzle pieces fit?

Thank you very much. Sorry they don't fit.

3 When students find others with similar pieces, instruct them to sit together and assemble their puzzle.

4 Once puzzles have been assembled, give the following instructions orally. Each group should appoint a note-taker to record their answers. Ask students to raise their hands when they have completed each instruction.

Write down three things you see in your puzzle.

Write down three colors you see in your puzzle.

What do you like about the picture?

What don't you like about the picture?

Count the following things: people, animals, different foods, furniture.

Point to something you know the word for in the target language. Write it down.

5.17 Raising Kids

Age Group
Middle school to adult

Language Level
Advanced

INTELLIGENCES DEVELOPED	OBJECTIVES
Bodily/kinesthetic	To develop problem-solving skills
Interpersonal	To help students further appreciate their parents/guardians
Linguistic	To develop basic mathematical skills
Logical/mathematical	To give students an opportunity to work with data and numbers
Visual/spatial	To give students an opportunity to work together

Materials Needed
• One copy of handout 5.17 for each student
• Answer key 5.17
• Colored markers
• Large sheets of paper

1 Make certain that students understand the concept of a pie chart. Provide simple examples if they have not covered this information in your class previously.

2 Divide students into groups (see activity 6.5 for suggestions) and give each student a copy of the handout.

3 Ask each student to complete the tasks. Give them colored markers and large sheets of paper for creating their pie charts.

4 After all students have finished, select one example from each group for checking (see answer key 5.17). Groups should make certain that all members have the correct answers.

EFL Version
There are two suggested ways of adapting this activity for an EFL context. You could give students the exchange rate for the dollar and have them calculate the amounts based on the currency being used by students. Alternatively, you might have students try to agree on a figure they think is right for the particular country in which they live. Use that figure to determine the proportional amounts and create a pie chart.

Scrap Artists 5.18

Age Group
Grades 3 to 5

Language Level
Intermediate

INTELLIGENCES DEVELOPED

Bodily/kinesthetic

Intrapersonal

Linguistic

Visual/spatial

OBJECTIVES

To foster creative expression

To reinforce language development through movement and the use of manipulatives

To give students an opportunity to work together

Materials Needed

• Scraps of varied textural items (cloth, tissue, wrapping paper, images from magazines and newspapers cut into interesting shapes)
• Colored construction paper
• Glue

1 Place materials on a central table. Divide the textural items into two categories: cloth, tissue, and wrapping paper; and magazine and newspaper cutouts.

2 Explain to students that they are going to create a collage. Have each student take one piece of colored construction paper on which to mount their collage. Instruct students to select the materials and shapes they like, arrange them on the paper, and glue them into place.

3 When students have finished, ask them to write a paragraph describing their creation. Explain to students that they must be very clear and specific in describing their piece; they should try to express what it is that makes their collage unique.

4 After students have completed their collages, randomly select five to seven examples and place them along the edge of the board. Give each collage a number. Then call upon students to read the descriptive paragraphs. Ask the other students in the class to listen to each composition and determine which collage is being described.

Search and Find 5.19

Age Group
Grades 1 and 2

Language Level
Beginning

INTELLIGENCES DEVELOPED

Bodily/kinesthetic

Intrapersonal

Linguistic

Visual/spatial

OBJECTIVES

To build self-esteem

To develop an enjoyment of reading and books

To reinforce language development through movement

To enhance language learning with visual aids

Materials Needed

• Several beginning-level picture books

1 Select some of your favorite children's books that feature many illustrations, few words, and plenty of repetition. Begin by reading an entire book to the students, showing them the pictures, and getting them to repeat some of the key words with you.

2 Ask a student to open the book to any page. Read the page out loud, close the book, and hand it to two students.

3 Ask the two students to find the page you have just read. Say the words on the page again, if necessary.

4 When the students find the page, ask them to read it back to you.

5 Continue the process until all students have had a turn.

5.20 Floor Plans

Age Group
Grade 5 to middle school

Language Level
Beginning

INTELLIGENCES DEVELOPED

Bodily/kinesthetic

Interpersonal

Linguistic

Logical/mathematical

Visual/spatial

OBJECTIVES

To foster creative expression

To reinforce language development with visual cues

To give students an opportunity to work together

Materials Needed
• Copies of handout 5.20 on different colors of paper
• Pieces of white poster board
• Glue
• Colored markers

1 Using the shapes on handout 5.20 as patterns, cut out the various sizes and colors of rectangles. Put all materials on a central table.

2 Get students into small groups using your favorite technique (see activity 6.5 for suggestions).

3 Encourage students to experiment with the different rectangles, arranging them to form the floor plan of a house.

4 Students then glue the rectangles into place on pieces of poster board and use colored markers to label each shape with the name of a different room in a house.

5 Finally, students make a list of at least ten items that would go in each room. Allow time for large group sharing.

6 Create a bulletin board with the floor plans, if possible.

Transportation Games 5.21

INTELLIGENCES DEVELOPED	OBJECTIVES	**Age Group**

Bodily/kinesthetic

Interpersonal

Linguistic

Visual/spatial

To develop vocabulary

To reinforce language development through movement

To improve listening skills

To reinforce language development with visual cues

To give students the opportunity to work together

Age Group
Grades 2 to 5

Language Level
Beginning

Materials Needed
- Copies of handout 5.21 or images of different forms of transportation from magazines and/or newspapers
- Scissors
- Glue
- Plain white paper
- A large rubber ball

1 Before class, create transportation picture cards using handout 5.21 or pictures from magazines and newspapers (you can have several different pictures for one mode of transportation).

2 Make certain that students know the transportation vocabulary. Introduce the required words one at a time. For example, introduce the word "plane." Give a picture of a plane to a student and say, "Isah has the plane." After you have passed out three or four cards, review the vocabulary by asking, "Who has the plane?" "Who has the car?" etc. You can also ask students to give the items to each other. For example, "Isah has the plane. Isah, give the plane to Petro." Add additional words until all students have mastered the vocabulary. Then select one of the following games.

Game 1

Tape a picture to the front of each student. Have students stand in a circle, with each student representing a mode of transportation. Say aloud, "I am going on a trip. I want to go by _____," and bounce the ball to the student with the appropriate picture. Then instruct that student to choose another mode of transportation and bounce the ball accordingly.

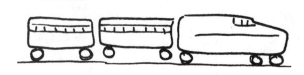

Game 2

This option is similar to the "Go Fish" card game. Have three cards for each mode of transportation. Put the cards in a stack and ask students to sit in small groups. Have each group appoint a scorekeeper. Give each group a stack of cards to mix up. All the cards should then be dealt, ensuring that each student has the same number of cards. The rules of the game are as follows:

1. Student A, to the immediate left of the dealer, goes first.

2. Student A asks for cards from any other student in the group. The cards asked for must be in Student A's hand (i.e., if Student A has one plane card he/she can ask for other plane cards). For example, "Give me all of your planes, please."

3. If the student asked has planes in his/her hand, he/she gives the planes to Student A and Student A continues, asking a different student for the same or different mode of transport.

4. If the student being asked for cards does not have planes in his/her hand, he/she says, "No transportation today." and Student A loses his/her turn. The student to the left of Student A takes a turn.

5. When a student gets three cards of the same form of transportation, he/she lays them down and receives a point.

6. The game continues until all cards have been laid down.

Vocabulary	
bicycle	train
car	sailboat
bus	tricycle
skateboard	motorcycle
plane	by foot

5.22 Travel Brochures Using the Internet

Age Group
High school to adult

Language Level
Advanced

INTELLIGENCES DEVELOPED
Bodily/kinesthetic
Interpersonal
Linguistic
Logical/mathematical

OBJECTIVES
To expand students' understanding of other countries and cultures
To introduce students to the Internet
To improve skills in planning, organizing, and goal setting
To give students an opportunity to work together

Materials Needed
• One copy of handout 5.22 for each student
• Computers with Internet access and printing capabilities

1 Take your class to the lab or computer room. Check if there are any restrictions on Internet printing or downloading, and make certain that students understand the rules.

2 Divide students into groups. The goal of this activity is for each group of students to create a travel brochure for a destination of their choice. Give each student a copy of handout 5.22 and instruct them to follow the directions.

3 While there are a number of options available for collecting information on various destinations, this activity will focus on using the Internet. Students will need to find their own websites as they are choosing their own topics to research.

Note: When you are working with lower level language learners, you will need to adapt the procedures outlined in handout 5.22 in the following ways:

Choose the curricular area to be researched.

Specify the tasks that students must complete and determine a schedule.

Search for websites that meet the curricular needs.

Evaluate each website for appropriateness (e.g., content, language level, and user-friendliness). Decide on how to direct students to use the site.

Bookmark selected sites.

Make a list of these selected sites for students.

Valentine's Day Cake 5.23

Age Group
Grade 5 to adult

Language Level
Intermediate to advanced

INTELLIGENCES DEVELOPED

Bodily/kinesthetic

Interpersonal

Linguistic

Logical/mathematical

Visual/spatial

OBJECTIVES

To build community

To develop logical sequencing skills

To give students an opportunity to see patterns in visual cues

To give students an opportunity to work together

Materials Needed

- One copy of handout 5.23, cut into strips
- A cake (baked in two, 8-inch layers—1 square and 1 round)
- One can of whipped cream
- One jar of raspberry jam
- A large piece of cardboard covered with foil
- A knife
- A rubber spatula
- Paper plates
- Plastic forks
- Napkins
- Scissors

1 Assemble all materials on a table in the front of the classroom.

2 Explain to the class that they are going to give you the instructions for making a Valentine's Day cake.

3 Cut the copy of handout 5.23 into strips. Hand out the strips, one per student. Explain to the students that they each have one vital piece of the instructions (if there are more students than command strips, have students share).

4 As a group, students must first decide in what order to give the instructions to you so that you can successfully make the cake.

5 Students then give you the instructions orally. Complete each step as it is given.

6 When the cake is fully assembled and all of the instructions have been used, everyone gets a slice!

The cat is chasing a ball.

The cat is sleeping on its side.

The cat is climbing a tree.

The cat is stretching.

The cat is eating.

The cat is cleaning itself.

The cat is rolling on its back.

The cat is fighting with the dog.

The cat is swatting at a bee.

The cat is playing with its owner.

The cat is licking its foot.

The cat is angry.

The cat is crying for food.

The cat is sleeping.

The cat has a mouse.

The cat is sharpening its claws.

The cat is jumping from a box.

The cat is playing with the clock.

The Cat Game

Pictures

DIRECTIONS

Work together with your group to make a piñata.

Day 1

1 First you are going to make paste. Get a small paper bowl, water, and flour or cornstarch from the central table. Put the starch in the bowl, stir, and add water gradually until the mixture reaches a glue-like consistency. (Add more starch to thicken.)

2 Get a balloon. Have one student inflate the balloon to the size your group wants the piñata to be. Tie the balloon shut.

3 Get scraps of newspaper. Cut the newspaper into large strips and dip them into the glue. Cover the entire balloon with three layers of the wet, sticky strips (papier-mâché). Let the mold dry for two or three days, turning it once so the bottom can dry.

After two or three days

1 Check your mold. It should be dry. If it is, poke a small hole in the top of the mold using scissors. In this way, you pop the balloon inside.

2 Then cut a hole in the top, big enough to allow candy to be dropped inside. Save the "lid."

3 Cut two pieces of string. Make two smaller holes at each side of the top and thread the string through the holes. Tape the string ends to the inside of the mold.

4 Decorate the mold with brightly colored paint and let it dry.

5 Cut the crepe paper into strips. Glue the strips to the mold. Start at the bottom and move towards the top. Leave about five inches free at the top.

6 Put candy or other prizes in the hole at the top. Glue the top shut using the lid.

7 Hang the piñata and have fun breaking it open!

Laundry Time

Pictures

DIRECTIONS

Cut out the strips and paste them together.

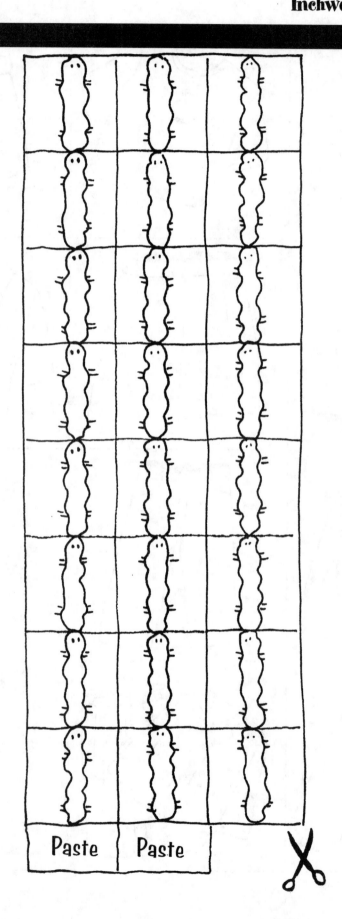

Paste   Paste

31	25	19	13	7	1
32	26	20	14	8	2
33	27	21	15	9	3
34	28	22	16	10	4
35	29	23	17	11	5
36	30	24	18	12	6
Paste	Paste	Paste	Paste	Paste	

DIRECTIONS

Measure yourself using the inchworm measuring tape.

My head is _____ inches around.

My neck is _____ inches around.

My arm is _____ inches long.

My wrist is _____ inches around.

My index finger is _____ inches long.

My leg is _____ inches long.

My foot is _____ inches long.

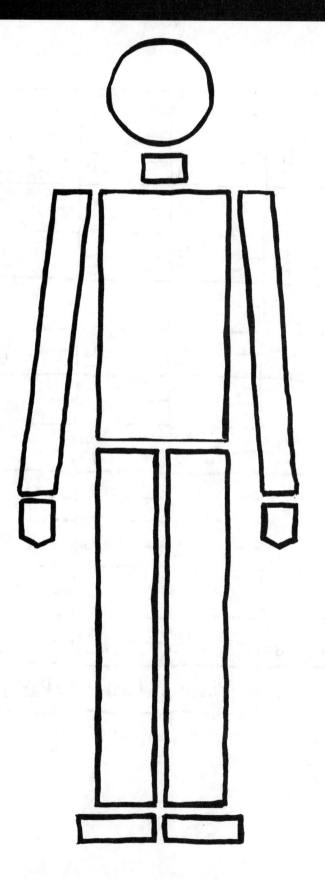

Multiple Intelligences and Language Learning © 2005 Alta Book Center Publishers, San Francisco, California
www.altaesl.com Permission granted to photocopy for one teacher's classroom use only

Measure Me

Using Measuring Tape

DIRECTIONS

Measure these different parts of your body and record your findings in the table.

Me	Measurement
My height	
Length of my arm	
Length of my longest finger	
Length of my leg	
Length of my foot	
Width of my hand	
Width of my smile	
Width of my shoulders	
Length of my arm span—from the top of my shoulder to the tip of my longest finger	
Distance around my wrist	
Distance around my head	
Distance from ear to ear	

DIRECTIONS

This page should be copied in three colors—red, yellow, and green.

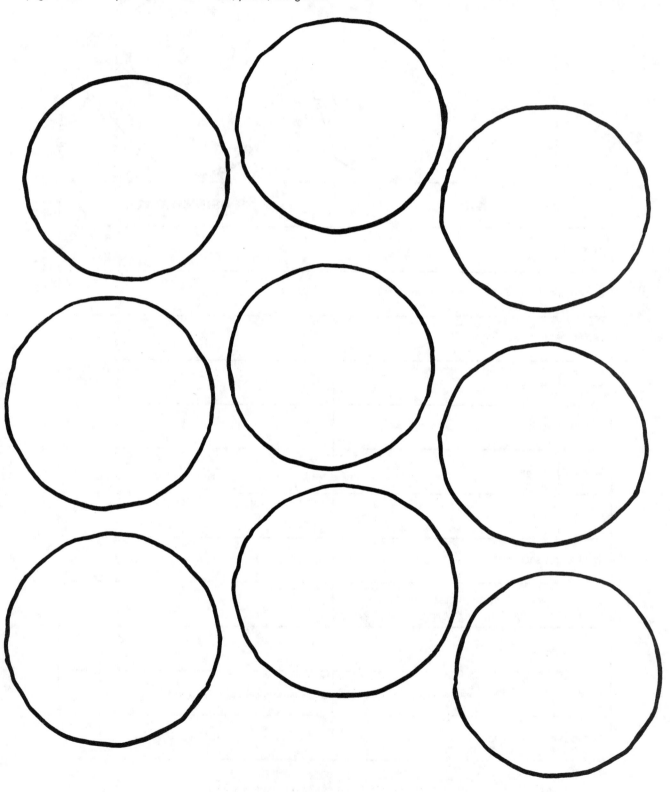

Stoplight Pattern

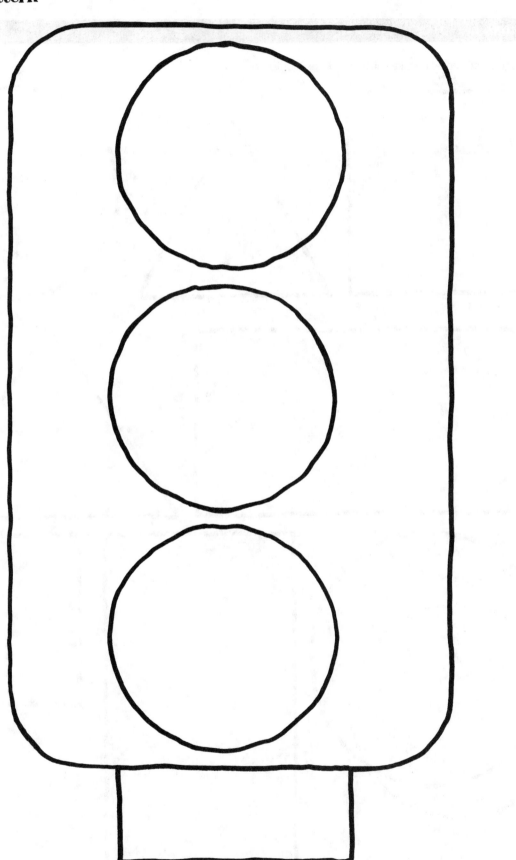

DIRECTIONS

This page should be copied on different sheets of colored paper.

DIRECTIONS

1 Study the information below.

2 Create a pie chart to represent the various costs of raising a child in the United States.

3 Figure out how much of the total will be spent on each category of items.

4 Be prepared to present your results to the entire group.

Problem

The American government estimates that it costs nearly $150,000 to raise a child to 18 years of age in the United States. Here is how the cost breaks down:

Clothing	8%
Healthcare	7%
Education and childcare	7%
Transportation	14%
Food	20%
Housing	33%
Other	10%

Source: Expenditures on Children by Families: 2000 Annual Report, U.S. Department of Agriculture Center for Nutrition Policy and Promotion, Misc. Publication No. 1528-2000.

How much is spent on each of the following:

Clothing _____

Healthcare _____

Education and childcare _____

Transportation _____

Food _____

Housing _____

Other _____

Pie Chart

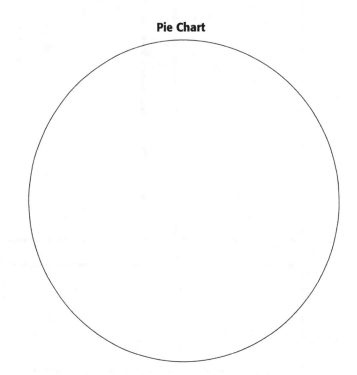

This page should be copied on different sheets of colored paper.

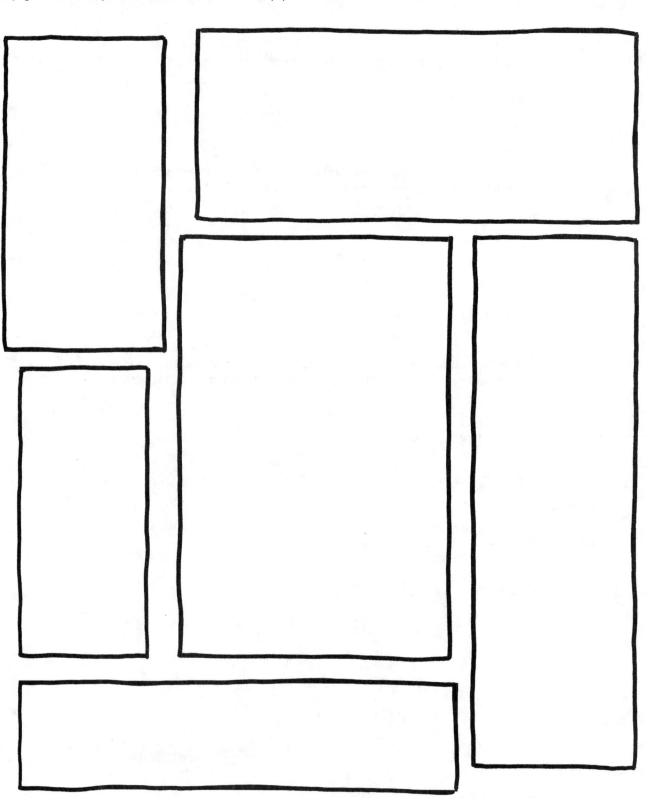

Transportation Games

Picture Cards

Travel Brochures Using the Internet

DIRECTIONS

Your task is to create a travel brochure for people who want to visit the destination your group has chosen. You will use the Internet to help you get the information you need. Here are the steps you should follow:

1 Choose a country or destination.

2 Do a subject search for your country or destination on the Internet.

3 Write down the names and addresses of the websites you find.

4 Visit the websites.

5 Read through the different sites until you find the information you want.

6 Bookmark the best sites for future reference.

Be sure to include a map and written description of your chosen location, along with answers to the following questions:

1 What's the climate like? What's the average temperature?

2 What should one wear?

3 What is the best way to get there from _____?

4 What is the cost of the ticket?

5 Where are good places to eat?

6 Where are good places to stay?

7 What is shopping like? For what items is _____ famous?

8 What is there to do? What kinds of activities are available?

9 What is the dominant language? Religion? Currency?

10 What are the major holidays and celebrations?

11 What is daily life like?

12 What is this location famous for?

Multiple Intelligences and Language Learning © 2005 Alta Book Center Publishers, San Francisco, California
www.altaesl.com Permission granted to photocopy for one teacher's classroom use only.

Valentine's Day Cake

Command Strips

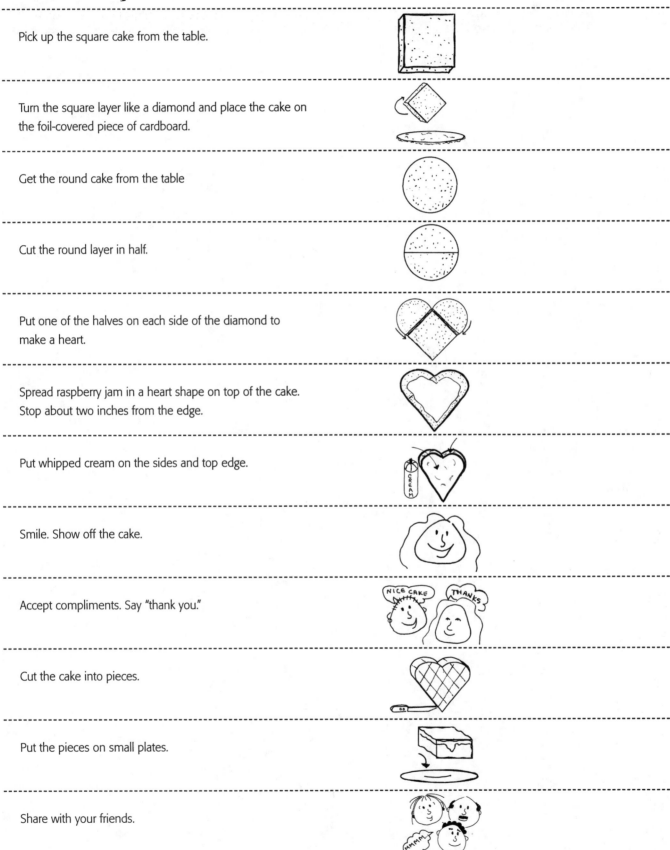

Pick up the square cake from the table.

Turn the square layer like a diamond and place the cake on the foil-covered piece of cardboard.

Get the round cake from the table

Cut the round layer in half.

Put one of the halves on each side of the diamond to make a heart.

Spread raspberry jam in a heart shape on top of the cake. Stop about two inches from the edge.

Put whipped cream on the sides and top edge.

Smile. Show off the cake.

Accept compliments. Say "thank you."

Cut the cake into pieces.

Put the pieces on small plates.

Share with your friends.

Personal Intelligences

"A community is like a ship; everyone ought to be prepared to take the helm."

— Henrik Ibsen (1828–1906)

"What a man really has is what is in him. What is outside of him should be a matter of no importance."

— Oscar Wilde (1845–1900)

The activities in this chapter help students develop their interpersonal and intrapersonal intelligences by:

working together with other students

learning to understand what other students think and value

learning how to be a good team member

accepting different roles and responsibilities in group work

learning how to evaluate one's own learning

exploring the learning process

clarifying one's own values and beliefs

6.1 *About My Community*

Age Group
Grade 5 to middle school

Language Level
High beginning to intermediate

INTELLIGENCES DEVELOPED

Interpersonal

Bodily/kinesthetic

Linguistic

OBJECTIVES

To help students learn more about their community

To give students an opportunity to interact with and get to know people in their community

To reinforce language development through movement

Materials Needed
• One copy of handouts 6.1A and 6.1B for each student or pair of students

1 Have students brainstorm and create a list of specific businesses in their community.

2 Give each pair (or individual student, if that is the preference) a copy of handout 6.1A. Tell students they have a week to visit and interview two of the businesses on the list created in step1.

3 Schedule a large group discussion for the day on which the assignment is due; you may use the questions on handout 6.1B for oral discussion or give them to students to answer first before facilitating a conversation.

Anagrams 6.2

INTELLIGENCES DEVELOPED	OBJECTIVES

Interpersonal

Bodily/kinesthetic

Linguistic

To develop vocabulary

To reinforce language development through the use of manipulatives

To give students an opportunity to work together

Age Group
Middle school to adult

Language Level
Intermediate

Materials Needed
- Cardboard or poster board
- Scissors
- Colored markers
- Board or flipchart
- Jar or bag

Version One: Large Group

1 Cut out small circles from cardboard/poster board and use colored markers to label each circle with either a consonant or a vowel. Make two sets of consonants and five sets of vowels. Place the circles in a jar or bag. (Note that you can use handout 2.13 for circle patterns.)

2 Divide students into pairs. Call on a pair of students to come to the front of the room and ask one partner to draw a handful of circles from the container.

3 Ask the student to read the letters out loud while his/her partner writes each letter on the board.

4 Give all students one minute to work in pairs and write down all the words they can make combining the letters on the board. Return the circles to the container.

5 After one minute, have students stop writing and call on another pair to come to the front and select letters. Repeat steps 3 and 4.

6 Conduct a large group sharing of all lists.

Version Two: Small Group

1 Cut out small circles from cardboard/poster board and use colored markers to label each circle with either a consonant or a vowel. Make two sets of consonants and five sets of vowels. Place the circles in a jar or bag. (Note that you can use handout 2.13 for circle patterns.)

2 Ask students to sit together in a circle. Have one student select a handful of letters from the container. The student should arrange the letters face up in the center of the circle.

3 Students, working individually, attempt to form words using the letters. When a student has a word, he/she should say it out loud. If the word is correctly spelled, he/she gets one point. All students keep track of their score.

4 When no one sees any more words, the lettered circles are returned to the container, mixed with the others, and new letters are drawn.

5 The first student to score 15 points (15 words) is the winner of that round.

6.3 Analogies

Age Group
Middle to high school

Language Level
Intermediate to advanced

INTELLIGENCES DEVELOPED	OBJECTIVES
Interpersonal	To foster creative expression
Linguistic	To develop vocabulary
Logical/mathematical	To develop logical thinking skills
	To give students an opportunity to work together

Materials Needed
• Board or flipchart

1 Create a list of analogies on the board. The analogies should match the language level of the students. Here are some ideas:

Singular to Plural

Child is to children as mouse is to _____ (mice).

Men is to man as boys is to _____ (boy).

Antonyms

Freeze is to melt as stop is to _____ (go).

Tall is to short as late is to _____ (early).

Synonyms

Heavy is to fat as thin is to _____ (skinny).

Late is to tardy as fast is to _____ (quick).

Homophones

Sew is to so as flower is to _____ (flour).

Pair is to pear as bear is to _____ (bare).

Product

Bread is to baker as lesson is to _____ (teacher).

Receptionist is to telephone as tailor is to _____ (clothing).

Wholes to Parts

Hand is to finger as foot is to _____ (toe).

Room is to window as loaf is to _____(slice).

Power

Gas is to car as humans is to _____(bicycles).

Electricity is to computers as batteries is to _____ (flashlights).

2 Ask students to complete the analogies, either individually or as a class.

3 After students complete all of the analogies, ask them to form partners and choose one or two analogy categories. For each chosen category, pairs need to write at least two appropriate analogies.

4 Ask partners to exchange their analogies with other partners and complete them.

Breakfast Please 6.4

INTELLIGENCES DEVELOPED	OBJECTIVES

Interpersonal

Bodily/kinesthetic

Linguistic

Logical/mathematical

To reinforce principles of nutrition

To reinforce food vocabulary

To give students an opportunity to work together

Age Group
Grade 5 to middle school

Language Level
High beginning to
intermediate

Materials Needed
• One copy of handout 6.4 for each group
• Board or flipchart
• Colored markers

1 With the entire class, brainstorm a list of items that might be on a restaurant's breakfast menu. Try to group the items into categories. Write the items on the board using a different colored marker for each category.

2 Ask students to think of interesting names for the items. For example, instead of simply saying "milk," students might say "creamy chocolate milk."

3 Have students determine a price for each item.

4 When the list is complete with prices, ask students to form small groups. Each student in the group is to choose three to five items from the menu, write down the items under his/her name, and total the prices. For example:

Carlos	
Creamy Chocolate Milk	$ .75
Super Scrambled Eggs	$ .99
Blueberry Bran Muffin	$1.25
Total	$2.99

5 One student in each group agrees to perform the role of server by totaling all the food costs and giving the "table" a bill.

6 Finally, students work together in their groups to answer the questions on handout 6.4.

6.5 Forming Groups

Age Group
All

Language Level
Beginning to advanced

INTELLIGENCES DEVELOPED	OBJECTIVES
Interpersonal	To teach students how to form groups and develop skills in working together
Bodily/kinesthetic	To reinforce language development through movement
Intrapersonal	To give students an opportunity to work together
Linguistic	

Materials Needed
• 3" x 5" colored cards (blue, yellow, green, etc.)
• Paper for making signs
• Deck of playing cards

Version One: Beginning

1 Number a set of 3" x 5" cards as follows: if you plan to have five groups of four students each, number four sets of cards 1–5. If you plan to have six groups of four students each, number four sets of cards 1–6, etc.

2 Give each student a card. Ask students to use the cards to form groups. All the number ones sit down together, number twos, number threes, and so on.

Version Two: Beginning

1 Form sets of 3" x 5" colored cards as follows: if you plan to have five groups of four students each, form four sets of different colored cards (for example, a set might have a blue, yellow, green, red, and white card). If you plan to have six groups of four students each, add another color to each set of cards, etc.

2 Give each student a card. Ask students to use the cards to form groups. All the blues sit down together, yellows, greens, and so on.

Post the following rules when asking students to form groups:

Move quickly and quietly.

Stay in your group.

Don't bother other groups.

Avoid speaking loudly.

Version Three: Beginning to Intermediate

1 Create a set of 3" x 5" vocabulary cards. Make sure the words are drawn from various categories/themes. You will need to make at least one card per student.

2 Give each student a card. Students must read the word on their cards and find other students whose words are somehow related. Students then form groups based on the related words. For example, *sandwich*, *soda*, *tablecloth*, *potato chips*, and *ants* may all sit down together under the theme *picnic*.

Note: Some connections will be obvious, but others may be subtle, leading students to see language relationships in new ways. You will want to have a general idea of how the cards fit together, even though students may configure themselves differently.

Version Four: Beginning to intermediate

1 Ask students to line up according to one of the following: their birthday and month (see note below); the length of their hair; their numerical street address; their height; or alphabetical order by their first name, last name, mother's name, last letter in their last name, etc.

2 Students then count off by fours or fives depending on the number of groups you would like to have. All of the ones sit together, the twos, threes, and so on.

Note: Avoid using the birth year with age-conscious adults. Also, if you have students who do not know their birthday and month on a western calendar, simply have them pick a month and day.

Forming Groups (continued) 6.5

Version Five: Intermediate to Advanced

1 Create a sign for each group of students. Each sign needs to be labeled with a conversation topic: sports, animals and pets, food, music, hobbies, literature, famous people, travel, science and outer space, etc. Post the signs around the classroom.

2 Ask students to stand in front of the sign that represents the subject they would most like to talk about.

3 Students sit down and talk with classmates who share their interests.

Version Six: Beginning to Advanced

1 Mix up a deck of playing cards and give one card to each student. Ask students to keep their cards facedown.

2 When all students have received a card, ask them to turn their cards over. Students must then find a classmate who has the same card but a different suit. For example, a student with a nine of clubs finds a student with a nine of spades. Once students have found a partner with a match, they should sit down together.

6.6 Getting to School

Age Group
Grade 5 to adult

Language Level
Intermediate

INTELLIGENCES DEVELOPED

Interpersonal

Bodily/kinesthetic

Linguistic

Logical/mathematical

OBJECTIVES

To develop skills in sorting and classifying data

To develop basic mathematical skills

To reinforce language development through movement

To give students an opportunity to work together

Materials Needed
• Board or flipchart
• Large sheets of butcher paper
• Colored markers
• Tape

1 Lead a large group discussion in which students discuss the distances from their homes to school.

2 After each student has decided his/her distance, they should write their names and the distances on the board or flipchart.

3 Students form groups of five or six. Show students a sample bar graph.

4 You can put this image on an overhead transparency or draw a simple model on the board or flipchart. Ask each group to talk about the bar graph. What do they think it is used for? How do they use it?

5 Once you feel that students understand the concept of a bar graph, give each group a large sheet of butcher paper and colored markers. Explain to students that they will be creating their own bar graphs using the distances from their homes to school. Walk around the room providing help and feedback.

6 Once all bar graphs have been completed, each group must write five to six questions about their data (on a separate sheet of paper).

7 Post the bar graphs around the room.

8 Ask two groups to join together and ask each other the questions they've written about their bar graph. Group 1, for example, asks Group 2 their questions. Group 2 would then study Group 1's bar graph and respond.

9 Have the groups switch roles and share their answers.

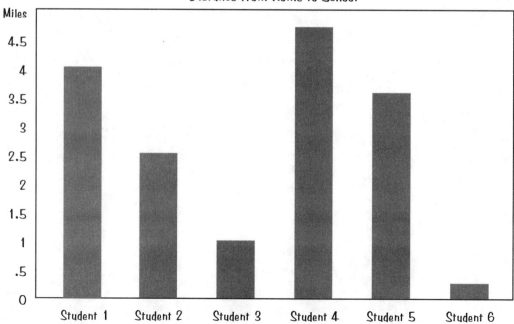

Distance from Home to School

Group Roles 6.7

INTELLIGENCES DEVELOPED	OBJECTIVES

Interpersonal

Linguistic

Logical/mathematical

To develop a better understanding of group process

To develop logical thinking skills

To develop skills in working together

To give students an opportunity to work together

Age Group
High school to adult

Language Level
Advanced

Materials Needed
- One copy of handout 6.7 for each group
- Scissors
- Envelopes

1 This activity can be used in conjunction with almost any other exercise that requires students to work in groups. Copy handout 6.7 and cut out each picture to make a set of roles for each group of five students. Place each set in an envelope.

2 Give an envelope to each group. Ask students to randomly select a role from the envelope.

3 Each student reads his/her role and the description. Then as a group they write appropriate phrases that their "role" might use to keep the group on task and make any group activity work better. Walk around the room giving feedback and helping with specific phrases.

4 After all groups are done, ask them to write the phrases they have come up with on the board.

5 Conduct a large group discussion. Ask students to answer the following questions:

Which roles are the easiest? Hardest?

Which roles do you prefer? Why?

Which roles do you usually play in a group? Why?

What other roles do you think might be needed in groupwork?

What role would be the most difficult for you? Why?

| Task-master | Encourager | Secretary | Checker | Reader |

6.8 Oral Directions

Age Group
High school to adult

Language Level
High beginning to
intermediate

INTELLIGENCES DEVELOPED	OBJECTIVES
Interpersonal	To raise student awareness of pronunciation problems
Bodily/kinesthetic	To help students speak clearly and comprehensibly
Linguistic	To give students an opportunity to work together
Visual/spatial	

Materials Needed
- One copy of handout 6.8 for each pair
- Scissors
- Plain white paper

1 Cut the handouts in half as marked. Divide students into pairs. Give one partner the top half of the handout (Version One) and the other a plain white sheet of paper.

2 Explain that the partner with the plain paper must follow the handout instructions read by his/her partner.

3 When partners have finished, ask them to read the instructions a second time, this time comparing them to the drawing. Are there mistakes? Is everything correct?

4 After completing Version One instructions, ask students to switch roles. Repeat steps 1–3 using the bottom half of the handout (Version Two).

Paper Airplanes 6.9

INTELLIGENCES DEVELOPED	OBJECTIVES
Interpersonal	To develop logical thinking skills
Bodily/kinesthetic	To reinforce language development through movement
Linguistic	To develop skills for seeing visual/spatial patterns and relationships
Logical/mathematical	To give students an opportunity to work together
Visual/spatial	

Age Group
Middle school to adult

Language Level
Intermediate to advanced

Materials Needed
• Plain white paper

1 Divide students into small groups. Give all students a piece of plain white paper and ask them to each make a paper airplane within their group. The planes do not have to be alike; encourage students to make different planes.

2 After students have finished, ask them to fly the planes within their groups and rank the planes in some way (distance traveled, fastest, most graceful, best designed, etc.).

3 Once the ranking has been completed, ask students to make guesses about why the airplanes performed differently. Students must create a chart presenting their results.

4 Using the chart, students determine the best paper airplane within their group.

5 In another class session or on the same day, have students, in their groups, write directions for making their best paper airplane.

6 Follow up with a large group discussion. Give each group a chance to present their results to the entire class.

6.10 Syllable Match

Age Group
High school to adult

Language Level
Intermediate to advanced

INTELLIGENCES DEVELOPED	OBJECTIVES

INTELLIGENCES DEVELOPED

Interpersonal

Bodily/kinesthetic

Linguistic

Visual/spatial

OBJECTIVES

To reinforce language development through movement

To recognize and work with different parts of a word

To develop vocabulary

To help students see patterns in words

To give students an opportunity to work together

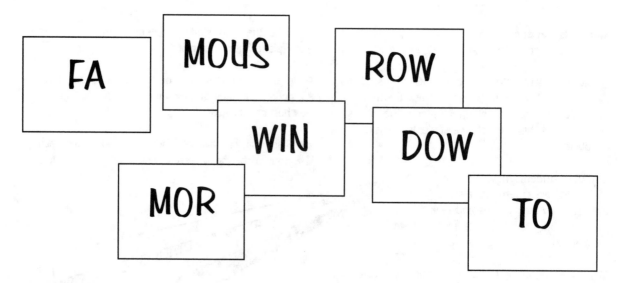

Materials Needed
- 3" x 5" cards
- Envelopes
- Board or flipchart

1 Write down a list of polysyllabic words. Write the syllables of each word on separate 3" x 5" cards (one syllable per card). Divide the syllable cards into envelopes, one per each pair of students.

2 Ask students to find a partner. Give each pair an envelope.

3 Partners work together to write down words that contain the syllables in their envelope. Syllables may be repeated in different combinations, but all syllables must be used at least once.

4 Ask the first pair finished to write their words on the board. Then ask the other pairs to compare their words and provide feedback.

5 Give several blank 3" x 5" cards and an empty envelope to each pair of students. Ask students to create four syllable cards for their own polysyllabic combination words and place the cards in the envelope.

6 Each pair numbers their envelope and exchanges it with another pair of students. Then repeat steps 2–3.

Tracking Water Usage 6.11

INTELLIGENCES DEVELOPED	OBJECTIVES

Interpersonal

Intrapersonal

Linguistic

To sensitize students to issues related to water conservation

To give students an opportunity to work with data collection

To give students an opportunity to work together

Age Group
Middle school to adult

Language Level
Intermediate to advanced

Materials Needed
- One copy of handout 6.11A for each student
- One copy of handout 6.11B for each group

1 Give each student a copy of handout 6.11A. Ask students to keep track of where and how they use water for one day and to return their completed handouts to class the following day.

2 When all students have recorded their water usage, divide them into groups and give each group a copy of handout 6.11B.

3 Based on their collective data, have each group determine approximately how much water they used in one day.

4 Once handout 6.11B is complete, ask students to answer the questions below.

5 Finally, ask the groups to share their findings with the entire class.

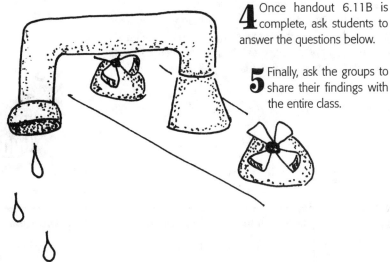

Questions

1. At what time of day is the most water used?

2. Who uses the most water?

3. On what activity is the most water used?

4. How much water is used in total?

5. What do you think you could do to save water? What do you think the people in your family or people who live with you could do to save water? Make three suggestions.

6.12 Your Time

Age Group
Grades K and 1

Language Level
Beginning

INTELLIGENCES DEVELOPED

Interpersonal

Bodily/kinesthetic

Linguistic

Logical/mathematical

OBJECTIVES

To give students meaningful practice in working with numbers

To give students practice in telling time with numbered clocks

To give students an opportunity to work together

Materials Needed
• One copy of handout 6.12 for each student

1 Divide students into groups and give each student a copy of handout 6.12.

2 Dictate the following times. There are two versions given; use the version that is preferred in the country you are teaching. After you dictate each time, let students discuss the time in their groups and then draw the hands on the appropriate clock on their worksheet. Students should check to make sure that they all agree.

3 Collect one finished handout from each group for checking and grading.

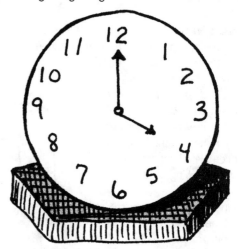

Dictation for a 24-Hour Clock	**Dictation for a 12-Hour Clock**
1. Zero eight hundred hours	1. Eight o'clock
2. Ten-fifteen	2. Ten-fifteen
3. Half past ten	3. Half past ten
4. Noon	4. Twelve noon
5. Nineteen-thirty	5. Seven-thirty
6. Sixteen-thirty	6. Half past four
7. Fourteen hundred hours	7. Two o'clock
8. Nine-twenty	8. Nine-twenty
9. Five forty-five	9. A quarter to six
10. Fifteen-fifteen	10. A quarter after three
11. Thirteen hundred hours	11. Eleven-thirty
12. Eighteen-thirty	12. Eleven forty-five

Weekly Menus 6.13

INTELLIGENCES DEVELOPED	OBJECTIVES
Interpersonal	To develop skills in planning healthy and nutritious meals
Linguistic	To develop an understanding of the costs of different foods
Logical/mathematical	To give students an opportunity to work together

Age Group
High school to adult

Language Level
Intermediate to advanced

Materials Needed
- One copy of handout 6.13 for each group
- Newspapers containing grocery store food ads/coupons

1 Divide students into small groups. Give each group a copy of handout 6.13 and a stack of newspapers.

2 Ask students to read and complete Steps One to Three on their worksheets.

3 When all groups are finished, have them share their results with the entire class.

SHOPPING LIST

milk
lettuce
tomatoes
rice
apples
chicken
tortillas
salt
beans

6.14 Autobio Poetry

Age Group
Middle to high school

Language Level
Beginning to intermediate

INTELLIGENCES DEVELOPED	OBJECTIVES
Intrapersonal	To develop an awareness of and value for individual differences
Interpersonal	To give students an opportunity to learn more about themselves
Linguistic	To give students an opportunity to learn about each other
	To build self-esteem
	To give students an opportunity to work together

Materials Needed
• One copy of handout 6.14 for each student

1 Give each student a copy of handout 6.14. Explain that they are going to learn how to write a poem about themselves. Reassure them that it will not be difficult and that each of them will be successful.

2 It is important to "walk" students through the first few steps until they can see what needs to be done. Begin by asking them to write their name where indicated on the handout. On the next line, have them write a word that describes them in terms of their relationship to another person. Give examples (e.g., brother, sister, uncle, aunt, friend, son, or daughter). Next, ask students to write down three things they love. Continue through the handout, checking to make sure that students understand the instructions.

3 When students have completed their poem, give them time to read it through and make corrections. Walk around the room providing feedback.

4 Ask students to form small groups and read their poem aloud to the rest of the group.

5 After all students have had a chance to share, write the following set of questions on the board and ask each group to answer them. Each group should appoint a secretary to record their answers.

In how many different ways did group members describe themselves?

Which members in your group love the same things?

Does anyone want to visit the same places as someone else?

Make a list of the different things your group members enjoy doing.

Acknowledgement: Thank you to Brenda Crooks, one of my former students at the University of Utah, for her inspiration for this activity.

Dear Abby 6.15

INTELLIGENCES DEVELOPED	OBJECTIVES

Intrapersonal

Interpersonal

Linguistic

Logical/mathematical

To develop problem-solving skills

To develop skills for handling conflict

To give students an opportunity to work together

Age Group
Middle school to adult

Language Level
Intermediate to advanced

Materials Needed
- One copy of handout 6.15A, 6.15B, or 6.15C for each pair or small group of students

1 Ask students to form pairs or small groups. Tell them about "Dear Abby" (see handouts for background information). Explain to them that they are going to write a "Dear Abby" letter that expresses their opinion on how to resolve a particular conflict.

2 Give each pair or small group a copy of handout 6.15A, 6.15B, or 6.15C. Ask them to follow the instructions.

3 When students have completed the handout, ask them to exchange letters and write responses. Walk around the classroom giving help and providing feedback as needed.

4 Follow up with a large group discussion.

6.16 Dreams

Age Group
Grade 3 to adult

Language Level
Intermediate to advanced

INTELLIGENCES DEVELOPED	OBJECTIVES
Intrapersonal	To give students an opportunity to learn more about themselves
Interpersonal	To develop an awareness of and value for individual differences
Linguistic	To develop vocabulary
Visual/spatial	To give students an opportunity to work together

Materials Needed
• One copy of handout 6.16A for each student
• One copy of handout 6.16B for each pair

1 Conduct a short discussion about dreams. Do students remember their dreams? If they do, invite examples of what they remember. Talk about the fact that some people believe that dreams reveal important information about the dreamer's life.

2 Give each student a copy of handout 6.16A. Ask each student to remember a dream they have had. Once they remember a dream, ask them to record some ideas from the dream in the dream bubble on the handout so that they will not forget the content. Then they should practice retelling their dream. Give them several days to complete the assignment.

3 On the day that you plan to work with the dreams in class, ask students to find a partner. Give each pair a copy of handout 6.16B. Explain that the handout contains a list of common dream themes along with some interpretations. Relate a short dream that you have had to the class. Then ask them to tell you what images were important in the dream. Using handout 6.16B, students tell you what your dream might signify.

4 Ask each student to retell their dream to their partner. Using handout 6.16B, their partner tries to tell them what some of the images in the dream could mean. Tell students not to worry if some of the themes of their dreams do not appear on the handout. If none of a particular student's themes are listed, the partner should attach his/her own meanings to the themes.

5 When each pair finishes, they join another pair to form a small group. Each person in the group tells his/her partner's dream and explains the possible meanings.

6 Follow up with a large group discussion.

Evaluate Your Own Work 6.17

INTELLIGENCES DEVELOPED

Intrapersonal

Linguistic

Logical/mathematical

OBJECTIVES

To develop skills for becoming independent learners

To help students understand more about their own learning processes

Age Group
Middle school to adult

Language Level
Intermediate to advanced

Materials Needed

• One copy of handout 6.17A or 6.17B for each student

1 Give each student a copy of handout 6.17A or 6.17B. Explain to them that this activity is going to help develop their skills in evaluating their own learning in the areas of reading or writing.

2 Students complete the handout individually.

3 When students are finished, they form small groups and share their responses.

Feelings 6.18

INTELLIGENCES DEVELOPED

Intrapersonal

Bodily/kinesthetic

Interpersonal

Linguistic

Logical/mathematical

Visual/spatial

OBJECTIVES

To give students an opportunity to learn more about themselves

To give students practice in recognizing their feelings

To foster creative expression

To develop logical thinking skills

To reinforce language development with visual cues

To give students an opportunity to work together

Age Group
Grades 1 to 4

Language Level
Beginning

Materials Needed
• One copy of handout 6.18 for each pair
• One copy of handout 6.18 for each student
• One overhead transparency of handout 6.18
• Envelopes
• Overhead projector

1 Using the handout copies you've made for each pair, cut apart the emotion words and pictures. Place each set of words/picture flashcards in an envelope.

2 Give each student an uncut copy of handout 6.18. Teach students the meaning of the emotion words through the following steps:

a Say each emotion word and demonstrate it.

b Ask students to demonstrate the emotion word as you point it out on an overhead projector.

c Ask students to say the words as you demonstrate.

d Ask students to demonstrate the words as you say them.

3 Have students put away their copies of the handout and sit down with a partner. Give each pair an envelope that you prepared in Step 1.

4 Students remove the flashcards from the envelope and match the words and pictures.

5 Students put away the pictures. One partner reads the words and the other demonstrates the feelings. Then they switch roles.

6.19 Gender Differences

Age Group
High school to adult

Language Level
Intermediate to advanced

INTELLIGENCES DEVELOPED

Intrapersonal

Bodily/kinesthetic

Interpersonal

Linguistic

Logical/mathematical

OBJECTIVES

To give students an opportunity to learn more about each other

To give students an opportunity to look closely at their personal beliefs

To reinforce language development through movement

To give students practice in sorting and analyzing data

To give students an opportunity to work together

Materials Needed
• One copy of handout 6.19A for each student
• One copy of handout 6.19B for each group

1 Give each student a copy of handout 6.19A. Each student interviews three classmates and records the information on his/her handout.

2 Students form groups of four to five. Give each group a copy of handout 619.B. Ask students to compile data collected from the interviews onto handout 6.19B. Students should decide on a secretary to record everything.

How Do You Prefer to Learn? 6.20

INTELLIGENCES DEVELOPED	**OBJECTIVES**

Age Group
Middle school to adult

Language Level
Intermediate to advanced

Intrapersonal

Interpersonal

Linguistic

OBJECTIVES

To help students understand more about their own learning processes

To develop an awareness of and value for individual differences

To give students an opportunity to work together

Materials Needed
• One copy of handout 6.20 for each student

1 Give each student a copy of handout 6.20. Instruct students to answer the questions on the handout.

2 Ask students to find a partner or form groups of three. One person should be the secretary and one person should be the presenter.

3 Students share their answers. The secretary records the answers. The presenter shares the results with the entire class.

Letters to Parents 6.21

INTELLIGENCES DEVELOPED	**OBJECTIVES**

Age Group
Middle to high school

Language Level
Beginning to intermediate

Intrapersonal

Interpersonal

Linguistic

Visual/spatial

OBJECTIVES

To give students experience in determining what is important to them

To give students an opportunity to work together

Materials Needed
• Board or flipchart
• One copy of handout 6.21 for each student

1 Ask each student to make a list of five things for which they are grateful.

2 Students find a partner and share their list.

3 Do a large group sharing and record students' various answers on the board.

4 Give each student a copy of handout 6.21 and ask them to write a letter to their parents (or to a grandparent, relative, friend) telling them the things for which they are grateful in their lives.

6.22 Personal Galleries

Age Group
High school to adult

Language Level
Intermediate to advanced

INTELLIGENCES DEVELOPED	OBJECTIVES
Intrapersonal	To learn more about art and artists
Interpersonal	To develop a better understanding of personal taste in art
Linguistic	To develop an awareness of and value for individual differences
Visual/spatial	To give students an opportunity to work together

Materials Needed
• Books on various artists
• Internet access (optional but helpful)

1 Explain to students that they are going to create a class art gallery. Ask each student to select a favorite artist for the gallery.

2 Each student finds examples of the selected artist's work and brings copies to class. (The Internet is a great resource for this!)

3 Students prepare a short report on the artist and art- work. The report should include the following:

   Artist's name

   Medium used

   Most significant works

   Where and when the artist was born

   Something about the artist's family

   Why the student likes the artist

   If the artist is still living

4 Each student gives an oral report on his/her artist of choice.

5 Create a bulletin board "showing off" the various pieces. You may also post the selections on the wall for students to view independently.

6 Follow up with a large group discussion about what students learned, liked best, and were most surprised by.

Personal Totem Poles 6.23

Age Group
Grade 3 to middle school

Language Level
Beginning to intermediate

INTELLIGENCES DEVELOPED	OBJECTIVES
Intrapersonal	To give students an opportunity to learn more about themselves
Bodily/kinesthetic	To develop an awareness of and value for individual differences
Linguistic	To foster creative expression
Logical/mathematical	To reinforce language development through movement
Visual/spatial	

Materials Needed

- One empty paper towel tube for each student
- One popsicle stick for each student
- One copy of handouts 6.23A and 6.23B for each student
- Crayons or colored markers
- Scissors
- Glue
- Cardboard
- Board or overheard projector

Note: It is a good idea for you to make a sample totem pole before beginning the activity with your class.

1 Start collecting empty paper towel tubes several weeks prior to beginning this activity. Ask students and other teachers to help you in your collection effort. You also need to buy popsicle sticks at a craft store or collect them during the summertime (when popsicles are a favorite with children!). Wash the popsicle sticks and store them in a bag.

2 Introduce totem poles to students. To do so, find pictures of totem poles in the library; photographs of real totem poles are ideal. Explain that Native American Indians of the Northwest Coast, such as the Kwakiutl and the Tlingit, are well known for their totem poles. Totem poles are hand-carved from large logs. Some totem poles are so large that doorways can be cut into the bottoms of them. Totem poles often tell the history of a family and display animals that are important to a family or individual person.

3 Tell students that they will be making personal totem poles in this activity. Students will work with three animals on their personal totem poles—a bear, a wolf, and an eagle. Show students the sample of your finished totem pole.

4 Give each student a copy of handouts 6.23A and 6.23B. Students first color each animal and write their name on the wings of the eagle. They then cut out

the animals (following the thick black lines) and glue them to their totem poles (the empty paper towel tubes) in this order: the eagle on top, the wolf in the middle, and the bear at the bottom.

5 Students cut out circles from cardboard (using the circle pattern on handout 6.23B) and glue a circle onto the bottom of each "totem pole" to create a stand.

6 The final step in the totem pole creation is to glue two halves of a popsicle stick to the back of the eagle's wings for support. See the example below.

7 Once the totem poles have been completed, students work individually to carry out the following tasks. You may want to write these instructions on the board or put them on an overhead transparency.

Each animal on your totem pole represents a strength you have. What are your strengths? Write down three strengths and the three animals that represent them.

Describe your totem pole. Where are the animals located? What colors are the eagle, bear, and wolf? Write down your description on a piece of paper.

Form a group of four to six people. Make sure you have your personal totem pole. When it is your turn, tell the other members of the group about your strengths and which animals represent them. Describe your personal totem pole in detail.

6.24 Read and Recite

Age Group
High school to adult

Language Level
Intermediate to advanced

INTELLIGENCES DEVELOPED	OBJECTIVES

Intrapersonal

Linguistic

To help students evaluate what it is they are learning

Materials Needed
- A reading passage (short story, expository prose, narrative, etc.)

1 Select an appropriate reading passage. It could either be a short story divided into sections or a piece of expository prose that explains a process. Narrative seems to be easy for most students, so it is also a good choice for this activity.

2 Follow these steps in the classroom:

a Read a portion of the passage aloud to your students.

b Stop. Students take quick notes, writing down what they remember.

c Students find a partner and read what they have written to their partner.

d Each pair then identifies elements they remembered similarly and differently.

e Students predict what they think will happen next.

f Students share their predictions in a large group.

g Read the next portion of the passage to your students and repeat steps a–f.

Self-Reflection 6.25

INTELLIGENCES DEVELOPED	**OBJECTIVES**

Intrapersonal

Linguistic

Interpersonal

To help students reflect on their behavior in various situations

To develop skills for getting along with others

Age Group
Middle to high school

Language Level
Intermediate to advanced

Materials Needed

• One copy of handout 6.25A or 6.25B for each student, depending on the situation

Note: This activity can be used at the time a conflict occurs as a way to help students through a specific situation, but is perhaps best employed as part of an on-going self-evaluation, encouraging students to reflect on their interactions with others.

Version One: For Students Involved in a Conflict

1 If you are working with students involved in a conflict, do this version. Make sure that the partners are good listeners and committed to helping the involved students accept responsibility for their parts in the interaction. Give each student a copy of handout 6.25A.

2 Students complete the handout individually.

3 Once students have completed the handout, they share their answers with the person with whom they are having a conflict. After participating in the activity, students involved in a conflict may find that the answers to the questions on the handout lead them to resolve the problem through discussion rather than confrontation.

Version Two: For General Student Self-Evaluation

1 If you are working with students who are not currently involved in a conflict, do this version. Give each student a copy of handout 6.25B.

2 Students complete the handout individually.

3 Once they have worked through all of the questions and written thoughtful responses, students find partners and share one important piece of information that they learned about themselves.

6.26 Task Evaluation

Age Group
High school to adult

Language Level
Intermediate to advanced

INTELLIGENCES DEVELOPED	OBJECTIVES
Intrapersonal	To develop skills for evaluating independent work
Linguistic	To develop skills for working independently
Logical/mathematical	

Materials Needed
• One copy of handout 6.26 for each student

1 This goal-setting activity focuses students on the importance of establishing goals for oneself and evaluating how one has achieved these goals. Explain to students that being able to determine on one's own what one has learned (the content) and how one has learned (the process) is an important part of learning. Tell them that you will be asking them to participate in task evaluation.

2 Give each student a copy of handout 6.26 and ask them to complete the first part before they carry out an activity. They should work alone if the activity in which they participate requires individual work; they should work together if the activity requires pair or group participation. In the case of group work, students may choose a secretary to record their responses.

3 Students then carry out the activity of your choice.

4 After students have completed the activity, have them complete the second half of the handout.

DIRECTIONS

Introduction to Store Personnel:

Hi, our names are [my name is] _____. We are students at _____ School. We are completing a school assignment about the businesses in our community and would be grateful if you could answer the following questions for us. Can you help us? We would really appreciate it!

1 How long has the business been located in this community?

2 How long have you worked here?

3 Who owns the business?

4 What do you like about working here?

5 When are your busiest hours?

6 Are your customers younger or older people?

7 Do you have regular customers? If so, do you know them by name?

Multiple Intelligences and Language Learning © 2005 Alta Book Center Publishers, San Francisco, California

About My Community

Reflections

DIRECTIONS

Answer the following questions individually or with a partner. Then share your answers with the class and record them on the board or a flipchart.

1 How much time did it take to complete this activity?

2 Did you have to visit any business more than once?

3 Were there any questions to which you could get no answers? Why?

4 Which was your favorite business?

5 What was the most difficult part of this assignment?

6 What was the easiest part of this assignment?

7 What did you like about this activity?

8 What did you not like about this activity?

DIRECTIONS

Work together in your groups. Answer the following questions:

1 Who ordered the most items? The fewest?

2 Whose breakfast was the most expensive? The cheapest?

3 What was the most popular item?

4 Whose breakfast was the most unique?

5 Whose breakfast was the healthiest?

6 What was the total bill for your group? Did your group agree with the bill that your server gave you?

Multiple Intelligences and Language Learning © 2005 Alta Book Center Publishers, San Francisco, California

Group Roles

Taskmaster: To keep the group focused and aware of time constraints.

Checker: To make certain that everyone understands each part of the task.

Encourager: To encourage group members to participate.

Reader: To read the text as it is written and help the secretary improve the quality of the group's written work.

Secretary: To record the group's ideas.

Version One

1 Write your name and the date in the upper right corner.

2 Draw a rectangular window in the middle of the paper.

3 Draw a chair to the left of the window.

4 Draw a person looking out of the window.

5 Draw a hat on the person's head.

6 Draw a door to the right of the window.

7 Draw a doorknob on the door.

8 Draw some flowers under the window.

9 Draw the sun in the sky and give it a smiling face.

10 Write your initials in the bottom left corner.

Version Two

1 Write your name in the top left corner.

2 Draw a circle around your name and another circle in the middle of the paper.

3 Draw a smaller circle inside the first circle.

4 Draw a triangle in the top left corner under your name.

5 Draw a larger triangle underneath it.

6 Draw two diagonal lines and two parallel lines in the bottom right corner.

7 Draw two perpendicular lines in the bottom left corner.

8 Draw question marks around the circles in the middle of the paper.

9 Draw two hearts on the left side of the paper.

10 Draw two diamonds on the right side of the paper.

Multiple Intelligences and Language Learning © 2005 Alta Book Center Publishers, San Francisco, California www.altaesl.com. Permission granted to photocopy for one teacher's classroom use only.

Tracking Water Usage
Individual Consumption

Use the sheet below to track your water consumption for one day. If someone else in your family uses water for an activity that involves you in some way, track that as well. For example, if someone in your family washes dishes after a meal you ate or washes clothes including yours, write that usage on the chart. Record the amount of time the water was used, who used the water, where it was used, and for what activity.

Total Time of Usage	Who	Where	Activity

DIRECTIONS

Total the water consumption in your group using everyone's information from handout 6.11A and the approximate amounts in the box at the bottom of this page.

Activity	Where	Amount Used

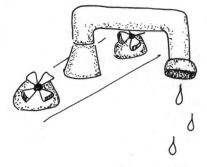

Approximate amount of water used in common activities:

Taking a bath	30 gallons
Taking a shower	20 gallons
Getting a drink of water	1/4 gallon
Washing one's hands	1 gallon
Brushing one's teeth	1/4 gallon
Flushing the average toilet	3 gallons
Cooking a meal	5 gallons

Multiple Intelligences and Language Learning © 2005 Alta Book Center Publishers, San Francisco, California

Your Time

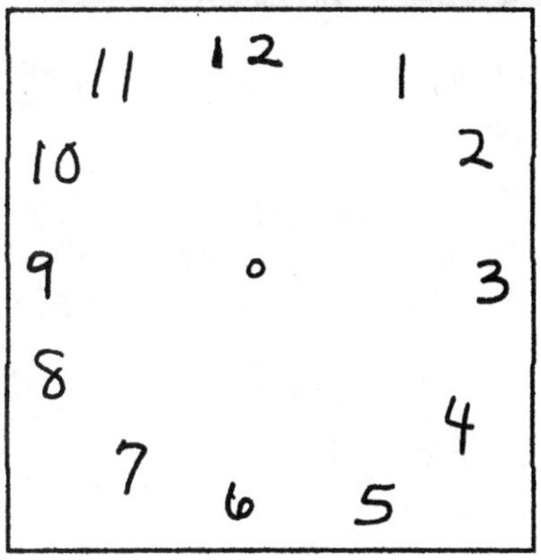

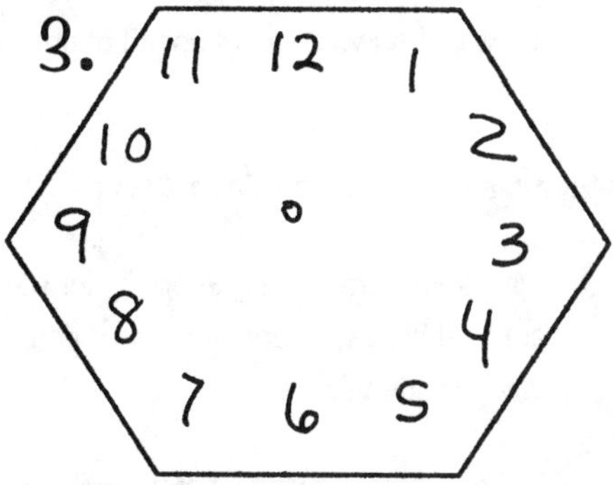

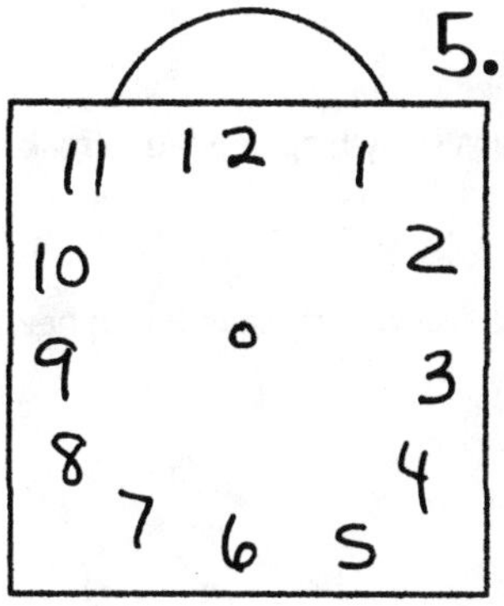

1.

2.

3.

4.

5.

6.

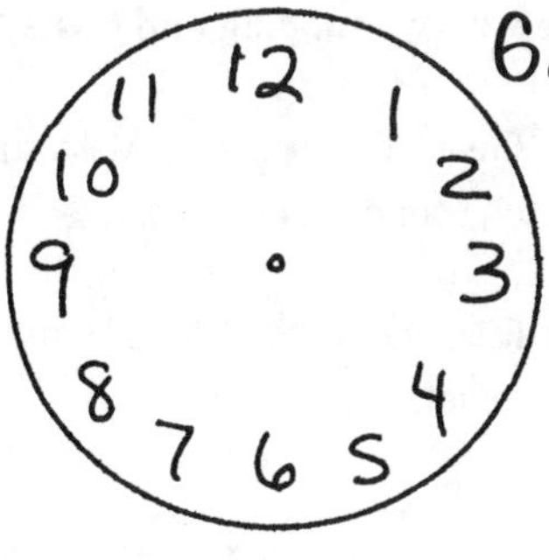

7.

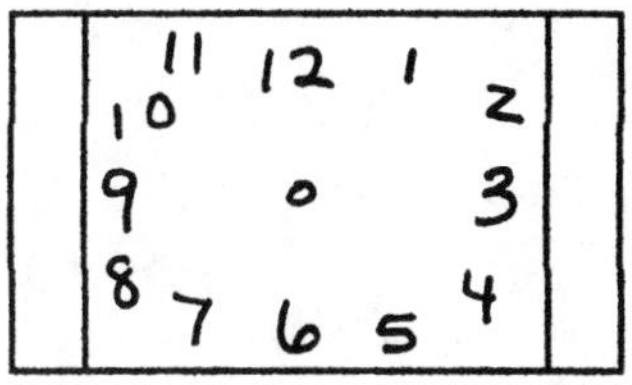

8.

9.

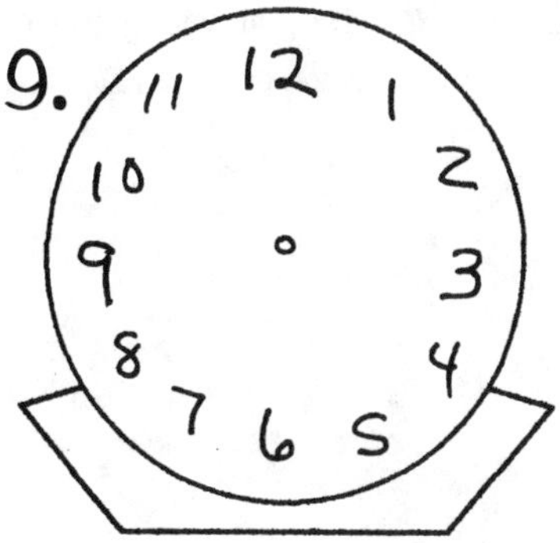

10.

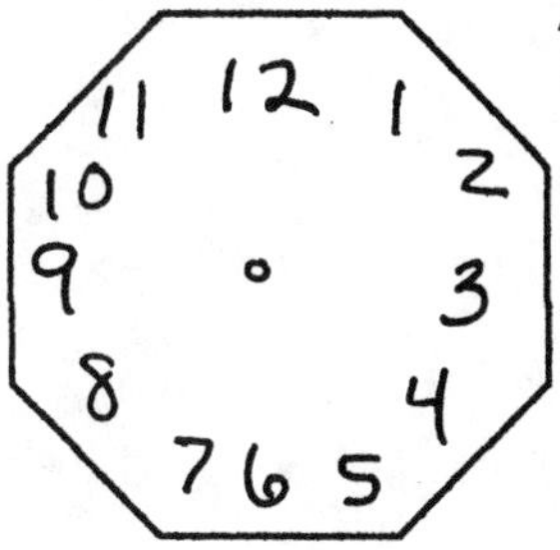

11.

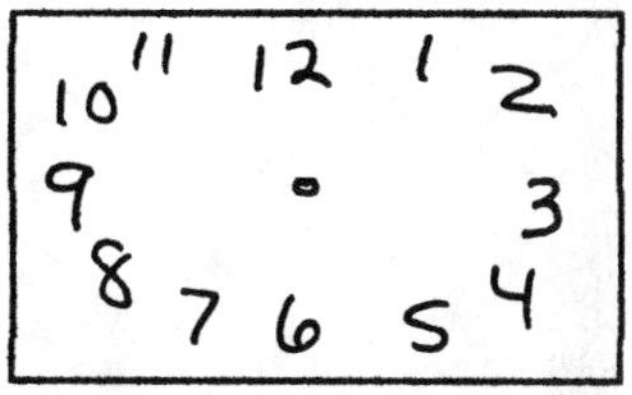

12.

6.13 Handout

Weekly Menus

DIRECTIONS

Imagine that you are a group of friends who are living together. You are all on a limited budget. None of you has very much money, so you have to plan your meals ahead of time and shop very carefully.

Step One: Menus and Food Groups

1 Within your group, decide on dinner menus for the next week. Make sure your meals are healthy; pay attention to the different food groups. Take individual preferences into consideration.

2 Make a chart showing what you will eat and what food groups are included.

Step Two: Shopping and Costs

1 Create a shopping list. Make sure the list contains everything needed to make the items on your dinner menus.

2 Estimate the cost of the items you need to buy. Use grocery store ads in newspapers for references.

Step Three: Write About It

1 Work together with your group to write a composition explaining the process you went through above. Be prepared to share your results with the entire class.

Multiple Intelligences and Language Learning © 2005 Alta Book Center Publishers, San Francisco, California

AUTOBIO POEM

_____

(first name)

_____

(relationship to another person)

Lover of _____, _____, _____

(list three things)

Who feels _____, _____, _____

(list three emotions)

Who needs _____, _____, _____

(list three things)

Who would like to visit _____, _____, _____

(list three places)

Who enjoys _____, _____, _____

(list three things)

Who likes to wear _____

(a descriptive clothing item)

Who lives in _____

(a descriptive place)

DIRECTIONS

Abigail Van Buren is known as "Dear Abby" in the newspaper. She is a woman who wrote a *syndicated column** in many English language newspapers in the United States and around the world. Though Abigail no longer writes the column, her daughter does under the same "Dear Abby" heading. The column is very popular. People write letters to "Dear Abby" complaining about problems they are having with other people. Their letters are answered and advice is given. For example, some people write "Dear Abby" complaining about problems they are having with their wives, friends, husbands, co-workers, children, boyfriends, or girlfriends. They are then told what to do. Read the letter below and write a response as if you were Abigail Van Buren.

Dear Abby,

I share an office with my colleague at work. I try to be a good officemate: I keep things neat and tidy, and try to respect his space. He, on the other hand, is a slob! His desk is a mess and stacks of books and papers are everywhere! When students come to talk to him, he frequently uses my desk and side of the office because there's no room on his side. Lately, he's even been piling stuff on my desk. A couple of times, when gathering materials, he's scooped up some of my papers by mistake. I've later found the papers among his things. These mishaps cause great difficulties for me. I've spoken to him repeatedly, asking that he please not use my desk and office space. He says that I'm being selfish and rude, and claims that because the two of us share the office, he has the right to use any space that's available. The situation is driving me crazy! What should I do?

Sincerely,

Miserable Officemate

*Syndicated column: a column that is sold and appears in many different newspapers at the same time. In other words, Abigail Van Buren wrote for a syndicate that sold her column to various newspapers.

Dear Abby

Version #2

Handout 6.15B

DIRECTIONS

Abigail Van Buren is known as "Dear Abby" in the newspaper. She is a woman who wrote a *syndicated column** in many English language newspapers in the United States and around the world. Though Abigail no longer writes the column, her daughter does under the same "Dear Abby" heading. The column is very popular. People write letters to "Dear Abby" complaining about problems they are having with other people. Their letters are answered and advice is given. For example, some people write "Dear Abby" complaining about problems they are having with their wives, friends, husbands, co-workers, children, boyfriends, or girlfriends. They are then told what to do. Read the letter below and write a response as if you were Abigail Van Buren.

Dear Abby,

My fiancé and I have been engaged for more than a year and are planning to marry next summer. Last week he told me that he still wants to get married, but that he wants a few months "off" to date other girls before we marry. I am devastated by his suggestion because I feel that he no longer loves me. He argues that it's only for a few months, and we will be married for the rest of our lives. What should I do?

Sincerely,

Devastated in Delaware

---

*Syndicated column: a column that is sold and appears in many different newspapers at the same time. In other words, Abigail Van Buren wrote for a syndicate that sold her column to various newspapers.

DIRECTIONS

Abigail Van Buren is known as "Dear Abby" in the newspaper. She is a woman who wrote a *syndicated column** in many English language newspapers in the United States and around the world. Though Abigail no longer writes the column, her daughter does under the same "Dear Abby" heading. The column is very popular. People write letters to "Dear Abby" complaining about problems they are having with other people. Their letters are answered and advice is given. For example, some people write "Dear Abby" complaining about problems they are having with their wives, friends, husbands, co-workers, children, boyfriends, or girlfriends. They are then told what to do. Read the letter below and write a response as if you were Abigail Van Buren.

Dear Abby,

My friend and I have many of the same classes in school and frequently study together. She's having a hard time in math, but I am doing very well. On several occasions I know that she has taken my notebook and simply copied the math homework. These homework assignments are corrected and graded. Last night she asked to see my notebook. I told her that I couldn't let her copy my homework because I felt it was cheating. She became very angry with me and now won't talk to me at all. She says that I am a bad friend and that if she fails the course, it will be my fault for not helping her. I feel so bad about this confrontation. I don't want my friend to be mad at me, but I feel that I cannot let her copy my homework. What should I do?

Sincerely,

Not Happy About Homework

---

*Syndicated column: a column that is sold and appears in many different newspapers at the same time. In other words, Abigail Van Buren wrote for a syndicate that sold her column to various newspapers.

Dream Journal

Listen to your partner describe his/her dream. Make notes about the themes and images in your partner's dream. Look at the themes below and see if you can find images from your partner's dream. Attach possible meanings to the images. Share the information with your partner.

Image or Theme from the Dream	Meaning of the Dream
an accident of any kind	unexpected change or upset in one's life
acting or an actor	desire for recognition
airplane	rapid movement
alcohol	relaxation, freedom from responsibility
aliens	distance, strangeness
alligator	fear
altar	sacrifice
ambulance	rescue
angels	compassion, higher consciousness
animals (domestic)	in general, the desire to be civilized, accepted, tamed
animals (wild)	freedom
apartment	focus on only part of oneself
applause	recognition
arm	strength, preparation
arrest	enforced stop in one's life
arrow	painful realization
ashes	something remaining
athlete	strength
attorney (lawyer)	resolution of conflict
avalanche	release of buried feelings
baby	rebirth
baggage (luggage)	opinions, material goods
baldness	sexual issues
ball	wholeness
bandage	protection
bar, tavern, or nightclub	pleasure
basement	below, the unconscious
bath, bathroom, hot tub, or shower	cleansing
beach	moving from unconsciousness to consciousness
beard	power

Multiple Intelligences and Language Learning © 2005 Alta Book Center Publishers, San Francisco, California

Image or Theme from the Dream	Meaning of the Dream
bed or bedroom	rest and privacy
bee	social life
bell	signal
bicycle	moving oneself forward
big	generosity
bill	something is due
boots	vigor
boss	control
boulder	barrier
boy	masculine power developing
boyfriend	an ideal
brakes	need to control
brain	reason
bread	shared resources
breasts	maternal love
bride	openness to being feminine
bridge	connection
briefcase or bag	professional identify
brother	masculine part of one's self
bubble	unreal
bugs	minor problems
bus	a shared journey
butterfly	beauty and freedom
cage	danger
camel	endurance
camera	experience, a need to distance
camping	the basics of life
cancer	destruction
candle	personal vision
candy	temptation
car	ego
carnival or party	freedom from restraint
carpet	protection
castle	fortification
cat	independence

6.16B Handout (continued)

Image or Theme from the Dream	Meaning of the Dream
cellular phone	accessible
cemetery	death or transformation
chains	lack of freedom
chair	need to establish a position
chicken	disorganization
chocolate	pleasure
Christ	restricted communication
Christmas	celebration and reunion
cigarette	addiction
city	civilized
climbing	growth
cloak or cape	protection
closet	looking for your identity
clothing (general)	exploration of new roles
clouds	transition
clown	healing
coal	potentiality
coffee	over excitement
cold	emotional chill
beige	neutrality
black	isolation
blue	harmony
brown	security
gray	peace
green	growth, healing
orange	emotion, stimulation
pink	love
red	vigor, passion
white	purity
yellow	intellect
computer	communication
cooking	nourishment
court	conflict
cow	docility
credit card	protection

Image or Theme from the Dream	Meaning of the Dream
cripple	limitations
cross	sacrifice
crowd	options
crystal	clarity
curtain	protection
dancing	joy
danger	change
dark	mystery
daughter	youth
death	an end to a cycle
dentist	desire for independence and power
desert	isolation
devil	temptation
diamond	purity
dining room or food	hunger
dinosaur	fantasy
dirt	fertility
dog	obedient, unconditional love
dolphin	intelligence
donkey	sturdiness
door	access
dove	peace
dragon	mystery
drowning	overwhelmed emotionally
drugs	need to heal
drunkenness	fear
dwarf	unrealized power
eagle	vision
earthquake	great change
egg	hope
elephant	wisdom
excrement	garbage from you past
eye	clarity
face	ego, self-image
falling	fear of failure

Image or Theme from the Dream	Meaning of the Dream
flatulence	defensiveness
fat	protection
fence	separation and differences
fire	need for inspiration
fish	need to know your emotions
flags	loyalty
flood	an overflow of emotion
flowers	beauty
fog	confusion, inability to see clearly
food	greed
foot	need to focus on basic beliefs
forest	desire to learn about one's self
frog	transformation and change
gambling	need for recognition
garbage	the need to get rid of things
garden	inner growth, self development
ghost	fear of memories
goose	aggression
gorilla or ape	innocence
gun	violence and aggression
hair	sensuality
hat	opinionated
heart	love, security
horse	speed and elegance
hotel	changing self
house	beliefs about oneself
hurricane	destruction
ice	inability to access feelings
island	fear of solitude
jewels	things that are pleasurable
keys	need to solve a problem
kissing	desire for intimacy
kitchen	productivity
knife	aggression
adder	desire to improve

Multiple Intelligences and Language Learning © 2005 Alta Book Center Publishers, San Francisco, California
www.altaesl.com Permission granted to photocopy for one teacher's classroom use only.

Image or Theme from the Dream	Meaning of the Dream
lightening	sudden vision
lion	courage, pride
lizard or other reptile	cold-blooded
locker	storage
magic or magician	change, transformation
mail	need to communicate
marriage	desire for union
mask	disguise
meat	essential nourishment
milk	desire for maternal love
mirror	self-identity
money	desire for security
motorcycle	virility
mountain	success
mouse	meekness, quiet
mud	stuck feelings
murder	fear of violence
music	harmony in life
nakedness	feeling vulnerable
ocean or water	overwhelming emotion
owl	wisdom
pain	conflict
parade	looking for options
pillow	comfort
pimples	sensitivity
pirate	rejection of social rules
plants	harmony, order
priest	spiritual well-being
prison	punishment
radio	communication
rat	cleverness
scar	emotional hurt
school	discipline
shower	cleansing
skating	grace

Image or Theme from the Dream	Meaning of the Dream
skiing	balance
skunk	passive aggression
sleeping	desire to learn something new
snow	clarity
soldier	confrontation
spaceship	desire to transcend physical limitations
sports	honor
sun	energy and light
sunrise	hope
sunset	release
surfing	exploring different feelings
swimming or swimming pool	emotions
tattoo	displaying oneself
teacher or teaching	knowledge, wisdom
test	desire to demonstrate one's knowledge and abilities
tiger	wild beauty
toilet	the need to release or cleanse one's self
tongue	pleasure of taste
tree	desire to change something
video games	skill and dexterity
volcano	repressed feelings
vomit	the need to get rid of something
walking	movement and change
war	fear of conflict
wart	ugliness, fear of ugliness
wasp	stinging anger
water	fluidity, change
witch	intuition and natural wisdom
wolf	instinct
worm	decay and insignificance

Note: The author has a personal interest in the interpretation of dreams. The information in the chart was compiled over many years as a result of reading about dream interpretation and talking to people experienced in working with dreams.

Multiple Intelligences and Language Learning © 2005 Alta Book Center Publishers, San Francisco, California www.altaesl.com Permission granted to photocopy for one teacher's classroom use only.

Evaluate Your Own Work

After Reading . . .

TITLE OF BOOK: _____

1 What type of book did you read?

2 Why did you choose this book to read?

3 Who is the author? Do you know anything about the author? If so, how did you find out about the author? Write down as much as you can about the author.

4 How long did it take you to read this book?

5 How often did you read this book? Did you have a regular schedule for reading?

6 What was this book about?

7 What did you like most about reading this book?

8 What did you like least about reading this book?

9 Write down two things you learned as a result of reading this book.

10 Would you recommend this book to a friend? Why or why not?

Evaluate Your Own Work

After Writing . . .

1 What did you write?

   a. a letter

   b. a paper for a class

   c. a short story

   d. a poem

   e. other _____

2 Why did you choose to write in the above format?

   a. I wanted to write in this format.

   b. It was required.

   c. I did it for personal reasons.

   d. other _____

3 How long did it take you to complete the writing project?

   a. less than one day

   b. two days

   c. three to five days

   d. other _____

4 How often do you write something that someone else will read?

   a. everyday

   b. every other day

   c. about once a week.

   d. only when it's required for a class

   e. about twice a month

   f. other _____

5 Do you have a regular schedule for writing?

   a. No, I don't.

   b. Yes, I write in the mornings.

   c. Yes, I write at night.

   d. Yes, I write about two days a week.

   e. other _____

6 What do you write about most often?

   a. my family

   b. my life

   c. my friends

   d. my hobbies

   e. other _____

7 What do you like most about writing?

8 What do you like least about writing?

9 What subjects or topics do you write about?

10 Do you consider yourself a good writer? Why or why not?

Multiple Intelligences and Language Learning © 2005 Alta Book Center Publishers, San Francisco, California
www.altaesl.com Permission granted to photocopy for one teacher's classroom use only.

Happy	Sad	Confused
Nervous	Shy	Sleepy
Angry	Afraid	Surprised

DIRECTIONS

Interview three of your classmates. Record the results using the corresponding opinion numbers in the box. Make sure to also circle *male* or *female*.

Opinion Numbers

0 = disagree

1 = neutral

2 = agree

Statements	Interview 1 Male Female	Interview 2 Male Female	Interview 3 Male Female
1 Women should not work outside the home.			
2 Men should help with the housework.			
3 Boys should be taught to clean and cook.			
4 Women should not be in politics.			
5 Women are not logical.			
6 Men shouldn't cry in public.			
7 A girl should not ask a boy for a date.			
8 Women are more patient than men.			
9 Men are more violent than women.			
10 Sons are easier to raise than daughters.			

Multiple Intelligences and Language Learning © 2005 Alta Book Center Publishers, San Francisco, California
www.altaesl.com Permission granted to photocopy for one teacher's classroom use only.

Gender Differences

Results

DIRECTIONS

Share the responses from your interview (handout 6.19A) with your group. Total the results for each statement. Then rank them on a separate sheet. Discuss the differences in the responses, if any, given by males and females. Share your ideas and opinions.

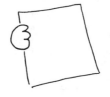

Opinion Numbers

0 = disagree

1 = neutral

2 = agree

Statements	Total Opinions	
	Female	**Male**
1 Women should not work outside the home		
2 Men should help with the housework.		
3 Boys should be taught to clean and cook.		
4 Women should not be in politics.		
5 Women are not logical.		
6 Men shouldn't cry in public.		
7 A girl should not ask a boy for a date.		
8 Women are more patient than men.		
9 Men are more violent than women.		
10 Sons are easier to raise than daughters.		

DIRECTIONS

Directions: Read each item carefully. Circle the answer that best describes you.

1 I prefer to learn new information . . .
   a. via pictures, overheads, charts, graphs, or videos.
   b. via lectures and audiotapes.
   c. by talking to and working with my classmates.

2 When I work with new information, I prefer to . . .
   a. get the details first.
   b. get the general ideas first.
   c. I have no preference.

3 When I have to make a decision, I like to . . .
   a. make it right away.
   b. have time to think about it.

4 When I first come into a classroom, I notice . . .
   a. how the furniture is arranged.
   b. if the room is warm and if there is good lighting.
   c. what people are there and where they are sitting.

5 When I have to solve a problem, I like to . . .
   a. read about it first and then try to figure it out on my own.
   b. talk about the problem and solution with my friends and colleagues.

Multiple Intelligences and Language Learning © 2005 Alta Book Center Publishers, San Francisco, California www.altaesl.com Permission granted to photocopy for one teacher's classroom use only.

Letters to Parents

_____
(date)

Dear _____,

I am writing you a letter in _____ [the target language] to tell you that I

am grateful for _____, _____

_____, _____

and _____.

Thank you.

Your _____,

_____
(sign your name)

Personal Totem Poles

Bear and Wolf

Bear

overlap and paste

Wolf

overlap and paste

overlap Bear

Eagle and Stand

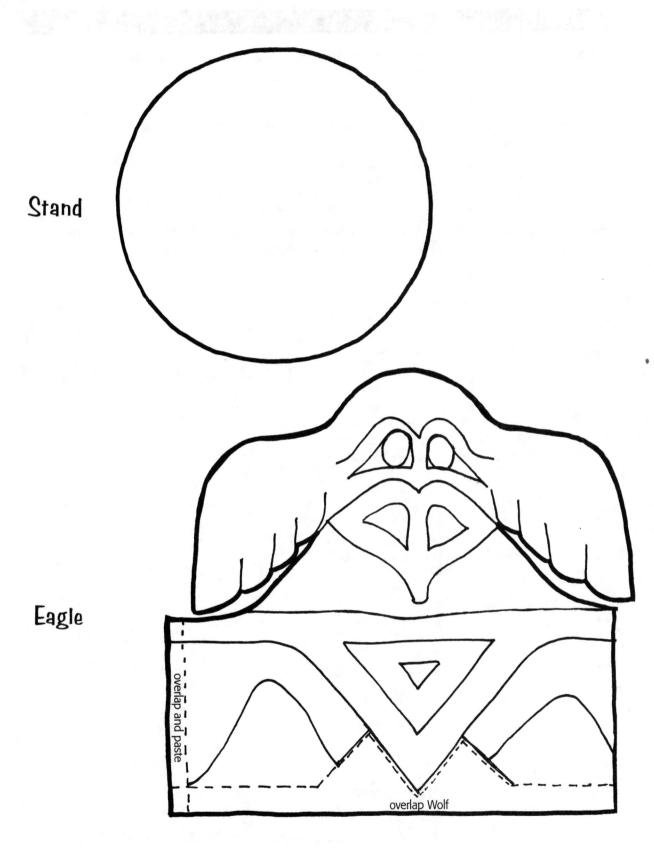

Stand

Eagle

overlap and paste

overlap Wolf

Self-Reflection
For Students Involved in a Conflict

Answer the following questions honestly and thoughtfully. Then share your answers with the person with whom you are having a conflict.

1 In this interaction, have I said things or behaved in ways that hurt other people? How do I know?

2 What are my goals in this interaction? What do I really want to happen (e.g., Do I want peaceful and happy encounters? Do I want others to see my point of view? Do I want others to take action because of my point of view? Do I want others to like me?)?

3 What specifically have I done to achieve my goals?

4 What do I think is the best option in resolving this conflict?

   a continue talking

   b let it go

5 What exactly is it about this conflict that makes me upset?

Self-Reflection

For General Student Self-Evaluation

DIRECTIONS

Answer the following questions honestly and thoughtfully. Then share your answers with another person.

1 In my interactions, do I say things or behave in ways that hurt other people? How do I know?

2 What are my goals for interaction in general? What do I really want to happen in my interactions (e.g., Do I want peaceful and happy encounters? Do I want others to see my point of view? Do I want others to take action because of my point of view? Do I want others to like me?)?

3 What specifically have I done to achieve my goals?

4 What do I think is the best option in resolving conflict?

  a continue talking

  b let it go

5 What exactly is it about conflict that makes me upset?

Multiple Intelligences and Language Learning © 2005 Alta Book Center Publishers, San Francisco, California
www.altaesl.com Permission granted to photocopy for one teacher's classroom use only.

Name _____

Before the Activity

1 What goal do you have for this activity (i.e., What do you want to learn?)?

2 How do you hope to accomplish this goal?

After the Activity

3 How well did you accomplish your goal?

1   2   3   4   5

Not so well   Very well

Comments:

Multiple Intelligences and Language Learning © 2005 Alta Book Center Publishers, San Francisco, California

Musical Intelligence

"Yes, music is the prophet's art; among the gifts that God hath sent, one of the most magnificent."

— Henry Wadsworth Longfellow (1807–1882)

The activities in this chapter help students develop their musical intelligence by:

humming, chanting, and whistling

identifying musical instruments

listening to and appreciating music

recognizing melodies and songs

singing and rapping

tapping and clapping in order to identify the rhythm of a song

learning about the structure of music

7.1 The Alphabet Song

Age Group
Pre-K to grade 2

Language Level
Beginning

INTELLIGENCES DEVELOPED	OBJECTIVES
Musical	To use music to teach the alphabet
Bodily/kinesthetic	To reinforce language development through movement
Interpersonal	To give students an opportunity to work together
Linguistic	

Materials Needed
• Large flashcards featuring the letters of the alphabet
• The tune to an alphabet song

1 This activity should be used to practice the letters of the alphabet after you've already introduced the letters to your students. Place alphabet flashcards in front of the class or tape them on the board or wall.

2 Sing an alphabet song while pointing to the letters. Sing the song a second time.

3 As you sing the song a third time, hand out a few flashcards to some students. When you sing the song a fourth time, ask the students who have flashcards to stand up when you sing their letters.

4 Give out more flashcards before you sing the song a fifth, sixth, and seventh time. Invite students to join in the singing when they can.

5 Continue the process until all flashcards have been given out. You may repeat this activity each day for several days until the song is learned and students are more familiar with the alphabet.

The Animal Song 7.2

Age Group
Grades 1 to 3

Language Level
Beginning to intermediate

INTELLIGENCES DEVELOPED	OBJECTIVES
Musical	To give students an opportunity to work with adjectives to describe animals
Interpersonal	To develop rhythm
Linguistic	To give students an opportunity to work together

Materials Needed
• One copy of handout 7.2A for each pair
• One copy of handout 7.2B for each pair

1 Teach students the song "I'm in Love With a Big Blue Frog." If you do not know the melody to this song, make up your own tune and use the lyrics below.

> **Lyrics**
>
> I'm in love with a big blue frog,
> a big blue frog,
> a big blue frog.
> I'm in love with a big blue frog,
> and a big blue frog loves me.

2 Sing the song several times out loud. Encourage students to join in when they can.

3 Put students in pairs and give each pair a copy of handouts 7.2A and 7.2B.

4 Each pair selects an animal from the list on handout 7.2A.

5 Using handout 7.2B, each pair then creates a poem for the selected animal. They need to fill in the blanks with adjectives that describe the animal.

6 In a large group sharing, discuss the different choices of adjectives students made.

7 Adapt the "blue frog" tune for each pair's chosen animal.

7.3 April Fool's Song

INTELLIGENCES DEVELOPED	OBJECTIVES
Musical	To develop rhythm
Bodily/kinesthetic	To develop skills in carrying a tune
Interpersonal	To reinforce language development through movement
Linguistic	To give students an opportunity to work together

Materials Needed
• One copy of handout 7.3 for each student

1 Explain April Fool's Day to students. Give examples of the harmless tricks/jokes people traditionally play on each other. Explain that telling small white lies and then quickly saying "April Fools!" once someone believes you is the fun of the day.

2 Give each student a copy of handout 7.3. Teach students the first few lines of the April Fool's Song. If you know the tune, sing it out loud. If you do not know the tune, have someone play the melody line on a piano or record it on a cassette/CD.

3 Students work in pairs to think of harmless tricks and jokes to tell on April Fool's Day.

4 Partners write out their ideas and sing them to the tune of the April Fool's Song.

The Birthday Song 7.4

INTELLIGENCES DEVELOPED

Musical

Linguistic

Visual/spatial

OBJECTIVES

To recognize and focus on each student in the classroom

To develop rhythm

Materials Needed

- Butcher paper
- Magazines
- Glue
- Scissors
- 3" x 5" colored cards
- Colored markers
- Tape

1 If you have your own classroom, create a birthday song bulletin board. If you don't have your own classroom, make a portable bulletin board using butcher paper. Divide the bulletin board into 12 sections, one section for each month. Think of creative ways to represent each month. This representation can be composed of pictures cut from magazines or original drawings done by you and your students. Glue the pictures next to their corresponding month.

2 Give each student a 3" x 5" card (you might use a different color of cards for each month) and a colored marker. Each student writes down his/her name and birth date and then tapes the card to the bulletin board under the appropriate month.

3 Teach students the "Happy Birthday" song in English. Designate one day each month as "birthday day." Students who are born in that month stand so that the class can sing to them. You might also want to provide a special treat.

7.5 Class Band

Age Group
Grades K to 2

Language Level
Beginning

INTELLIGENCES DEVELOPED	OBJECTIVES
Musical	To develop rhythm
Bodily/kinesthetic	To develop an appreciation of music
Interpersonal	To reinforce language development through movement
Linguistic	To give students an opportunity to work together

Materials Needed
- A collection of small instruments (e.g., wooden spoons, cups, glasses, bells, whistles, wooden sticks, etc.)
- A rhythmic musical selection
- Cassette or CD player

1 Collect small commercial and homemade instruments until you have enough for each student in the class or designated group to participate (you may find it easier to work with one group at a time).

2 Separate students into groups by instrument. For example, put all the cups, glasses, and wooden spoons together (the wooden spoons tap on the dishware), the bells and whistles together, and the wooden sticks together.

3 Clap your hands in rounds of four. Ask students to count with you and "play" (i.e., tap) their instruments each time you clap. Repeat the beat in sequences of four with students playing along and counting.

4 After students have developed skills in working with a four-beat rhythm, change to three-, two-, and six-beat tempos.

5 Finally, using a cassette or CD player, play a musical selection with a strong rhythm. Encourage students to "play" along with the music, using their instruments to ring, whistle, tap, etc. to the beat. Students without musical instruments can clap as they count.

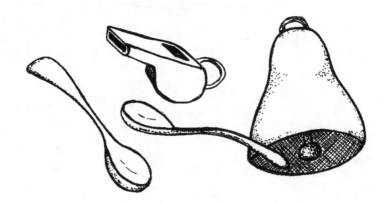

Class Choreography 7.6

INTELLIGENCES DEVELOPED	OBJECTIVES
Musical	To reinforce language development through movement
Bodily/kinesthetic	To give students practice in giving and following commands
Interpersonal	To develop rhythm
Linguistic	To give students an opportunity to work together

Age Group
Middle school to adult

Language Level
Intermediate to advanced

Materials Needed
• Musical selections
• Cassette or CD player

1 Have students form teams. Ask each team to choose a musical selection that all team members like and choreograph a dance, mime, skit, or role-play to that selection.

2 After students have developed their dance or movement sequence, help them come up with vocabulary words to describe what they are doing, such as *turning, bending, jumping, circling*, etc.

Note: Children often prefer dancing; high school and adult students often prefer working with mime or role-play. Role-playing requires the use of more language, so it should be reserved for intermediate- or advanced-level students.

7.7 Favorite Music

Age Group Middle school to adult	**INTELLIGENCES DEVELOPED**

Age Group
Middle school to adult

Language Level
Intermediate to advanced

INTELLIGENCES DEVELOPED

Musical

Intrapersonal

Linguistic

OBJECTIVES

To give students an opportunity to think about their musical likes and dislikes

To develop an appreciation of music

Materials Needed
- Cassette and/or CD player
- Board or flipchart

1 Ask students to bring their favorite musical selections to class. Specify whether students should bring cassettes or CDs, and plan to have the appropriate equipment on hand.

2 Give each student a few minutes to play his/her favorite piece to the class. Ask students if they recognize any of the instruments in the selection. Make a list of instruments on the board.

3 Ask students to create a short presentation on a musical selection. Write the presentation guidelines on the board and review them with students.

4 Students give their presentations to the class.

Presentation Guidelines

- Your presentation should be about five minutes long, including the time for listening to the musical selection.

- Give the name of the group/singer and the title of the song.

- If there are words to the musical selection, tell the class your favorite words from the song. Write the words on the board.

- Explain why you like the song. How does it make you feel?

- Explain what instruments are being used in the song. Draw a picture of one of the instruments or bring a picture to class.

- What is your favorite time to listen to the selection? Morning? Evening? Weekends?

- Play about two minutes from the selection.

Filipino, Polynesian, and Indonesian Dance 7.8

INTELLIGENCES DEVELOPED	OBJECTIVES
Musical	To develop rhythm
Bodily/kinesthetic	To develop cooperation among students
Interpersonal	To improve muscle coordination
Linguistic	To give students an opportunity to work together

Age Group
Grade 3 to middle school

Language Level
Beginning to intermediate

Materials Needed
- Two long poles (6 to 7 feet or 2 to 2 1/2 meters in length)
- Two smaller pieces of wood

1 Describe the Tinikling bird to students. This bird has long, skinny legs. When it walks through grasses, stems, and fallen trees, it must be careful not to get its legs caught. Explain to students that they are going to have a similar challenge. They are going to learn a dance that will require careful footwork.

2 Teach students to use the poles. Clap to demonstrate the rhythm of the poles. Have students clap with you. The rhythm is the following:

Beat 1: Clap hands together.

Beat 2: Strike upper legs.

Beat 3: Strike upper legs again.

3 Place poles about one foot or 30 centimeters apart. Place two small boards under the pole's ends. Demonstrate the same rhythm with the poles as you demonstrated with clapping. Have students clap as you demonstrate the rhythm with the poles. The rhythm is the following:

Beat 1: Strike poles together.

Beat 2: Strike poles on small pieces of wood.

Beat 3: Strike poles on small pieces of wood.

4 Ask for student volunteers to demonstrate with the poles. Have other students clap as they demonstrate.

5 Ask for a 2nd and 3rd set of volunteers.

6 Teach students to hop—left foot, right foot—both outside and inside the poles while the poles are stationary.

7 Teach students to dance with the poles. The dance sequence is as follows.

Step 1: Hop on left foot outside the poles.

Step 2: Hop on right foot inside the poles.

Step 3: Hop on left foot inside the poles.

Step 4: Hop on right foot outside the poles.

Repeat on the other side.

8 Next demonstrate the dance with the poles in rhythm (Step 3), using students who can work the poles.

9 Students try the dance with the poles in rhythm. They begin with a slow pole rhythm. Students not dancing should follow your lead in clapping the rhythm.

10 Finally, teach students the chant below. Once the students know the chant, help them coordinate the chant with the rhythm of the poles and the dance movements.

Do	Chant
Large hop left	We can dance!
Small hop right	We can hop!
Small hop left	We can clap!
Large hop right	We can't stop!

7.9 Language Learning Rap

Age Group
Grade 5 to middle school

Language Level
Intermediate

INTELLIGENCES DEVELOPED	OBJECTIVES
Musical	To develop a sense of rhythm
Bodily/kinesthetic	To reinforce language development through movement
Interpersonal	To give students an opportunity to work together
Linguistic	

Materials Needed
• Rap lyrics

1 Make an overhead transparency of the rap you are going to teach. Review the vocabulary in the rap with students before teaching the rhythm. A modified cloze activity works well for this.

2 As soon as students are familiar with the vocabulary, teach the rhythm of the rap by tapping lightly on a table, desk, or floor and having students follow. For the rap shown here, do a one-two tap with the "I say" lines being said just before the tapping

3 Insert the words to the rap while tapping out the rhythm. It is best to insert the words slowly, line by line within the rap itself. Encourage students to join in, saying the words to the rap as soon as they can. Set a rhythm for the rap that feels comfortable to you.

4 Encourage students to create their own raps and teach them to their classmates.

Language Learning Rap

I say	(tap, tap)
(tap, tap)	I say
I say	(tap, tap)
(tap, tap)	Five, six, seven, eight
One, two, three, four	We use language to get things done.
I say	There's a language class for everyone!
(tap, tap)	I say
I say	(tap, tap)
(tap, tap)	I say
One, two, three, four	(tap, tap)
Learning language is such fun.	Nine, ten, eleven, twelve
There's a language class for everyone!	I say
I say	(tap, tap)
(tap, tap)	I say
I say	(tap, tap)
(tap, tap)	Nine, ten, eleven, twelve
Five, six, seven, eight	Join our class and you'll have fun.
I say	There's a language class for everyone!

Country Line Dancing 7.10

INTELLIGENCES DEVELOPED	OBJECTIVES

Musical

Bodily/kinesthetic

Interpersonal

Linguistic

To improve listening skills

To develop rhythm

To reinforce language development through movement

To give students an opportunity to work together

Age Group
Grade 5 to adult

Language Level
Intermediate to advanced

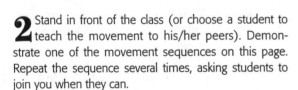

Materials Needed
• Country music
• Cassette or CD
  player

1 Ask students to form lines. There should be about five students in each line.

2 Stand in front of the class (or choose a student to teach the movement to his/her peers). Demonstrate one of the movement sequences on this page. Repeat the sequence several times, asking students to join you when they can.

3 Play the music and perform the movement sequence with the music.

Note: Once students know the sequence, have them vary the movements or have different lines start at different times. Students can also create their own sequences and teach these sequences to each other.

Sequence 1

• Begin with your feet together.
• Step left and snap your fingers.
• Step right and snap your fingers.
• Repeat on both sides.
• Jump with feet together.
• Step left, cross behind with the right foot, step left with the left foot again, and bring both feet together.
• Step right, cross behind with the left foot, step right with the right foot again, and bring both feet together.
• Repeat the entire sequence.

Sequence 2

• Begin with your feet together.
• Step right and slid the left foot over to meet the right
• Step left and slide the right foot over to meet the left
• Repeat on both sides, three times.
• Stand with your feet together.
• Bend your knees at the same time as you raise your arms and snap your fingers over your head.
• Resume normal stance.
• Bend your knees again at the same time as you snap your fingers with your arms at your sides.
• Resume normal stance.
• Repeat both knee bend/snap moves three times.
• Step right and turn on the right foot, lifting the left foot off of the ground.
• Repeat the entire sequence.

7.11 Modified Square Dancing

Age Group Grade 5 to middle school	**INTELLIGENCES DEVELOPED**
Language Level Intermediate to advanced	

INTELLIGENCES DEVELOPED

Musical

Bodily/kinesthetic

Interpersonal

Linguistic

OBJECTIVES

To improve listening skills

To develop rhythm

To reinforce language development through movement

To give students an opportunity to work together

Materials Needed
• Square dancing music
• Cassette or CD player

1 Find a musical selection to which students can square dance. Square dancing music is readily available and can be purchased at almost any music store. If you cannot find actual square dancing music, an American country/western selection with a clear, fast-paced, four-beat rhythm will work.

2 Ask students to form pairs, then have four pairs join, forming a group of eight students. Pairs should stand facing inward, one pair on each side, thus creating a "square."

3 Teach students the basic steps to square dancing (see sequence). Give the instructions out loud and first clap out the rhythm without the music. In square dancing, the shortened instructions on how to move are known as "calls." "Calls" are in bold-faced type in the "Square Dancing Sequence" on the right. Music for square dancing has a four-beat tempo.

4 Once students have learned the basic steps with the clapping and calls, play the music. Students begin clapping. Speak loudly so that your calls can be heard over the music.

Square Dancing Sequence

• **All move center:** Students clap four times and move to the center of the square and back on the fourth clap.

• **Slide left:** Students clap four times and slide to their left on the fourth clap.

• **Slide right:** Students clap four times and slide to their right on the fourth clap.

• **Circle left and home:** One student in each pair is designated the lead. He/she raises his/her left hand, turns right, touches left palm to right palm with the student on the immediate left and circles around until both return to their original positions. The process continues with the next pair until all leads have circled around.

• **Circle right and home:** One student in each pair is designated the lead. He/she raises his/her right hand, turns left, touches right palm to left palm with the student on the immediate right and circles around until both return to their original positions. The process continues with the next pair until all leads have circled around.

• **Circle around:** One student in each pair is designated the lead. The lead students raise their left hands and turn right, touching palm-to-palm with each student on their right. Instead of circling around and returning home, students continue around the circle, touching palm-to-palm and alternating left and right hands.

• **All hands and circle left:** All eight students join hands and circle left.

• **All hands and circle right:** All eight students join hands and circle right.

Mood Music 7.12

INTELLIGENCES DEVELOPED	OBJECTIVES

Musical

Intrapersonal

Linguistic

To expose students to a variety of music

To give students an opportunity to learn more about themselves

To develop an appreciation of music

Age Group
High school to adult

Language Level
Beginning to advanced (depending on how the activity is structured)

Materials Needed
• One copy of handout 7.12 for each student
• Musical selections that vary greatly in style and tempo
• Board or flipchart

1 Select several pieces of music that are very different from each other. Cue up the exact location for listening to each selection (you should plan on playing about 20–30 seconds from each selection). The selections chosen for listening do not have to be at the beginning of the pieces.

2 Conduct a large group discussion about students' musical listening experiences. What are three reasons why they listen to music? What are three feelings that music evokes? Write students' responses on the board.

3 Give each student a copy of handout 7.12. Explain that they are going to listen to different kinds of music.

4 Play the first selection. Encourage students to relax and listen. Then have them complete the questions on their handout. Repeat for the other selections.

7.13 Music Cloze

Age Group
Middle school to adult

Language Level
Intermediate to advanced

INTELLIGENCES DEVELOPED	OBJECTIVES

Musical

Interpersonal

Linguistic

To give students an opportunity to learn a song

To give students an opportunity to work together

Materials Needed

- Cassette or CD player
- Musical selection
- One copy of the complete lyrics for each student
- One copy of a cloze exercise (of the lyrics) for each student
- Overhead projector

Version One

Select a song that covers content you have been teaching in class or reinforces a grammar point that you want students to practice. Songs with repeated words and refrains work best. Write out the words to the song. Then rewrite the words in a modified cloze exercise format, deleting every ___nth word. Make a copy for every student.

2 In class, explain to students what the song is about. Identify difficult words or concepts. Then ask students to listen as you play the song.

3 Hand out the cloze exercise. Have students listen to the song again and write down the missing words in the exercise.

4 Students form pairs. Repeat the process above, asking students to listen to the song and compare/discuss the answers in their exercise with their partner.

5 Put a copy of the cloze exercise on an overhead projector and ask students to give you the answers. Leave blanks in places where no students have the answers.

6 Ask students to circle the words they are missing. Have them listen to the song a third time. Hand out the completed song and have students check their answers.

Version Two

1 Select a song and listen to it. Write out the words to the song. Then create two cloze worksheets (A and B). Each worksheet complements the other, i.e., what is supplied in Worksheet A is missing from Worksheet B and vice versa. Together, each pair of students will have all the information needed to complete both worksheets.

2 In class, explain to students what the song is about. Identify difficult words or concepts. Then ask students to listen as you play the song.

3 Students form pairs. Hand out one copy of Worksheet A and B to each pair. Students listen to the song again and write down the missing words in the blanks.

4 Students share their version (A or B) of the worksheet with their partners to complete it.

5 Once they have their worksheets completed, students listen to the song one final time and check their answers.

Music Library 7.14

INTELLIGENCES DEVELOPED

Musical

Bodily/kinesthetic

Intrapersonal

Linguistic

OBJECTIVES

To introduce students to different types of music

To help students explore their own interests in music

Age Group
Grade 5 to high school

Language Level
Intermediate

Materials Needed
- Cassette or CD player
- Headphones
- Cassettes or CDs featuring different types of music
- Copies of handout 7.14

1 Create a music library in your classroom. Designate a small table as the listening center. The table should have a cassette or CD player, headphones, a selection of cassettes or CDs featuring various types of music (from different cultures and eras—classical, country, punk, classic rock and roll, blues, jazz, big band, Latin, etc.), and copies of handout 7.14.

2 Tell students that they can go to the "music library" when they have free time and listen to their preferred music. Ask them to complete a copy of handout 7.14 each time they visit.

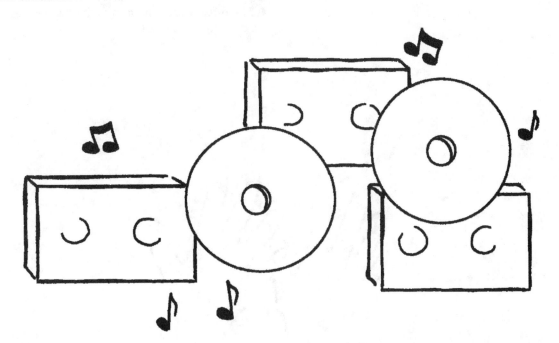

7.15 Partner Clapping Game

Age Group
Pre-K to grade 2

Language Level
Beginning to intermediate

INTELLIGENCES DEVELOPED

Musical

Bodily/kinesthetic

Interpersonal

Linguistic

OBJECTIVES

To develop rhythm

To reinforce language development through movement

To give students an opportunity to work together

Materials Needed
- Copies of handout 7.15 or one copy on an overhead transparency

1 Teach students the rhymes on handout 7.15. You may give them copies of handout 7.15 or place the handout on an overhead transparency. Say the rhymes over and over again, clapping out the rhythm. Have students join in when they can.

2 Ask students to find a partner and sit on the floor facing each other. Teach the following:

- Hand claps: Clap hands together.
- Leg claps: Clap hands on knees or thighs.
- Partner claps: Students clap their left hand with the right hand of their partner and vice versa.
- Double partner claps: Students clap both hands of their partner.
- Crossover partner claps: Students clap both hands of their partner, right to right, left to left.

3 Once students can do these moves together and have memorized the rhymes, put the rhymes and the clap sequences together.

Piggybacking 7.16

INTELLIGENCES DEVELOPED	OBJECTIVES	**Age Group** Grade 5 to high school

Musical

Interpersonal

Linguistic

To give students an opportunity to write a song

To develop rhythm

To give students an opportunity to work together

Age Group
Grade 5 to high school

Language Level
Intermediate

Materials Needed
- A tune known by all students
- Water-based markers
- One overhead transparency for each group of students
- Overhead projector

1 Place students in small groups of three or four. Ask them to think of a tune to a song that they all know. It doesn't matter if they know all of the words or even know different words—the melody is the only important aspect. Groups practice humming the tune together.

2 Each group makes up new words to the song, using the same tune.

3 When they finish writing the words, give each group an overhead transparency and a water-based marker. Groups designate a secretary to write their original words on the transparency.

4 Each group shares their new song by displaying their lyrics on an overhead projector and singing their song with the class.

7.17 Poetry TPR

Age Group
Grades 2 to 5

Language Level
Beginning

INTELLIGENCES DEVELOPED

Musical

Bodily/kinesthetic

Interpersonal

Linguistic

OBJECTIVES

To reinforce language development through movement

To develop rhythm

To give students an opportunity to work together

Materials Needed
• One copy of handout 7.17A for each student
• One copy of handout 7.17B for each student
• Scissors
• Crayons or colored markers
• Cardboard or paper to make flashcards

1 Introduce the animals on handout 7.17A. Give each student a copy of the handout and ask them to choose their favorite animal, cut it out, and color it. Make certain that all animals are selected.

2 Make flashcards of the adjectives and descriptive phrases in the poem on handout 7.17B (*furry, big horn,* etc.). Display the flashcards at the front of the class and have students select the flashcards that describe their animal. Make sure each student has at least one flashcard.

3 Give each student a copy of handout 7.17B. Read the poem clearly. Each time students hear their animal or the words on their chosen flashcards, instruct them to stand up and wave their picture or flashcard.

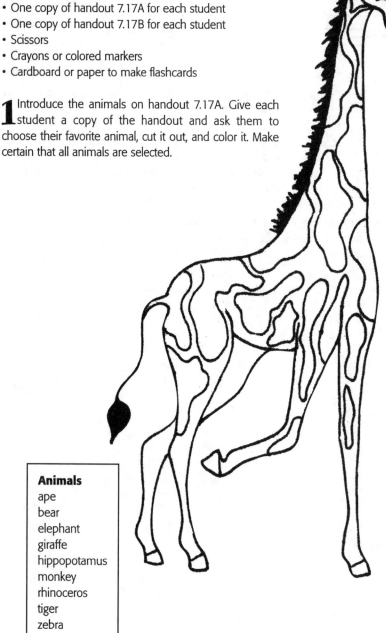

Animals
ape
bear
elephant
giraffe
hippopotamus
monkey
rhinoceros
tiger
zebra

Adjectives and descriptive phrases
big horn
furry
black
very plump
black stripes
white stripes
largest cat
long trunk
long tail
not very tall
long neck
very tall
body like a man
walk on two legs
very big
black pig

Rounds 7.18

INTELLIGENCES DEVELOPED	OBJECTIVES	Age Group

Musical

Interpersonal

Linguistic

To develop rhythm

To give students an opportunity to work together

Age Group
Grade 1 to middle school

Language Level
Beginning

Materials Needed
• Words to a familiar song
• Board or overhead projector

1 Choose a song to which many students know the tune, such as "Skip to My Lou," "Michael Row your Boat," or "Old MacDonald." Write the words to the song on the board or an overhead projector transparency.

2 Review the words; anticipate any words that might be difficult for students and teach the words according to your favorite method.

3 Sing the song. Encourage students to join you when they feel they can.

4 Once all students are singing, teach the rounds as follows: first divide the song into equal parts. For example, if the words to the song are written in couplets, two couplets could form one part. You may also count lines. Explain to students that each part of the song is called a round. Number each round in chronological order and divide students into groups equal to the number of rounds in the song. Give each group a number. For example, if you have divided a song into three parts, you will also have three groups.

5 Group 1 goes first. Group 1 sings Round 1 and continues to Round 2. Group 2 sings Round 1 as Group 1 sings Round 2. Group 3 sings Round 1 when Group 2 sings Round 2 and Group 2 sings Round 3. Groups will end the song at different times.

7.19 Rhythm Clapping Games

Age Group
Grades K to 2

Language Level
Beginning

INTELLIGENCES DEVELOPED

Musical

Bodily/kinesthetic

Interpersonal

Linguistic

Logical/mathematical

OBJECTIVES

To develop skills in recognizing rhythm in a song

To develop skills in counting from 1–10

To reinforce language development through movement

Materials Needed
• Musical selections

1 Select several pieces of rhythmic music from a variety of genres (e.g., reggae, jazz, blues, country western, classical, rock). Use about one minute from each of the different selections. The music can have words or be purely instrumental. If you can pre-record the selections on a single cassette or CD, managing this activity will be easier.

2 Students listen to the selection briefly (about 15–20 seconds). Begin clapping to the rhythm of the song. Clap to the side, clap high, clap low, etc. Ask students to join in when they can. Count as you clap (e.g., "1, 2, 3 and 1, 2, 3" or whatever the rhythm is). Vary the counting from ascending to descending and from even numbers to odd numbers.

3 After about a minute, change selections and repeat the process. After working successfully through several songs, vary the movements per piece. You may want to call on an outgoing student to come to the front and work with you. He/she can suggest variations on the movement.

4 Once you have gone through all of the selections, ask for one or two student volunteers to lead their classmates. These students should take the lead in movement and counting. Once they get started, help them as needed.

Up and Away 7.20

INTELLIGENCES DEVELOPED	OBJECTIVES	Age Group

Musical

Bodily/kinesthetic

Linguistic

To reinforce language development through movement

To develop rhythm

Age Group
Grades K to 3

Language Level
Beginning

Materials Needed
- Musical selection that has a fast and upbeat rhythm
- Cassette or CD player

1 Perform the poem "Stretching" for your students. If you cannot recite the poem from memory, present the poem on an overhead projector or write it on the board. As you read or recite, do the physical movements described by the poem.

2 After you have gone through the poem once, do the movements and ask students to follow you. If you have access to a cassette or CD player, add a musical selection in the background. The selection should have a fast and upbeat rhythm. Use the music to inform the movement and set the pace as you read or recite the poem. Encourage students to follow your movements.

3 Have students move on their own or ask a student volunteer to lead them. Encourage students to repeat the words to the poem as they stretch.

> **Stretching**
>
> I put my left arm in the air
> and stretch and stretch so high.
> I put my right arm in the air
> and stretch to reach the sky.
> I move my arms in circles,
> both large and very small.
> I stretch and stretch again
> until I feel so tall.
> I put my arms down by my side
> and bend my knees a bit.
> I turn around and take a bow
> and finally, that's it.

7.2A Handout

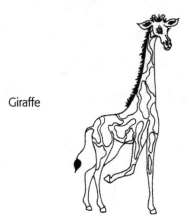

Giraffe

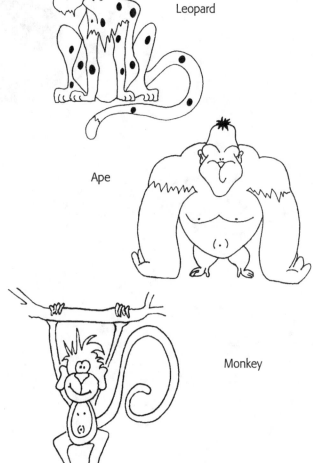

Tiger

Rhinoceros

Lion

Bear

Leopard

Elephant

Ape

Hippopotamus

Zebra

Monkey

The Animal Song
Lyrics

I'm in love with a _____, _____, _____

                   (adjective)   (adjective)   (animal)

a _____, _____, _____

   (adjective)   (adjective)   (animal)

a _____, _____, _____

   (adjective)   (adjective)   (animal)

I'm in love with a _____, _____, _____

                   (adjective)   (adjective)   (animal)

and a _____, _____, _____ loves me.

     (adjective)   (adjective)   (animal)

Melody Line

There's a   big go -rilla in the chi-cken coop Ap-ril Ap-ril   Fools

Lyrics

Your hair is the color of tomato soup.

April, April Fools!

There's a gorilla in the chicken coop.

April, April Fools!

The cat's in the middle of the custard pie.

April, April Fools!

There's a dog in the kitchen and he's ten feet high.

April, April Fools!

Multiple Intelligences and Language Learning © 2005 Alta Book Center Publishers, San Francisco, California www.altaesl.com Permission granted to photocopy for one teacher's classroom use only

Mood Music

Questionnaire

Name _____

Music Selection 1

Describe this music in three words or less:

How did this music make you feel?

Would you listen to this music again? When?

Would you buy this music?

Music Selection 2

Describe this music in three words or less:

How did this music make you feel?

Would you listen to this music again? When?

Would you buy this music?

Music Selection 3

Describe this music in three words or less:

How did this music make you feel?

Would you listen to this music again? When?

Would you buy this music?

7.14 Handout

Music Library

Response Sheet

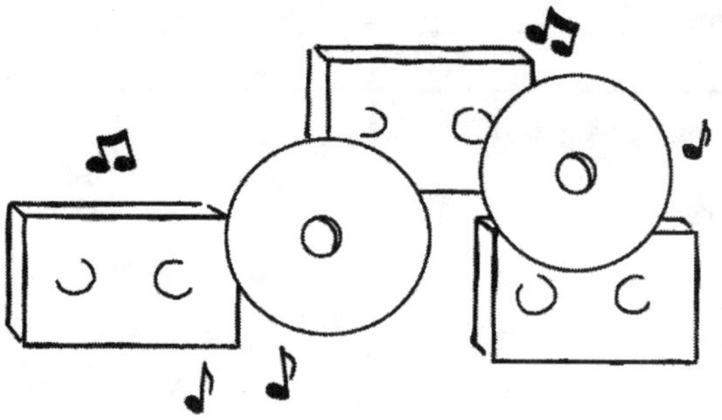

Name ________________________________

Date ____________________

Number of times you have visited the music library: ________

What music did you listen to? ____

____

Did you like this music? Why? Why not? ____

____

Why did you choose this music? ____

____

If someone gave you enough money, would you buy this music? ________

If yes, why? ____

____

If no, why? ____

____

How do you feel when you listen to this music? ____

____

What other music would you like to have in the music library? (Please give the name of the group or singer and the title of the cassette or CD.) ____

____

Partner Clapping Game
Rhymes

Sequence 1

One, Two, Here's My Shoe

Rhymes	Clap Sequence
One, two, here's my shoe.	2 leg claps, 2 hand claps
Three, four, shut the door.	4 double partner claps
Five, six, pick up sticks.	2 leg claps, 2 hand claps
Seven, eight, lay them straight.	4 double partner claps
Nine, ten, a big fat hen.	2 hand claps, 3 double partner claps

Sequence 2

Ghosts and Goblins

Rhymes	Clap Sequence
Ghosts and goblins	2 leg claps
out at night;	2 hand claps
they give me	2 leg claps
a terrible fright.	2 hand claps
Who can see them?	2 crossover partner claps right
Who will tell?	2 crossover partner claps left
Who can say now	2 double partner claps
all is well?	2 leg claps
Ghosts and goblins	2 leg claps
out at night;	2 hand claps
they give me	2 leg claps
a terrible fright.	2 hand claps

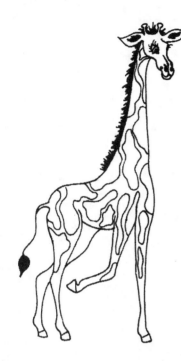

I'm a rhino and so it goes
I have a big horn on my nose.

I am an animal all furry and black.
Tell me please what you think about that.

I am a horse and very plump,
with black and white stripes on my rump.

They say that I'm the largest cat.
I have black stripes on my back.

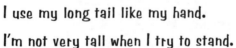

I'm an animal with a big, long trunk.
Many people call me an elephant.

I use my long tail like my hand.
I'm not very tall when I try to stand.

I've a long, long neck and am very tall.
I might not hear you if you call.

I have a body like a man.
I walk on two legs when I can.

I am a hippo and very big.
Sometimes I'm called a big, black pig.

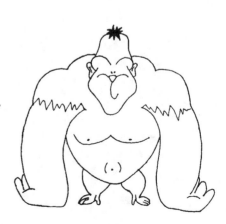

Naturalist Intelligence

"I believe in God, only I spell it Nature."
— Frank Lloyd Wright (1867–1959)

The activities in this chapter help students develop their naturalist intelligence by:

developing an appreciation of plants

encouraging an appreciation of diversity among animals

discovering patterns in nature

observing details in nature

recognizing different plants and animals

addressing environmental concerns

observing animals

learning about the care of animals and pets

learning about the life cycle of plants

8.1 Animal Talks

Age Group
Grades K to 2

Language Level
Beginning

INTELLIGENCES DEVELOPED

Naturalist

Bodily/kinesthetic

Intrapersonal

Linguistic

OBJECTIVES

To develop animal and animal parts vocabulary

To develop color, shape, and size vocabulary

To foster an appreciation of animals

To recognize differences among animals

To reinforce language development through movement

To help students understand more about their own learning processes

Materials Needed
- A large three-sided box
- Scissors or box cutter
- Pictures of animals
- Tape

1 Cut out the back panel of a large box. On the front of the box write "Animal Talks." Place the three-sided box in the front of the classroom. Place a chair in the middle of the box.

2 Lay pictures of animals face down on a table. Animals can be repeated (i.e., different types of dogs, cats, or horses can appear on separate pictures). Ask each student to take a picture and hold it against his/her body so it is not visible to classmates.

3 A student volunteer sits in the box and gives a two- to three-sentence talk about his/her animal or mimes an action characteristic of that animal. Classmates then take turns guessing the animal. When they guess correctly, the student in the box turns the picture around.

4 Tape the "guessed" picture to a bulletin board or the classroom wall.

5 Have five or six students do the above steps each day until all students in the class have had a chance to lead the activity.

Autumn Leaves 8.2

Age Group
Grade 3 to middle school

Language Level
Intermediate

INTELLIGENCES DEVELOPED

Naturalist

Bodily/kinesthetic

Interpersonal

Linguistic

Visual/spatial

OBJECTIVES

To foster creative expression

To reinforce language development through movement

To give students an opportunity to work together

Materials Needed
- Leaves
- Twigs
- Aprons or old shirts
- Tempera paints
- Plain white paper

1 Ask students to bring a collection of leaves and twigs to class. They should also bring an old shirt or apron if the school or program does not routinely provide these (large, plastic garbage bags can also be used). Designate a table for everyone to work with the paint.

2 Begin with a short demonstration. Dip a leaf lightly into tempera paint and press it on a sheet of white paper to make a print. Dip several more leaves and twigs into different colors of paint, carefully arranging them on the paper.

3 Ask students to create their own prints.

4 When they have finished, students write descriptions of their prints, focusing on the colors used, the shapes of leaves and twigs, and the placement of the items on the paper.

5 If you have your own classroom, create a bulletin board with the prints and essays. If you don't have a bulletin board, have students post the prints and essays on the wall.

6 Once the prints are posted, follow up with these questions:

Which print has the most colors? What colors are used?

What color is used most often?

Which is the most unusual print?

Which prints are almost the same?

What colors are the twigs?

Where are the twigs most commonly placed?

What is the most common placement of the leaves?

8.3 Calendar of Weather

Age Group
Grade 5 to adult

Language Level
Beginning to intermediate

INTELLIGENCES DEVELOPED	OBJECTIVES
Naturalist	To develop weather vocabulary
Linguistic	To foster an appreciation of the environment
Logical/mathematical	To develop logical thinking skills
Visual/spatial	To give students an opportunity to work together

Materials Needed
• One copy of handout 8.3 for each student

1 Give each student a copy of handout 8.3. Students write the month and dates in the appropriate spaces.

2 Ask students to keep a weather log for one month by recording the weather each morning. If the weather fluctuates during the day (i.e., it might be sunny in the morning and rainy in the afternoon), students need to record multiple observations. Remind students of their daily task.

3 When the month is over, ask students to bring their weather calendars to class. Students form groups and check their answers to ensure that their records match.

4 Write the following questions on the board. Each group selects a secretary to record the answers:

How many sunny days were there last month?

On how many days did it rain?

On which days was it windy?

Did it snow on any days?

What other kinds of weather were there?

What was the warmest day of the month? The coolest?

What weekend had the "best" weather?

Did you and the members in your group agree on your record keeping? If not, on which days did you observe different weather?

Camping Out 8.4

INTELLIGENCES DEVELOPED	OBJECTIVES
Naturalist	To develop vocabulary for talking about the environment
Bodily/kinesthetic	To foster an appreciation of the environment
Interpersonal	To reinforce language development through movement
Linguistic	To give students an opportunity to work together

Age Group
Grade 5 to middle school

Language Level
Intermediate

Materials Needed
- Pictures of outdoor scenes from around the world
- Flashlight
- Light, white cloth
- Marshmallows (optional)

1 If you have a large class, you may want to divide students in half and work with two groups. Ask students to sit on the floor in a circle. Show them pictures of many different outdoor scenes from around the world. Pass the pictures around so that all students can have a closer look.

2 Stand a flashlight in the center of the circle, turn it on, and cover it with a very light, white cloth (this will serve as an imaginary campfire). Ask students to imagine that they are camping in the woods. You might pass around a bag of marshmallows for students to enjoy and explain that marshmallows are treats often associated with camping.

3 Ask students to brainstorm different ways they can protect nature while camping in the woods, i.e., don't litter, put out fires, stay on the trails, etc. Encourage them to introduce facts and detailed reasons for protecting nature.

4 Have students break into small groups and explain that each group will be in charge of a national park. The group members' task is to develop guidelines for tourists who come to visit and stay in the campgrounds. Ask each group to come up with 10 guidelines and appoint a secretary to record them. Instruct groups to use the imperative.

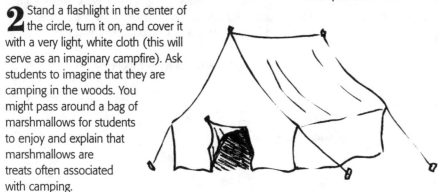

8.5 Drawing Animals

Age Group	**INTELLIGENCES DEVELOPED**	**OBJECTIVES**
Grade 5 to adult	**Naturalist**	To develop animal and animal parts vocabulary
Language Level	Interpersonal	To develop color, shape, and size vocabulary
Intermediate	Linguistic	To foster an appreciation of animals
	Visual/spatial	To recognize differences among animals
		To develop visual awareness
		To give students an opportunity to work together

Materials Needed
- One copy of handout 8.5A on an overhead transparency
- One copy of handout 8.5B for each group
- Plain white paper
- Colored markers
- Overhead projector

1 Place a transparency of handout 8.5A on an overhead projector. Students match the animal pictures in Column 1 to the animal names in Column 2. Write the answers on the transparency.

2 Give each student a sheet of plain white paper. Students choose one of the animals from handout 8.5A and draw it. Write the words below on the board.

3 When students finish their drawings, have them label their pictures with the appropriate body parts from the vocabulary list. Walk around the room checking students' work.

4 Students form small groups or work with a partner. Give each group a copy of handout 8.5B. Each group appoints a secretary to record answers.

5 Check answers as a large group.

Vocabulary List
back
ears
face
front legs
hind legs
hoofs
mouth
neck
nose
paws
tail

Folded Leaf Patterns 8.6

Age Group
Grades 3 to 5

Language Level
Beginning

INTELLIGENCES DEVELOPED	OBJECTIVES
Naturalist	To develop vocabulary for talking about leaves
Interpersonal	To develop color, shape, and texture vocabulary
Linguistic	To foster an appreciation of trees
Logical/mathematical	To foster creative expression
Visual/spatial	To develop logical thinking skills
	To give students an opportunity to work together

Materials Needed
- Copies of handout 8.6A
- One copy of handout 8.6B for each student
- Leaves
- Plain white paper
- Crayons or colored markers
- Board or overhead projector
- Scissors

1 Before the start of class, collect as many differently shaped leaves as possible. Photocopy handout 8.6A and cut apart a leaf pattern for each student. Place the leaves, leaf patterns, plain white paper, and crayons or colored markers on a central table.

2 Put students in small groups at tables; if this is not possible, have them put their desks in circles or simply find a partner.

3 Ask each student to come to the table, collect materials (i.e., one leaf, one leaf pattern, a piece of paper, and some crayons or colored markers) and return to his/her group.

4 Write the following instructions on the board or put them on an overhead transparency:

a Fold your paper in half and then in half again. Next, fold your paper on the diagonal as in the example below:

b Unfold the paper. Line up the leaf pattern on one of the diagonal folds. Trace around the leaf pattern. Do this for each diagonal fold.

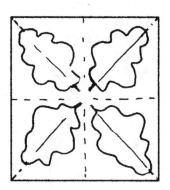

c Decorate the leaf patterns and background with different colors.

5 Once students have completed their projects, give each student a copy of handout 8.6B. Students answer the questions.

6 Check answers in a large group sharing.

7 If you have your own classroom, create a bulletin board. Then ask students to read answers 4–6 on their handouts out loud and have other students guess which student's project is being described.

1.   **2.**   **3.**

8.7 Magic Plants

Grades K to 2

Language Level
Beginning

INTELLIGENCES DEVELOPED	OBJECTIVES

Naturalist

Linguistic

Visual/spatial

To develop vocabulary for talking about plants

To foster creative expression

To foster an appreciation of plants

To recognize differences among plants

Materials Needed
- Plain white paper
- Colored markers

1 Explain to students that they are going to create their own "magic plant." Pass out plain white paper and ask students to each draw a picture of their plant.

2 Students describe two of their plant's magical powers. As students list examples, write key words on the board.

3 When you have finished with the discussion, ask students to say the new words with you and write them in their notebooks. You may want to focus on six or seven students each day until you have cycled through the entire class.

Mighty Plants 8.8

INTELLIGENCES DEVELOPED	OBJECTIVES
Naturalist	To develop vocabulary for talking about trees
Bodily/kinesthetic	To develop color, shape, and texture vocabulary
Interpersonal	To foster an appreciation of trees
Linguistic	To reinforce language development through movement
Visual/spatial	To give students an opportunity to work together

Age Group
Middle to high school

Language Level
Intermediate

Materials Needed
• Pictures of many different types of trees

Note: National Arbor Day in the United States is April 25th. If you live in the United States, it is ideal to do this lesson around that time. If you are teaching in another country, find out if the country in which you are teaching has an arbor day. If you are teaching students from many different cultures and language backgrounds, ask them to find out if their own countries of origin have similar holidays. U.S. National Arbor Day gets some attention in the news media.

1 If possible, take your class to a library or computer lab to do research on trees. Try to find out the many ways in which trees help people and animals. Encourage students to make sketches of the different types of trees they find in their research.

2 Place pictures of many different types of trees in front of the classroom on the edge of the board or tape them to the wall. Give each tree a number.

3 Ask students to form pairs and select a tree. Students write a description of their selected tree. They write the number of the selected picture (tree) next to the description.

4 Collect as many different descriptions as possible. Read the descriptions out loud and ask students to guess the number of the tree described.

8.9 Natural Categories

Age Group
Middle school to adult

Language Level
Intermediate

INTELLIGENCES DEVELOPED	OBJECTIVES
Naturalist	To develop vocabulary for talking about animals and plants
Bodily/kinesthetic	To foster an appreciation of animals and plants
Interpersonal	To recognize differences among animals and plants
Linguistic	To foster creative expression
Visual/spatial	To reinforce language development through movement
	To give students an opportunity to work together

Materials Needed
- One copy of handout 8.9A for each group
- One copy of handout 8.9B for each group
- Scissors
- Glue
- Butcher paper

1 Divide students into groups. Give one copy of handouts 8.9A and 8.9B to each group, along with several pairs of scissors. Instruct students to cut out the category headings on handout 8.9A and the words on handout 8.9B. The words should then be divided evenly among the group members.

2 Students place the different words under the most appropriate categories.

3 When all group members agree on the placement of the words, give each group a large piece of butcher paper. Students glue the category headings and corresponding words to the paper.

Nature's Collage 8.10

Age Group
Grade 5 to adult

Language Level
Intermediate

INTELLIGENCES DEVELOPED	OBJECTIVES
Naturalist	To develop vocabulary for talking about animals and plants
Bodily/kinesthetic	To foster an appreciation of animals, plants, and the environment
Interpersonal	To recognize differences among animals and plants
Linguistic	To develop logical thinking skills
Logical/mathematical	To reinforce language development through movement
Visual/spatial	To give students an opportunity to work together

Materials Needed
- One large sheet of butcher paper or newsprint
- Plain white paper
- Crayons or colored markers
- Scissors
- Glue
- Small pieces of paper (sticky notes work great)

1 Give students plain white paper and ask them to draw pictures of their favorite animals, plants, or trees. Encourage them to draw more than one item. When they are finished, students cut out their drawings.

2 Tape a large piece of butcher paper or newsprint to the classroom wall. Divide students into groups and assign each group a section of the wall. Explain that each group is going to create a collage of the pictures they have drawn. They need to decide where to put all of the things they have drawn so that when they finish, the collage will look like one picture. They can draw other items directly on the paper, such as mountains, lakes, roads, etc.

3 When students finish the collage, conduct a large group sharing. Find out what each student contributed. Have students tell you as much about the items they contributed as they can.

4 Finally, give students small pieces of paper or sticky notes. Ask them to write down the names of the items they drew and stick the notes on the collage next to or above the items.

8.11 Nature's Showcase

Age Group
Grades K to 2

Language Level
Beginning

INTELLIGENCES DEVELOPED	OBJECTIVES
Naturalist	To develop vocabulary for talking about plants
Bodily/kinesthetic	To develop color, shape, and texture vocabulary
Linguistic	To foster an appreciation of plants
Visual/spatial	To foster creative expression
	To develop visual awareness
	To reinforce language development through movement

Materials Needed
- One copy of handout 8.11 for each student
- Leaves, stems, twigs, blossoms, roots, grass, bark, and anything else that you may gather outside that is related to plants and trees

1 Before the start of class, collect as many diverse plant-related items as you can (leaves, stems, twigs, blossoms, flowers, roots, grass, bark, etc.).

2 Display the collection on a table in your classroom. Mark all items with a number.

3 Give each student a copy of handout 8.11. As you discuss each item and identify it, instruct students to write the name of the item on their handout along with a few descriptive words. Give students the opportunity to touch each item. Write the names of the items and important words on the board.

4 If possible, take a trip outside and have students collect items for the next display.

Nature's Signposts 8.12

INTELLIGENCES DEVELOPED	OBJECTIVES

Naturalist

Bodily/kinesthetic

Linguistic

Visual/spatial

To develop vocabulary for talking about the world around us and the environment

To foster an appreciation of plants and nature

To develop visual awareness

To reinforce language development through movement

Age Group
Grades 3 to 5

Language Level
Intermediate

Materials Needed
- Gardening magazines or magazines about animals
- Glue
- Scissors
- Black and yellow construction paper

1 Put the magazines, glue, scissors, and construction paper on a central table. Ask each student to cut out a picture of an item in nature (a flower, an animal, a mountain, etc.) from one of the magazines and mount it on black construction paper.

2 Students then cut around the mounted picture again, so that when the picture is turned over one sees a black "silhouette" of it. Students glue just the top of the picture to a piece of yellow construction paper, the black side (silhouette) facing out.

3 Each student writes a description of the picture he/she selected and makes a short presentation in front of the class. The student displays his/her silhouette and gives two or three hints as to its source. If the class cannot guess the item, the student flips the picture up to reveal the original magazine image.

8.13 Pointillism

Grade 5 to high school

Age Group
Grade 5 to high school

Language Level
Intermediate

INTELLIGENCES DEVELOPED	OBJECTIVES
Naturalist	To observe details in nature
Interpersonal	To foster an appreciation of nature and the environment
Linguistic	To develop visual awareness
Visual/spatial	To give students an opportunity to work together

Materials Needed

- Examples of pointillism by French Neo-Impressionist Georges Seurat
- Photos taken with a digital camera
- Tempera paints in blue, green, brown, gold, orange, white, and red
- Plain white paper
- Cotton swabs

1 Explain to students that pointillism was made popular by the French Neo-Impressionist painter, Georges Seurat. Pointillism's effect is created by thousands of tiny dots that are blended by the eye into one image. Today, TV images and photos taken with a digital camera are composed in much the same way.

2 If possible, take students outside or to a park. If you cannot easily plan an outdoor field trip, have students look at pictures of parks, forests, or other outdoor areas. Ask students to notice the different shades of green, the bark on the trees, and the different colors of blue in the sky.

3 In the classroom, give students dishes of tempera paints, plain white paper, and cotton swabs. Students dab colors on the paper à la pointillism. Ask them to make a branch, a leaf, a cloud, the sky, etc.

4 Students compare their work to Seurat's. Ask questions to help students. Where are the leaves darker and lighter? What about the bark on a tree? What happens to the color of the object when the dots are closer together? Where are the most dots in your picture? The least?

5 Conduct a large group discussion for students to share their creations and discoveries.

Puddles 8.14

Age Group
Grade 3 to middle school

Language Level
Intermediate

INTELLIGENCES DEVELOPED	OBJECTIVES
Naturalist	To develop vocabulary for talking about water and puddles
Bodily/kinesthetic	To introduce concepts related to water and absorption
Interpersonal	To foster an appreciation of nature and the environment
Linguistic	To develop logical thinking skills
Logical/mathematical	To reinforce language development through movement
Visual/spatial	To give students an opportunity to work together

Materials Needed
- A collection of different kinds of surface material, such as dirt, cork, glass, paper, wood, cotton, etc.
- A small pitcher of water

1 Conduct a large group brainstorm about puddles and how they are formed.

2 Place the collection of kinds of surface material on a central table. Have students look at all of the items on the table. Write the names of the items on the board.

3 Ask students to predict on which surfaces puddles will and will not form. Have them try to tell you why and write their predictions on the board.

4 Ask for student volunteers to try to create puddles on the various surfaces by pouring small amounts of water onto them. As students conduct the experiments, have them test their predictions for accuracy.

8.15 Rain Helpers

Age Group
Grades 3 to 5

Language Level
Intermediate

INTELLIGENCES DEVELOPED
Naturalist
Interpersonal
Linguistic
Visual/spatial

OBJECTIVES
To develop weather vocabulary
To foster creative expression
To give students an opportunity to work together

Materials Needed
- Copies of handout 8.15
- One large sheet of white paper
- Crayons or colored markers
- Glue
- Scissors

1 Make one copy of handout 8.15 for each student. Cut out the umbrella patterns before class.

2 Put students in small groups of three or four. Give each group a large sheet of white paper. Give each student a set of umbrella patterns. Tell students that they each need to make an umbrella from the pre-cut shapes, color it, and mount it in some way onto the white paper.

3 After all umbrellas have been glued to the paper, have students color and add the rain using the raindrop patterns from handout 8.15.

4 When the projects are complete, put the following questions on the board for each group to answer:

Describe the picture that you and your classmates created.

When was the last time you remember it raining?

Was the rain hard or soft? How long did it last?

How can you tell if it's going to rain?

What do the clouds look like when it's going to rain?

Describe two different types of clouds. Which ones do you see most often?

Spring Flowers 8.16

INTELLIGENCES DEVELOPED	OBJECTIVES	Age Group

Naturalist

Linguistic

Visual/spatial

To develop vocabulary for talking about flowers

To develop colors vocabulary

To develop an understanding of the relationship between one-dimensional patterns and the finished three-dimensional product

To foster creative expression

Age Group
Grades 3 to 5

Language Level
Intermediate

Materials Needed
- One copy of handout 8.16A for each group
- One copy of handout 8.16B for each group
- One copy of handout 8.16C for each student
- Magazines with pictures of flowers
- Scissors
- Glue
- Colored construction paper
- Straws
- Aprons or old shirts
- Newspaper
- Tempera paints in brown and green
- Small dishes for the paint
- Small sponges
- Tape

Note: This activity can be used as a culminating exercise for a unit on plants. Students will be making a small basket with spring flowers. It is a good idea for you to make a sample project before beginning the activity with your class.

1 Assemble all materials on a central table, including a copy of handout 8.16B (the basket instructions) for each group. Go through all of the materials on the table, explaining what each item is so that students do not get confused.

2 Divide the class into small groups of no more than four students. Give each group a copy of handout 8.16A. Show students a sample of the finished project. Explain that there are three different stages in this project plus the final assembly. Assign each group a specific order for the

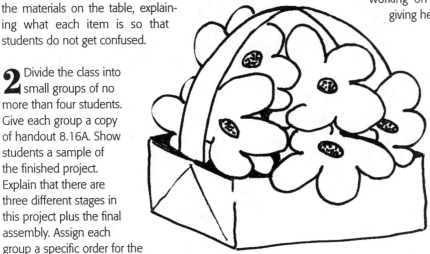

stages on which they are to work (e.g., Group 1 works on Stage 3, Stage 2, and Stage 1 in that order. Other groups are ordered differently.). Having each group work on the project in a different order makes managing the activity and the materials easier.

3 Ask each group to choose one student to collect materials for each stage. Call on these students to collect materials for the stage on which their group has been assigned to work. Remind students to return the materials to a central table when the group is not using them. Only one person from each group should be at the materials table at any given time. When students finish the stage on which they are working, they can move to the next stage, collecting new materials according to the handout.

4 Once all stages have been completed, students do the final assembly.

5 When the projects have been fully assembled, give each student a copy of handout 8.16C. Ask students to work in pairs within their groups to complete their individual copies of the handout. While students are working on the questions, walk around giving help and suggestions.

6 Conduct a large group sharing once all students have answered the questions.

7 Assemble all baskets on a table, windowsill, or desk. You may also want to take a picture of each group with their finished basket and post the pictures on a bulletin board.

8.17 Surprise, Surprise!

Age Group
Grades 1 to 3

Language Level
Beginning

INTELLIGENCES DEVELOPED	OBJECTIVES
Naturalist	To develop vocabulary for talking about animals and plants
Interpersonal	To develop color, shape, and size vocabulary
Linguistic	To foster an appreciation of animals and plants
Logical/mathematical	To recognize differences among animals and plants
Visual/spatial	To foster creative expression
	To give students an opportunity to work together

Materials Needed
- One copy of handout 8.17 for each pair
- One copy of handout 8.17 on an overhead transparency
- Overhead projector

1 Ask students to find a partner and give each pair a copy of handout 8.17. Students need to identify categories and then put the pictures in those categories by numbering them (e.g., all those pictures marked "1" might be birds). Students can create the categories in many different ways—let them surprise you.

2 When students are finished, conduct a large group sharing. Display a copy of the handout on an overhead projector. Ask students to give you their numbers and categories.

Decorating Trees 8.18

Age Group
Grades 1 to 3

Language Level
Beginning

INTELLIGENCES DEVELOPED

Naturalist

Interpersonal

Linguistic

Visual/spatial

OBJECTIVES

To develop vocabulary for talking about trees

To recognize differences among trees

To develop color, shape, size, and texture vocabulary

To foster an appreciation of plants and trees

To give students an opportunity to work together

Materials Needed
- Pictures of trees
- Plain white paper
- Colored markers
- Scissors
- Glue
- Colored construction paper

1 Show students pictures of many different kinds of trees. Make certain that some of the trees are evergreens. Ask students what kinds of trees people often have in their homes during the Christmas season. Students will often choose one of the evergreen examples, but if they do not, it's okay.

2 Give each student a piece of plain white paper. Ask them to draw one of the trees and draw decorations on the tree. Students may color their trees.

3 Students then cut out or around their individual trees and mount them to colored pieces of construction paper.

4 If possible, tape all the trees to a bulletin board. Conduct a large group discussion about the trees students created, using some of the questions below:

On what occasion do people decorate trees?

What different kinds of trees do people decorate?

What do they put on the trees?

Have you decorated a tree? When?
Who helped you?

What is your favorite tree decoration?

8.19 Trees and More Trees

Age Group
Grades 3 to 5

Language Level
Beginning

INTELLIGENCES DEVELOPED	OBJECTIVES

Naturalist

Linguistic

Visual/spatial

To give students an opportunity to learn more about plants

To recognize patterns in nature

To recognize different kinds of trees

To develop visual awareness

Materials Needed
• Plain white paper
• Crayons or colored markers

1 Give each student a piece of plain white paper and ask them to fold the paper into four equal sections. Then have them draw a different tree in each section. Each tree must be a representation of one they've seen in real life.

2 Below each tree, ask students to write the following:

Two or three sentences or words describing the tree they have drawn

A statement giving the location where they have seen the tree

A number indicating how old they believe the tree is

Something they like about the tree

3 If possible, create a bulletin board with the pictures. See if you and your students can decide on how many different trees were drawn.

TV Topics 8.20

INTELLIGENCES DEVELOPED	OBJECTIVES

Naturalist

Linguistic

Visual/spatial

To give students an opportunity to learn more about geography and the world in which we live

To develop vocabulary for talking about the environment

To foster appreciation of the environment

To develop visual awareness

Age Group
Grade 5 to high school

Language Level
Intermediate to advanced

Materials Needed
• Country, city, and world maps

Note: For good or for ill, television is as much a part of the 21st-century environment as the natural world of animals and plants. Since many students watch television, it is a good idea to encourage them to use the medium to reinforce important ideas and concepts in the classroom. Here are suggestions for using television to spur language learning and heighten students' media awareness.

1 Ask students to list their favorite TV programs and mark the locations of the settings on a map.

2 Students answer the following questions:

Does the setting of the program have anything to do with the plot?

What is the weather like?

What does the area look like?

Are there mountains? Lakes? The ocean? How do you know?

3 Have each student make a list of all of the places mentioned by the class along with an important fact that they learned about each place.

4 Ask students to watch a news program for a week and make a list of people who are in the news and why they are in the news. Where are these people from? Mark the locations on a map.

8.3 Handout

Calendar of Weather

Write the month for which you are recording weather in the space provided. Write the dates in the upper right-hand corner of each box.

Month:						
Sunday	Monday	Tuesday	Wednesday	Thursday	Friday	Saturday

Drawing Animals

Matching

Match the animals with the words. Write the appropriate letter in the blank space.

_____ 1.

_____ 2.

_____ 3.

_____ 4.

_____ 5.

_____ 6.

_____ 7.

_____ 8.

_____ 9.

_____ 10.

a. Bear

b. Zebra

c. Hippopotamus

d. Giraffe

e. Ape

f. Tiger

g. Monkey

h. Elephant

i. Lion

j. Rhinoceros

DIRECTIONS

Work with a partner or a small group. Write answers to the following questions. Be prepared to share your answers.

1 What do the zebra, giraffe, and tiger have in common?

2 What do the monkey and lion have in common?

3 What does the elephant have that no other animal has?

4 Explain what is unique about the giraffe.

5 Which animals' ears are the most remarkable?

6 What does the lion have that no other animal has?

7 What does the rhinoceros have that no other animal has?

8 How is the ape different from the other animals?

9 Which animal is the smallest? The largest?

10 Which animals do you think look the most alike?

Multiple Intelligences and Language Learning © 2005 Alta Book Center Publishers, San Francisco, California
www.altaesl.com Permission granted to photocopy for one teacher's classroom use only.

Pattern

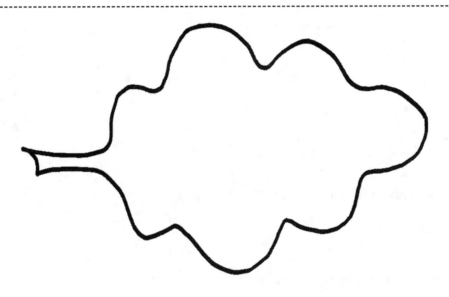

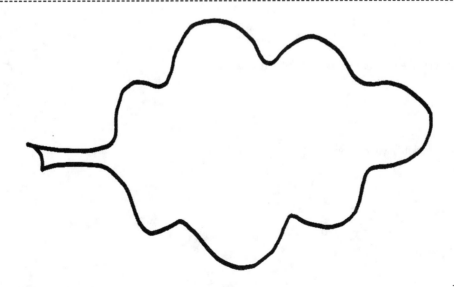

DIRECTIONS

1 Describe the shape of your leaf. Is it big or small? Is it long or short? Fat or skinny? Rough or smooth?

2 Do you think this leaf comes from a tree, flower, or bush?

3 What do you think the different shades of green on a leaf mean? Are leaves always green?

4 What colors are the leaf patterns in your project?

5 What colors are used in the background?

6 How many colors did you use for your leaf patterns? For the background?

7 Describe two other projects done by your classmates.

8 How is your project different from the projects by your classmates?

9 Write a short description of your project.

Multiple Intelligences and Language Learning © 2005 Alta Book Center Publishers, San Francisco, California

Headings

Cut out the category headings below.

Types of Fish

Parts of a Fish

Mammals

Parts of an Animal

Flowers

Trees

Cut out the words below. Divide them equally among the group members. Take turns putting the words under the category headings on handout 8.9A. When all group members agree on the placement of the words, glue the words and headings on a large piece of butcher paper.

trout	scale	giraffe	trunk
tulip	blue	spruce	apple
bass	catfish	marlin	fin
rose	geranium	petunia	dog
cat	cherry	elm	oak
maple	dogwood	iris	salmon
gill	lion	monkey	pine
cedar	bear	zebra	ear
tusk	hoof	tail	violet
daffodil	ponderosa	quaking	aspen
plum	chrysanthemum	rhinoceros	paw

Multiple Intelligences and Language Learning © 2005 Alta Book Center Publishers, San Francisco, California

Nature's Showcase

Listen as the teacher talks about the items on the display table. Write down the word for each item. Describe the item in two or three words.

1

2

3

4

5

6

7

8

9

10

Spring Flowers
Collecting Materials

DIRECTIONS

Stage 1

Collect the following from the central table (remember, only one person from your group should collect materials):

Magazines

Scissors

Glue

1 piece of colored construction paper

5–7 plastic straws

Find and cut out 8–10 pictures of flowers from the magazines. Mount (glue) the flower pictures onto colored construction paper. Cut out the mounted flowers. Glue the mounted flowers on the straws. Other flowers can be used as ground cover during final assembly.

Stage 2

Collect the following from the central table (remember, only one person from your group should collect materials):

Aprons or old shirts

Newspaper

Brown and green tempera paints

2 small dishes

2 small sponges

Put on an apron or old shirt to keep paint from getting on your clothes. Pour a small amount of tempera paint into the dishes. Use sponges to smear the paint on the newspaper in random patches.

Stage 3

Collect the following from the central table (remember, only one person from your group should collect materials):

Handout 8.16B

2 pieces of colored construction paper

1 colored marker

Scissors

Tape

Form the basket following the instructions on handout 8.16B. Write your names on the outside of the basket and tape the basket together as directed.

Final Assembly

Crumple up the painted newspaper from Stage 2. Place the newspaper into the basket. Stick the straws with flowers into the newspaper. Glue them into place if necessary. Paste other flowers onto the newspaper or the basket. Admire your finished work!

DIRECTIONS

Step 1

To form the basket, crease a piece of construction paper on all four sides, 2 1/2" from the edge. The paper should look like this:

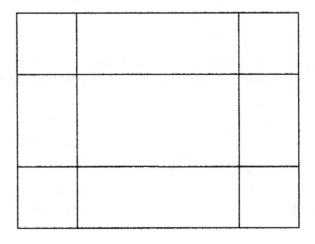

Step 2

Crease the corners of the paper so it looks like this:

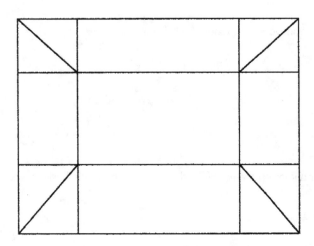

Step 3

Fold up the sides to form a box shape. Tape the edges. This is your basket!

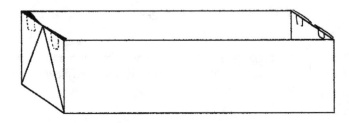

Step 4

To form the handle to your basket, cut a strip of construction paper 3" x 11". Fold it in thirds lengthwise. Tape it together. Tape it onto the edges of the basket.

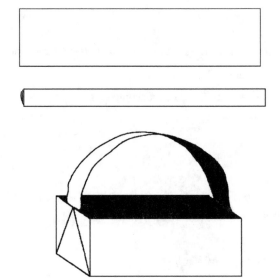

Multiple Intelligences and Language Learning © 2005 Alta Book Center Publishers, San Francisco, California

Spring Flowers

Questions

Work with your group to answer the following questions. You may talk to the members of your group and get help with your answers, but each member of the group should complete an individual question sheet.

1 How many baskets did the class make?

2 What are the colors of the baskets?

3 How many different flowers are in the basket you made?

4 What are the colors of the flowers?

5 Do you know the names of any of the flowers? If so, what are they?

6 Are there any flowers in your basket that you don't know the names of?

7 Have you seen these flowers before? If so, where have you seen them?

8 Describe your favorite flower. Why do you like this flower?

DIRECTIONS

Create categories for the pictures, then number the pictures according to their category.

Category 1 =   Category 4 =

Category 2 =   Category 5 =

Category 3 =   Category 6 =

Appendices

2.6 Holiday Scramble

January	February
baby confetti New Year old, white-haired man Times Square in New York	cards saying *Be Mine* Chinese New Year* chocolate candy in red, heart-shaped boxes day for sweethearts human dragon* Presidents' Day Valentine's Day

March	April
green green river Irish leprechauns parade in Chicago St. Patrick's Day	bunny rabbit Christian holiday Easter eggs in a basket

May	June
flowers in cemeteries Memorial Day remembering family members who have died fireworks	

July	August
flags Independence Day in the U.S. parades	

September	October	
day to stop working Labor Day	black cats Columbus Day fasting* ghosts Halloween	pumpkins Ramadan* witches family dinners pilgrims

November	December	
Thanksgiving turkey and dressing Veteran's Day	brightly-wrapped packages Christian holiday Christmas decorated evergreen trees dreidel Hanukkah	kinara** Kwanzaa** menorah reindeer Santa Claus zawadi**

* The dates of these holidays and/or corresponding holidays vary according to the Chinese and Muslim lunar calendars.

** Kwanzaa is celebrated from December 26th to January 1st.

Miles to Go 2.11

1. Delta 1290 or American 2340
2. United 242 and United 809
3. Yes, you can fly from Seattle to New York (American 2160) or Denver to New York (American 2185 or Northwest 27).
4. United 745 and Delta 1261
5. Take United 271 from Los Angeles. You will make a connection in Salt Lake City (American 2218). Your wait time will be 1 hour and 30 minutes.
6. 6 hours and 15 minutes
7. United 744 from Los Angeles to Cincinnati is direct, so there is no need to use different airlines. United 271 from Los Angeles to Salt Lake City, connecting to Delta 1340 to Cincinnati is another option.
8. 5 hours and 25 minutes.
9. The flight is 5 minutes shorter. American 2160 is 5 hours and 20 minutes. United 242 is 5 hours and 25 minutes.
10. Options are United 271 connecting to United 921, Delta 1153, American 2340, or Delta 1290. The direct option is Delta 1261.
11. Take United 745 to Denver, then Northwest 38 to Dallas. Another option is United 271 to Salt Lake City, connecting to Delta 1153 to Denver, and connecting to Northwest 38 to Dallas.
12. Delta, American, and Northwest offer no flights from Los Angeles to Salt Lake City; United offers one flight (United 271). No options are available in the afternoon or evening.
13. The next available flight from Los Angeles to Salt Lake City is the same flight the next day.
14. Northwest 38

Across and Down 3.1A

Answers for row equations:

	Addition	**Subtraction**
Row 1	4 + 2 = 6	4 − 2 = 2
Row 2	2 + 4 = 6	2 − 4 = −2
Row 3	0 + 6 = 6	0 − 6 = −6
Row 4	3 + 3 = 6	3 − 3 = 0
Row 5	1 + 5 = 6	1 − 5 = −4

Answers for column equations:

	Addition	**Multiplication**
Column 1	1 + 4 = 5	4 x 1 = 4
Column 2	2 + 3 = 5	3 x 2 = 6
Column 3	1 + 4 = 5	4 x 1 = 4
Column 4	2 + 3 = 5	3 x 2 = 6
Column 5	1 + 4 = 5	4 x 1 = 4
Column 6	3 + 2 = 5	2 x 3 = 6

3.1B Across and Down

Answers for row equations:

	Subtraction	**Multiplication**
Row 1	4 − 6 = -2	4 x 6 = 24
Row 2	7 − 3 = 4	7 x 3 = 21
Row 3	7 − 3 = 4	7 x 3 = 21
Row 4	5 − 5 = 0	5 x 5 = 25
Row 5	4 − 6 = −2	4 x 6 = 24
Row 6	5 − 5 = 0	5 x 5 = 25
Row 7	5 − 5 = 0	5 x 5 = 25
Row 8	7 − 3 = 4	7 x 3 = 21
Row 9	9 − 1 = 8	9 x 1 = 9
Row 10	8 − 2 = 6	8 x 2 = 16
Row 11	7 − 3 = 4	7 x 3 = 21
Row 12	8 − 2 = 6	8 x 2 = 16
Row 13	10 − 0 = 10	10 x 0 = 0

Answers for column equations:

	Addition	**Multiplication**
Column 1	8 + 5 = 13	8 x 5 = 40
Column 2	7 + 6 = 13	7 x 6 = 42
Column 3	10 + 3 = 13	10 x 3 = 30
Column 4	8 + 5 = 13	8 x 5 = 40
Column 5	8 + 5 = 13	8 x 5 = 40
Column 6	8 + 5 = 13	8 x 5 = 40
Column 7	10 + 3 = 13	10 x 3 = 30
Column 8	9 + 4 = 13	9 x 4 = 36
Column 9	7 + 6 = 13	7 x 6 = 42
Column 10	11 + 2 = 13	11 x 2 = 22

3.4 Easy Subtraction

First row: 1, 20, 0, 35, 30

Second row: 2, 5, 11, 44, 13

Third row: 15, 53, 44, 14, 31

3.5C Easy to Figure

1. $499.00
2. $279.00
3. The dresser is cheaper than the sofa.
4. The total cost is $137.00.

3.5D Easy to Figure

1. The sofa costs $149.00 more than the table.
2. Corn is the cheapest item. The computer is the most expensive item.
3. Food items: $23.61
4. Clothing items: $455.39
5. Kitchen items: $258.46
6. Furniture items: $2148.99, assuming furniture items are: chair, bed, chest of drawers, dresser, lamp, sofa, stool, and table
7. Answers will vary.
8. Answers will vary.

Grocery Store Math 3.6

Grocery Item	Amount Needed	Regular Price	Total Regular Price	Sale Price	Total Spent	Total Saved
Hamburger	2 lbs.	99¢ per lb.	$1.98	89¢ per lb.	$1.78	20¢
Rice	2 boxes	$1.29 per box	$2.58	$1.25 per box	$2.50	8¢
Pasta	1 package	79¢ per package	79¢	75¢ per package	75¢	4¢
Shampoo	1 bottle	$3.79 per bottle	$3.79	$3.56 per bottle	$3.56	23¢
Tomatoes	2 cans	59¢ per can	$1.18	4 cans/$1.00	50¢	68¢
		$1.49 per head	$2.98	99¢ per head	$1.98	$1.00
		79¢ per bag	79¢	75¢ per bag	75¢	4¢
		89¢ per can	$2.67	75¢ per can	$2.25	42¢
		$1.79 per can	$3.58	$1.69 per can	$3.38	20¢
		$3.69 per bottle	$3.69	$3.49 per bottle	$3.49	20¢
		$2.79	$2.79	$2.59	$2.59	20¢
		$2.59	$2.59	$2.37	$2.37	22¢
		$1.29	$1.29	$1.19	$1.19	10¢
		$2.39 per box	$4.78	$2.19 per box	$4.38	40¢
					GRAND TOTAL SAVED	$4.01

3.7 How Much Money Can I Make?

Taking the offer for 1¢ for the first day will give you the most money.

Day 1 = 1¢

Day 2 = 2¢

Day 3 = 4¢

Day 4 = 8¢

Day 5 = 16¢

Day 6 = 32¢

Day 7 = 64¢

Day 8 = $1.28

Day 9 = $2.56

Day 10 = $5.12

Day 11 = $10.24

Day 12 = $20.48

Day 13 = $40.96

Day 14 = $81.92

Day 15 = $163.84

Day 16 = $327.68

Day 17 = $655.36

3.8 Missing Pieces

Problem #1

1. 18, 4, 15, 250, 16, 450, 850, 4,850, 75
2. 18, 4, 15, 16
3. Five numbers
4. 250, 450, 850, 4850, 75
5. First step: calculate 75% of $4,850.00. The answer is $3,637.50. Then add up all of Philip's earnings. The total is $1,550.00. Next, subtract the amount Philip saved from $3,637.50. Philip needs to save $2,087.50 more.
6. He needs $3,637.50.
7. Multiply $4,850.00 by .75 or 75%.
8. He has $1,550.00. He does not have enough.

Problem #2

Multiply 15 hours by $6.00 in order to find out how much Philip makes in a week. The answer is $90.00. Now multiply $90.00 by .50 or 50%. Philip saves $45.00. Divide $2,087.50 (the amount of money he still needs) by $45.00. This equals $46.38. Philip must work approximately 46 weeks more before he will have enough money to get his car.

3.9 Mystery Products

Largest product = 832 x 68

Smallest product = 268 x 34

3.12 Odd Addition

Row 1: 16

Row 2: 65

Row 3: 25

Row 4: 54

Row 5: 29

Row 6: 65

Row 7: 52

Row 8: 89

Row 9: 99

Row 10: 56

Purchase Power 3.15

1. $9.50 x 5 = $47.50
2. $8.50 x 6 = $51.00
3. The ballet is more expensive at $40.00. The symphony is $8.50; $31.50 cheaper than the ballet.
4. $5.00 x $8.00 = $40.00
5. Six raffle tickets cost $30.00. $30.00 divided by 4 = $7.50.
6. Two seniors = $14.00; seven adults = $84.00; five children = $30.00; total = $128.00.
7. Four lectures x $9.00 = $36.00. $36.00 − $7.00 savings = $29.00 paid. $29.00 is 80.5% of $36.00 (divide 29 by 36), so the savings is 15.5%.
8. The ticket number is on the raffle ticket. The number needs to match the number drawn in the raffle in order to win.
9. Reserved seat numbers appear. In most countries, people going into a movie theater may sit wherever they want.
10. It is the reserved seat number. It could mean row number ten in seat seven.
11. $6.00 x 10 children = $60.00
12. Answers vary by student (i.e., music concerts, theater, art exhibits, the opera).
13. A string quartet is four people with string instruments such as the violin that play together.
14. Movie theaters and the amusement parks are open everyday and usually use the same tickets everyday. The focus of the raffle ticket is the number, not the date.

Ten Times 3.17

1. $10.00 x 10 = $100.00
2. $40.00 x 10 = $400.00 for the ballet; $8.50 x 10 = $85.00 for the orchestra. The difference is $315.00.
3. $12.00 x 100 = $1,200.00
4. $50.00 for 10, $500.00 for 100.
5. $12.00 x 10 adults = $120.00. $7.00 x 10 senior citizens = $70.00. It will cost $50.00 more.
6. For the adults, it will cost $9.50 x 10 = $95. For the senior citizens, it will cost $6.00 x 10 = $60.00. The difference between $95.00 and $60.00 is $35.00; the adults will pay $35.00 more.
7. For multiplying by 10, add a zero and move the decimal one place to the right i.e., $2.50 x 10 = $25.00. For multiplying by 100, add two zeros and move the decimal two places to the right.

The Yard Sale 3.18

1. The family would make $1,495.00; this is enough for their vacation.
2. Mother: $330.00, Father: $510.00, Oldest brother: $130.00, Middle brother: $100.00, Youngest brother: $60.00, Sister: $80.00.
3. The motorcycle is the most expensive item; it is being sold by the father.
4. No. They would be short $240.00.

4.8 Map Reading

1. Belgium, Germany, Italy, Luxembourg, Spain, and Switzerland
2. Mexico and Canada
3. South America. Brazil, Bolivia, Chile, Columbia, and Ecuador
4. Argentina extends farther south than South Africa. While both countries' northernmost point lies at ~22° S, Argentina's southernmost point lies at ~54° S while South Africa's southernmost point lies at ~34° S.
5. The Pacific Ocean is to the west; the Atlantic Ocean is to the east.
6. Austria, France, Germany, and Italy
7. Four
8. Mumbai is in India. India is in South Asia
9. Rio de Janeiro is in Brazil. Buenos Aires is in Argentina.
10. Miami, Florida is farther south than Florence, Italy. Miami lies at ~26° N while Florence lies at ~44° N.
11. Algeria, Egypt, Libya, Morocco, and Tunisia.
12. Iraq, Israel/The West Bank, Saudi Arabia, Syria
13. Toronto is in Canada. It is in the southeastern part of the country.
14. Beijing is farther north than Taipei. Beijing lies at ~ 40° north of the equator while Taipei lies at only ~ 25° north of the equator.

4.17 Scrambled Sentences

1. Mammals have hair.
2. Most mammals are born alive.
3. Whales are sea mammals.
4. Whales are also the largest mammals.
5. Some mammals like camels live in the desert.
6. Young mammals are fed milk from their mothers.
7. Cats and dogs are mammals.
8. Humans are also mammals.

4.21 Spelling Puzzles

1. road
2. green
3. rain
4. sky
5. frog
6. hand
7. fog

Word Maze 4.24A

```
P E N C I L U I O C O M P U T E R U T S
C A S D F G H C R A S R I U Y T R E W Q
Z H N O T E B O O K S G F D S A R E W Q
Q W A R T Y U M O P L K J T N E D U T S
A S D L G H J P L M N B E R A S E R N B
N O T E K O O U H U Y T P A M E R T T T
C H A Y H G R T H A I R E P O O L K J D
D E S K J Y H E G R F E A W S Q A K J E
Z X C V B N M R K J H G C D S A R E W S
R U L E R G R C H A I R H P O O L K J K
B O O K H A I R G R F E E W S P A P E R
A S D F B L A C K B O A R D X Z P E N B
S C I S S O R S G R F E E S T U D E N T
M A R K E R S T H A I T E A C H E R J D
```

Word Maze 4.24B

```
C A T S C I L T U R T L E S U S E R E G
C A S D F G H C R A S O I U Y T R E L I
Z H N O T T B O R K N G F D S A R E E R
A S D L G H J P E M N B E R A S E R P A
K A N G A R O O H U Y T P I G S R T H F
C H A Y H G R T H A I T E D O G S A F
D E G O L D F I S H F E U W S Q A K N E
Z X C V B N M R K J H G C R S A R E T S
Z E B R A G R C H A R R H P T O L K S K
T H A M S T E R S R F E E W S L I O N S
A S D F M O N K E Y O A R D X Z E E N B
H O R S E S R S G R F E E S T T I G E R
S N A K E R S T H A I T E A C H C O W S
S D U Y E W T O R K A R E M N G C R B O
```

Word Maze 4.24C

```
O S D F B L A R K C H I C K E N Z P E N
B O W L U I O C O M M U T E E U T S L G
C A S D F G H C I A E R I U Y T R E W R
Z H N O T E B L O K S A F D S A R E W A
C H I C K E K M O P L K T T N E D U T T
A S D L G H J P L M N B E R A S E N N U
D I S H K O O U H U Y T P L A T E T I I
C H A Y H G R T H A I N K P O O L K J T
D D S K J Y H E G R F A N W S Q A K J Y
Z X C V B N M R K J H P I D S A R E W S
S A L A D G R C H A I K S P O O N K J K
F O R K H A I R R G R I E E W S P A P E
K N I F E L A R K B U T T E R Z P E N
P L A T E T T I G R F E E S T F R U I T
F I S H H R S T H A I T E A C B R E A D
O S D F B L F U U I T T T E N A P K I N
```

Word Maze 4.24D

```
B E L T L A R S C H I K K E S D P E N B
H O S E U I O A O M M U T E W R T S L L
D A S D F G H N I A E R I U E E R E W O
R H N N T E B D O K S A E D A S R E W U
E H I C K E K A O P L K T T T S D U T S
S S D L G H J L L S K I R T E E N N E E
S H O E S O O S H U Y T P L R T E T I I
C H A Y H G R T H A I N K P O O L K J T
D D S K J Y H E G S F A N W S L E V I S
P A N T S N M R K J H P I D S A R E W S
S A L D D G R C H A I I S P O M N K J K
S O C K S H A P R R S R R E E W S P A P
K N F F E L A R E L U T T T R R K P G N
T S H I R T S G I F E E S T F I U I T
P I S L I P T T H P I T E A C B R A A D
O S D F B L S R U I T T T E N B T A I N
```

345

4.24E Word Maze

```
M R U G G B L A R K E R H C K E N Z T E
I W W L O I O C O T M U E E E U T S E N
C A S D O G H O I A E R I S Y T R E L D
R H N O K E T B R O K S A F S S U R E T
O H I C C E K M O C L K T T N E G U V A
W S D L A H J P L M A B E R A S R N I B
A I N K S I N K H U Y S P L A R E D S L
V H A Y E G R T H A I N E P E L L K I E
E T O V E Y H E S T O V E S S Q A K O Y
D E S K D N M R K J H P S D S A R E N S
S A L D R T A B L E I E S P Y O N K J K
M I R R O R I R R G R I E L A M P A P E
K N I F L A R K D U T T E R R Z P E N J
P L T T S T F R I D G E E S T F R R I T
F S S H E R S T H A I T E A C B R R A D
C H A I R L F R I I T O I L E T P B E D
```

4.24F Word Maze

```
B S A L V A D O R D A L I A L I Z P E J
I O I L U I O C O M M U T E E U T S L O
L A C D F G H C I A E R I U Y T R E W H
C H A C K E K M O P L K T T N E D U T K
L S M I C H A E L J O R D A N S E N N E
I C H A R L E S D E G A U L L E E T I N
N N J M Y H G R T H A I N K P O O L K N
T D O M A R I L Y N M O N R O E A K M E
O X R V B C M R K J H P I D S A R E A D
N A D R L S T E I N I K S P O N N K D Y
F O A K H A I J R G R I E E W S P A O E
K N N F E L R A G G A J K C I M Z P N N
P L A T E T T I G G F E E S T F R U N T
B R I T N E Y S P E A R S C B R R A D
G E O R G I A O K E E F F E E N A P K I
```

4.24G Word Maze

```
P S D J A P A N E S E I C K E N Z I E H
O O W L U I O C O M M U T E E U T N L U
R A S D F R E N C H E N A V A J O D W N
T H N O T E B L O K S A F D S A R O W G
U H I C K E K M O P L K T T N E D N T A
G S D L G H J P L M N B E H A S E E N R
U I S H K O O U H U Y T P L A T E S I I
E H A Y H C H I N E S E P O I L I J A A
S D S K J Y H E N G F A N W S Q A A J N
E X C V B N M E K J H P I A S A R N W S
E N G L I S H N H A I K S R O O N K J K
D O R K H A I G R G R I E A W S P A P E
K N I E E L A L K B U T T B R R Z P E N
P L A T P T T I G R F E E I T F R U I T
F I S G E R M A N Y T T E C C B R E A D
O S D F B L F H U I S P A N I S H K I N
```

5.17 Raising Kids

Clothing:	8% = $12,000		Food:	20% = $30,000
Healthcare:	7% = $10,500		Housing:	33% = $49,500
Education and Childcare:	7% = $10,500		Other:	10% = $15,000
Transportation:	14% = $21,000			

Inventory A: ESL/EFL Students: Grade 5 to Middle School

DIRECTIONS

Read each statement. Write 0 if you disagree. Write 2 if you agree. Write 1 if you are somewhere in between. Total the number of points you have in each intelligence. Compare your scores. Which score is the highest (strongest intelligence)? Which is the lowest (weakest intelligence)?

```
0 = disagree
1 = somewhere in between
2 = agree
```

Linguistic Intelligence

___ 1. I read often.
___ 2. I write notes and letters.
___ 3. I tell jokes.
___ 4. I remember people's names.
___ 5. I like poems.
___ 6. I know many words.

Logical/Mathematical Intelligence

___ 1. I do math in my head.
___ 2. I am good at chess and/or checkers.
___ 3. I like to categorize.
___ 4. I like number games.
___ 5. I like to solve problems.
___ 6. I ask many questions.

Visual/Spatial Intelligence

___ 1. I read maps easily.
___ 2. I enjoy art activities.
___ 3. I draw well.
___ 4. I like to look at pictures.
___ 5. I love books with illustrations.
___ 6. I like puzzles.

Bodily/Kinesthetic Intelligence

___ 1. I cannot sit quietly for a long time.
___ 2. I like to dance.
___ 3. I am good at sewing and building.
___ 4. I am good at a sport.
___ 5. I enjoy working with my hands.
___ 6. I like to run and walk.

Interpersonal Intelligence

___ 1. I am often a leader.
___ 2. I can name two friends.
___ 3. I like to study with friends.
___ 4. I like people.
___ 5. I have many friends
___ 6. I like parties.

Intrapersonal Intelligence

___ 1. I like to go places alone.
___ 2. I prefer to study alone.
___ 3. I know a lot about myself.
___ 4. I keep a diary.
___ 5. I set goals and achieve them.
___ 6. I learn from my mistakes.

Musical Intelligence

___ 1. I can hum tunes to many songs.
___ 2. I sing well.
___ 3. I play a musical instrument
___ 4. I sing in a choir.
___ 5. I know when music is off-key.
___ 6. I often listen to music.

Naturalist Intelligence

___ 1. I like plants.
___ 2. I have a pet.
___ 3. I know many different flowers.
___ 4. I know many different animals.
___ 5. I like to hike.
___ 6. I notice trees and plants.

Inventory B: ESL/EFL Students: High School

Read each statement. Write 0 if you disagree. Write 2 if you agree. Write 1 if you are somewhere in between. Total the number of points you have in each intelligence. Compare your scores. Which score is the highest (strongest intelligence)? Which is the lowest (weakest intelligence)?

```
0 = disagree
1 = somewhere in between
2 = agree
```

Linguistic Intelligence

____ 1. I like to talk about books that I read.

____ 2. I write notes and letters to my friends.

____ 3 I like to tell jokes.

____ 4. I notice advertisements for things I want to buy.

____ 5. I talk to my friends on the phone.

____ 6. I have a good vocabulary.

Logical/Mathematical Intelligence

____ 1. I often do math in my head.

____ 2. I am good at chess, checkers, or number games.

____ 3. I am good at solving problems.

____ 4. I like to analyze things.

____ 5. I am good at seeing patterns.

____ 6. I like to do crossword puzzles.

Visual/Spatial Intelligence

____ 1. I am good at using maps.

____ 2. I like to decorate.

____ 3. I like to draw.

____ 4. I like to look at pictures.

____ 5. I love books with illustrations.

____ 6. It is easy for me to see spatial relationships.

Bodily/Kinesthetic Intelligence

____ 1. It is hard for me to sit for a long time.

____ 2. I like to dance.

____ 3. I am good at sewing, woodworking, building, or mechanics.

____ 4. I participate in sports.

____ 5. I learn best through hands-on activities.

____ 6. I enjoy running and walking.

Interpersonal Intelligence

____ 1. I am often chosen as a leader.

____ 2. I enjoy talking to friends.

____ 3. I prefer to study with my friends.

____ 4. I like to support my friends.

____ 5. I have many friends.

____ 6. I enjoy parties with my friends.

Intrapersonal Intelligence

____ 1. I sometimes prefer to go places alone.

____ 2. I would rather study alone than with someone.

____ 3. I can identify and describe my talents.

____ 4. I remember my dreams and like to talk about them.

____ 5. I like to set goals and achieve them.

____ 6. I learn from my mistakes.

Musical Intelligence

____ 1. I know the tunes to many songs.

____ 2. I am a good singer.

____ 3. I play a musical instrument or sing in a choir.

____ 4. I can tell when music is off-key.

____ 5. I often tap rhythmically on the table or desk when I am listening to music.

____ 6. I often sing songs or listen to music.

Naturalist Intelligence

____ 1. I like houseplants.

____ 2. I have or would like to have a pet.

____ 3. I know the names of many different flowers.

____ 4. I know the names of many different animals.

____ 5. I like to hike and be outdoors.

____ 6. I notice the trees and plants in my neighborhood.

Inventory C: ESL/EFL Students: Adults

Multiple Intelligences and Language Learning © 2005 Alta Book Center Publishers, San Francisco, California
www.altaesl.com Permission granted to photocopy for one teacher's classroom use only.

DIRECTIONS

Read each statement. Write 0 if you disagree. Write 2 if you agree. Write 1 if you are somewhere in between. Total the number of points you have in each intelligence. Compare your scores. Which score is the highest (strongest intelligence)? Which is the lowest (weakest intelligence)?

```
0 = disagree
1 = somewhere in between
2 = agree
```

Linguistic Intelligence

___ 1. I like to read and talk about books.

___ 2. I often write notes and letters to my friends and family.

___ 3 I like to tell jokes at parties.

___ 4. I notice advertisements in magazines, on TV, and on billboards.

___ 5. I like to talk to my friends on the phone.

___ 6. I have a good vocabulary.

Logical/Mathematical Intelligence

___ 1. When I have to, I can do arithmetic easily in my head.

___ 2. I am good at creating a budget and sticking to it.

___ 3. I am good at chess, checkers, or number games.

___ 3. I am good at solving day-to-day problems.

___ 4. I like to analyze things.

___ 5. I generally get along well with other people.

___ 6. I am good at and like to do crossword puzzles.

Visual/Spatial Intelligence

___ 1. If I get lost in a new place, I can use a map to help me.

___ 2. I like to decorate my house or apartment.

___ 3. I often doodle (make small drawings and patterns on paper).

___ 4. I like to look at pictures.

___ 5. I love books with illustrations.

___ 6. It is easy for me to see spatial relationships.

Bodily/Kinesthetic Intelligence

___ 1. It is hard for me to sit for a long time.

___ 2. I get my best ideas when I am jogging, walking, or doing physical things.

___ 3. I am good at sewing, woodworking, building, or mechanics.

___ 4. I like sports and play at least one sport.

___ 5. I learn best through hands-on activities.

___ 6. I enjoy outdoor activities.

Interpersonal Intelligence

___ 1. I am often chosen as a leader.

___ 2. I enjoy talking to friends.

___ 3. I like to invite people to my house or apartment.

___ 4. I like to support my friends.

___ 5. I am a good listener.

___ 6. I like to have parties with my friends.

Intrapersonal Intelligence

___ 1. I sometimes prefer to go places alone.

___ 2. I have hobbies that I enjoy pursuing on my own.

___ 3. I can identify and describe my talents.

___ 4. I remember my dreams and like to talk about them.

___ 5. I like to set goals and achieve them.

___ 6. I like to have time to reflect on my work.

Musical Intelligence

___ 1. I know the tunes to many songs.

___ 2. I have a very expressive voice.

___ 3. I play a musical instrument or sing in a choir.

___ 4. I can tell when music is off-key.

___ 5. I often tap rhythmically on the table or desk when I am listening to music.

___ 6. I like to listen to music.

Naturalist Intelligence

___ 1. I like houseplants.

___ 2. I have or would like to have a pet.

___ 3. I know the names of many different flowers.

___ 4. I know the names of many different animals.

___ 5. I like to hike and be outdoors.

___ 6. I notice the trees and plants in my neighborhood.

Inventory D: Prospective Second Language Teachers

DIRECTIONS

Read each statement. Write 0 if you disagree. Write 2 if you agree. Write 1 if you are somewhere in between. Total the number of points you have in each intelligence. Compare your scores. Which score is the highest (strongest intelligence)? Which is the lowest (weakest intelligence)?

```
0 = disagree
1 = somewhere in between
2 = agree
```

Linguistic Intelligence

____ 1. I like to write papers and articles.

____ 2. Almost everyday, I read something just for pleasure.

____ 3. I often listen to the news on the radio or to cassettes of lectures, books, etc.

____ 4. I read billboards and advertisements.

____ 5. When I read stories, I create clear images about the characters and places in my mind.

____ 6. I use illustrations, charts, posters, and quotations frequently to add information to the papers I write.

____ 7 If I hear a song or a commercial jingle a few times, I can usually remember the words.

____ 8. I am a good letter writer.

____ 9. I encourage others to spend time reading and writing.

____ 10. I have written something that I like.

Logical/Mathematical Intelligence

____ 1. I feel more comfortable believing an answer is correct when it has been measured, calculated, or demonstrated in some way.

____ 2. I can calculate numbers easily in my head.

____ 3. I like my classes to be consistent with rules, routines, assignments, and other expectations clearly stated.

____ 4. I like playing games such as hearts, bridge, gin rummy, chess, or checkers.

____ 5. I like or have liked math classes in school.

____ 6. I believe that most things have logical and rational explanations.

____ 7. I like brainteaser games.

____ 8. I am interested in new developments in the sciences.

____ 9. I am good at solving problems.

____ 10. I like to measure things exactly.

Visual/Spatial Intelligence

____ 1. I pay attention to the colors I wear.

____ 2. I pay attention to the colors others wear.

____ 3. I like to use visual aids in the classes I teach.

____ 4. I like to draw.

____ 5. I like to read articles containing many charts and illustrations.

____ 6. I prefer textbooks with illustrations, graphs, charts, and pictures.

____ 7. I like doing puzzles and mazes.

____ 8. I notice the seating arrangement in a room almost immediately.

____ 9. It is easy for me to find my way around unfamiliar cities.

____ 10. I like to take photographs on trips and vacations.

Bodily/Kinesthetic Intelligence

____ 1. Many of my hobbies involve some form of physical activity.

____ 2. I like to use activities in my classes that require students to get out of their seats and move around.

____ 3. I find it difficult to sit for long periods of time.

____ 4. I like to be involved in many forms of outdoor activities.

____ 5. I often get my best ideas when I am jogging, walking, or doing other physical activities.

____ 6. When learning a new skill, I have to actually try it out in order to absorb it.

____ 7. I like doing things that involve working with my hands.

____ 8. I participate or have participated in one or more sports.

____ 9. I like to dance.

____ 10. I like to go on rides at amusement and theme parks.

Multiple Intelligences and Language Learning © 2005 Alta Book Center Publishers, San Francisco, California www.altaesl.com. Permission granted to photocopy for one teacher's classroom use only.

Inventory D (continued)

0 = disagree
1 = somewhere in between
2 = agree

Interpersonal Intelligence

___ 1. I like to listen to other people's ideas.

___ 2. I try to incorporate others' ideas into my own thinking.

___ 3. I would prefer going to a party with strangers over spending the evening alone.

___ 4   I like to discuss my problems with my friends.

___ 5. My friends often seek help from me in solving their problems.

___ 6. I like to entertain friends and give parties.

___ 7. I like to meet new people.

___ 8. I like to teach others how to do things.

___ 9. I consider myself to have strong leadership qualities.

___ 10. I frequently assume leadership roles and related positions.

Intrapersonal Intelligence

___ 1. I often spend time reflecting on things that have happened in my life.

___ 2. I plan for quiet time in my life.

___ 3. I consider myself to be independent and not necessarily swayed by the opinions of others.

___ 4. I keep a personal journal and record my thoughts and activities.

___ 5. I prefer to study and learn new material on my own.

___ 6. When hurt or disappointed, I find that I bounce back quickly.

___ 7. I can articulate the primary values that govern my life.

___ 8. I prefer to generate my own methods and procedures for learning new materials.

___ 9. I often create new activities and materials to supplement my classes.

___ 10. I have hobbies and interests that I enjoy doing on my own.

Musical Intelligence

___ 1. I have a very expressive voice when I am in front of a class or in other groups.

___ 2. I often incorporate music or chants into my lesson plans.

___ 3. I can tell if someone is singing off-key.

___ 4. I know the melodies to many different songs.

___ 5. When I listen to music, I have no difficulty identifying or following the rhythm.

___ 6. If I hear a new song a couple of times, I can usually remember the melody.

___ 7. I often sing in the shower.

___ 8. I frequently listen to music.

___ 9. Listening to music I like makes me feel good.

___ 10. When I hear a piece of music, I can harmonize with it easily.

Naturalist Intelligence

___ 1. I like to be outdoors.

___ 2. I like to observe what is happening around me when I am outdoors.

___ 3. I like to hike and camp outdoors.

___ 4. I know the names of many different plants.

___ 5. I know the names of and can describe most of the plants and animals in my neighborhood.

___ 6. I like or have liked biological and life science courses in school.

___ 7. I support ecologists' efforts to preserve our environment.

___ 8. Knowledge of the world and how it works is important to me.

___ 9. I often look at the sky and can recognize different types of clouds and the weather they bring.

___ 10. I believe that all natural phenomena can be studied and explained.

Pre-K to Grade 2

Grades 3 to 5

Beginning

2.4   Family Trees
2.19 Spelling Maze
2.24 Word Pictures
3.1   Across and Down
3.3   Data Graphs
3.4   Easy Subtraction
3.5   Easy to Figure
3.10 Next in Line
3.11 Numbered Messages
3.14 Problem Solving for Children
3.17 Ten Times
4.2   Calendar Daze
4.6   It Looks Like…
4.9   Match Me Up
4.12 Family Gift Boxes
4.13 Preference Clocks
4.14 Puppets
4.15 Ringing Bells
4.22 Visual Names
4.23 Weaving
5.2   Class Moves
5.4   Coins and Coupons
5.6   Group Chain
5.11 Measure Me
5.12 Murals for Parents
5.20 Floor Plans
5.21 Transportation Games
6.1   About My Community
6.4   Breakfast Please
6.5   Forming Groups
6.18 Feelings
6.23 Personal Totem Poles
7.2   The Animal Song
7.4   The Birthday Song
7.8   Filipino, Polynesian, and
      Indonesian Dance
7.17 Poetry TPR
7.18 Rounds
7.20 Up and Away
8.3   Calendar of Weather
8.6   Folded Leaf Patterns
8.17 Surprise, Surprise!
8.18 Decorating Trees
8.19 Trees and More Trees

Intermediate

2.1   Alphabet Question Book
2.3   Family Matters
2.4   Family Trees
2.13 Numbered Words
2.15 Scrolled Stories
2.20 Storytelling
2.24 Word Pictures
3.1   Across and Down
3.3   Data Graphs
3.4   Easy Subtraction
3.5   Easy to Figure
3.10 Next in Line
3.11 Numbered Messages
3.12 Odd Addition
3.14 Problem Solving for Children
3.16 Recipes for Math
3.19 What's Inside?
3.20 Your Change
4.2   Calendar Daze
4.7   Learning Gameboard
4.14 Puppets
4.16 Rooms in My House
4.18 Self Service
4.19 Semantic Mapping
4.21 Spelling Puzzles
4.22 Visual Names
5.1   The Cat Game
5.3   Classroom Shopping
5.8   How to Make a Piñata
5.11 Measure Me
5.12 Murals for Parents
5.16 Puzzle Partners
5.18 Scrap Artists
5.23 Valentine's Day Cake
6.1   About My Community
6.4   Breakfast Please
6.5   Forming Groups
6.6   Getting to School
6.16 Dreams
6.23 Personal Totem Poles
7.2   The Animal Song
7.3   April Fool's Song
7.8   Filipino, Polynesian, and
      Indonesian Dance
7.9   Language Learning Rap
7.10 Country Line Dancing
7.11 Modified Square Dancing
7.14 Music Library
7.16 Piggybacking
8.2   Autumn Leaves
8.3   Calendar of Weather
8.4   Camping Out
8.5   Drawing Animals
8.10 Nature's Collage
8.12 Nature's Signposts
8.13 Pointillism
8.14 Puddles
8.15 Rain Helpers
8.16 Spring Flowers
8.20 TV Topics

Advanced

2.3   Family Matters
2.20 Storytelling
3.19 What's Inside?
4.19 Semantic Mapping
4.21 Spelling Puzzles
4.22 Visual Names
5.3   Classroom Shopping
5.23 Valentine's Day Cake
6.5   Forming Groups
6.16 Dreams
7.10 Country Line Dancing
7.11 Modified Square Dancing
8.20 TV Topics

Middle School

Adult

Beginning

2.2 Antonym Crisscross
3.11 Numbered Messages
4.1 All Boxed Up
4.11 Memory Pictures
4.17 Scrambled Up
4.24 Word Mazes
5.2 Class Moves
5.4 Coins and Coupons
6.5 Forming Groups
6.8 Oral Directions
7.12 Mood Music
8.3 Calendar of Weather

Intermediate

2.5 Fashion Show
2.8 Interactive Writing
2.9 Letter Writing
2.10 Memories
2.11 Miles to Go
2.14 The Prize
2.16 Sentence Autobiographies
2.18 Shopping Patterns
2.22 Valuing Diversity
3.6 Grocery Store Math
3.8 Missing Pieces
3.11 Numbered Messages
3.13 Problem Solving for Adults
3.15 Purchase Power
3.18 The Yard Sale
3.19 What's Inside?
3.20 Your Change
4.3 Can You Believe Your Eyes?
4.4 Events in History
4.5 Food Pyramids
4.8 Map Reading
4.11 Memory Pictures
4.17 Scrambled Up
4.19 Semantic Mapping
4.20 Shared Writing
4.24 Word Mazes
5.3 Classroom Shopping
5.23 Valentine's Day Cake
6.2 Anagrams
6.5 Forming Groups
6.6 Getting to School
6.8 Oral Directions
6.9 Paper Airplanes
6.10 Syllable Match
6.11 Tracking Water Usage
6.13 Weekly Menus
6.15 Dear Abby
6.16 Dreams

6.17 Evaluate Your Own Work
6.19 Gender Differences
6.20 How Do You Prefer to Learn?
6.22 Personal Galleries
6.24 Read and Recite
6.26 Task Evaluation
7.6 Class Choreography
7.7 Favorite Music
7.10 Country Line Dancing
7.12 Mood Music
7.13 Music Cloze
8.3 Calendar of Weather
8.5 Drawing Animals
8.9 Natural Categories
8.10 Nature's Collage
8.13 Pointillism

Advanced

2.5 Fashion Show
2.8 Interactive Writing
2.9 Letter Writing
2.10 Memories
2.11 Miles to Go
2.18 Shopping Patterns
2.22 Valuing Diversity
3.6 Grocery Store Math
3.13 Problem Solving for Adults
3.15 Purchase Power
3.19 What's Inside?
4.3 Can You Believe Your Eyes?
4.4 Events in History
4.5 Food Pyramids
4.8 Map Reading
4.11 Memory Pictures
4.17 Scrambled Up
4.19 Semantic Mapping
4.20 Shared Writing
4.24 Word Mazes
5.3 Classroom Shopping
5.17 Raising Kids
5.22 Travel Brochures Using the Internet
5.23 Valentine's Day Cake
6.5 Forming Groups
6.7 Group Roles
6.9 Paper Airplanes
6.10 Syllable Match
6.11 Tracking Water Usage
6.13 Weekly Menus
6.15 Dear Abby
6.16 Dreams
6.17 Evaluate Your Own Work
6.19 Gender Differences
6.20 How Do You Prefer to Learn?
6.22 Personal Galleries
6.24 Read and Recite
6.26 Task Evaluation

7.6 Class Choreography
7.7 Favorite Music
7.10 Country Line Dancing
7.12 Mood Music
7.13 Music Cloze

Armstrong, T. (1994). Multiple Intelligences in the Classroom. Alexandria, VA: Association of Supervision and Curriculum Development.

Binet, A. & Simon. T. (1905). Méthodes nouvelles pour le diagnostique du niveaux intellectuel des anormaux [New methods for the diagnosis of the intellectual level of the abnormal]. L'année psychologique, 11, 236-45.

Ceci, S.J. (1990). On Intelligence . . . . More or Less: A Bio-ecological Theory of Intellectual Development. Englewood Cliffs, NJ: Prentice-Hall.

Campbell, L. (1997). How teachers interpret MI theory. Educational Leadership, 55, 1: 15-19.

Christison, M.A. (1997). An introduction to multiple intelligences theory and second language learning. Understanding Learning Styles in the Second Language Classroom. (Ed.) J. Reid. pp. 1-4. Englewood Cliffs, NJ: Prentice-Hall/Regents.

Christison, M.A. (1998). Applying multiple intelligences theory in preservice and inservice TEFL education programs. English Teaching Forum, 36, 2, 2-13.

Csikzentmihalyi, M. (1996). Creativity: Flow and the Psychology of Discovery and Invention. New York: Harper Collins.

Csikzentmihalyi, M. (1997). Finding Flow: The Psychology of Engagement with Everyday Life. New York: Basic Books.

Feldman, D.H. (1980). Beyond Universals in Cognitive Development. Norwood, NJ: Ablex.

Fodor, J. (1983). Modularity of Mind. Cambridge, MA: MIT Bradford Press.

Gardner, H. (1983). Frames of Mind: The Theory of Multiple Intelligences. New York: Basic Books.

Gardner, H. (1999). Intelligence Reframed. New York: Basic Books.

Gardner, H. (1993). Multiple Intelligences: The Theory in Practice. New York: Basic Books.

Gardner, H. (1999). Intelligence Reframed: Multiple Intelligences for the 21st Century. New York: Basic Books.

Goleman, D. (1995). Emotional Intelligence. New York: Bantam Books.

Goleman, D. (1998). Working With Emotional Intelligence. New York: Bantam Books.

Hoerr, T.R. (1997). Frog ballets and musical fractions. Educational Leadership, 55, 1: 43-46. Alexandria, VA: Association of Supervision and Curriculum Development.

Jencks, C. (1977). Who Gets Ahead: The Determinants of Economic Success in America. New York: Basic Books.

Kail, R. and Pellegrino (1985). Human Intelligence: Perspectives and Prospects. New York: W.H. Freeman and Company.

Lazear, D. (1991a). Seven Ways of Knowing: Teaching for Multiple Intelligences: A Handbook of Techniques for Expanding Intelligence. Palantine, IL: Skylight Publishers.

Lazear, D. (1991b). Seven Ways of Teaching. Palantine, IL: Skylight Publishers.

Lazear, D. (1994a). Seven Pathways of Learning. Palantine, IL: Skylight Publishers.

Lazear, D. (1994b). Multiple Intelligence Approaches to Assessment: Solving the Assessment Conundrum. Tucson, AZ: Zephyr Press.

Marzano, R.J., and R.S. Brandt, C.S. Hughes, B.F. Jones, B.Z. Presseisen, and S.C. Rankin (1988). Dimensions of Thinking: A Framework for Curriculum and Instruction. Alexandria, VA: ASCD.

Piaget, J. (1970). Piaget's theory. In P. Mussen (Ed.), Carmichael's Manual of Child Psychology. New York: Wiley.

Reid, J. (1995). Learning Styles in the ESL/EFL Classroom. Boston, MA: Heinle and Heinle Publishers.

Reid, J. (1997). Understanding Learning Styles in the Second Language Classroom. Englewood Cliffs, NJ: Prentice Hall/Regents.

Salovey, P. and Mayer, J. (1990). Emotional intelligence. Imagination, Personality and Cognition, 9, 185-211.

Sternberg, R.J. (1984). Toward a triarchic theory of human intelligence. Behavioral and Brain Science, 7, 269-315.

Sternberg, R.J. (1985). Beyond IQ. Cambridge, England: Cambridge University Press.

Teele, S. (1992). The Teele Inventory of Multiple Intelligences. Available from the author, P.O. Box 7302, Redlands, CA 92374.

Teele, S. (2000). Rainbows of Intelligence: Exploring How Students Learn. Thousand Oaks, CA: Corwin Press.

Vos Savant, M. (1995). Ask Marilyn. Parade Magazine, May 21, 1995, 20.

Weinreich-Haste, H. (1985). The varieties of intelligence: an interview with Howard Gardner. New Ideas in Psychology, 3, 4: 47-65